Praise for Melvin Litton:

In one of Melvin Litton's stories in his latest book of short stories *Son of Eve and Other Tales*, a still-born child is buried without ceremony in a back yard and foreshadows a murder in an old house years later, maybe in the same place. There is cinematic sudden violence, Kansas-centric tales of careworn nuclear families fierce with promise and love, forbidden darknesses of wind, longing and the chill of regret that seeps through generations. These stories come from the resurrected flatlands of Charlie Starkweather's ghost. They remind me of the "Dirty Realism" of Raymond Carver and Carson McCullers, and not to wring the obvious out of a reference, Sam Shepard. Litton is able to scour the horizons of his tales with scathingly simple phrases: "(the sun) drops like an empty bottle beyond the tall weeds." The spirit of place is in every story. The final chapter is an eloquent paean to his past working life and his perspective belongs to not only the retiree, but the writer who assembled his bones throughout the long years. He worked construction, he made things, it gave a rhythm and ritual to his life that is reflected in every sentence.

-John Macker, author of *Atlas of Wolves* (2019) and *The Blues Drink Your Dreams Away, Selected Poems, 1983-2018* (Finalist for an Arizona/New Mexico Book Award)

Praise for Melvin Litton:

"Melvin Litton's brilliant, eccentric *Son of Eve* is both transcendent and awash in forbidden depths. There's a beauty to his language, and also a darkness that at times gives pause; a folksiness that belies the stirring volatility and complexity just beneath the surface. Some phrases stop you with their beauty and insight: "ghostly, erratic, yet real as a heartbeat in pause" describes a neon sign above a subterranean bar in the title story. In some ways, Litton's work calls to mind authors as unlike as Allen Ginsberg and Jim Harrison. Idiosyncratic, earthy and unearthly, gorgeous and forbidding, there is no "less is more" in this collection of stories, only a fearless, and occasionally elegiac *telling* that will stay with you long after you have closed the book."

-Patricia Traxler, *In the Skin* (Spartan Press, 2020)

SON OF EVE & OTHER TALES

Melvin Litton

Spartan Press

Spartan Press
Kansas City, MO
spartanpresskc@gmail.com

First Edition 1 3 5 7 9 10 8 6 4 2
ISBN: 978-1-950380-64-0
LCCN: 2019950063

Cover and interior images: Melvin Litton
Author photo: Brian Byers
All rights reserved. No part of this publication may be reproduced or transmitted in any form or by any means, electronic or mechanical, including photocopying, recording or by info retrieval system, without prior written permission from the author.

Acknowledgments:

I wish to thank editors Jason Ryberg and Will Leathem at Spartan Press for turning my tales of the nearly real into an actual book.

The following stories appeared in other publications: Son of Eve (*Bards & Sages "Best Indie Speculative Fiction"*); The Player (*Folilate Oak*); The Fair / Cactus Flower *(Floyd County Moonshine)*; Beneath the Cedars / Weeds / The Ever Pond *(Chiron Review)*; The Is of Things *(Pif Magazine)*; Prospects / Jack Straw Says *(Mobius Journal)*; Black Moon *(The Broadkill Review)*: and Snakes! (Spartan Press "Uneasy")

For Debra and our sons
Matt and Reuben

TABLE OF CONTENTS

Son of Eve / 1
Lion Jack / 23
The Player / 39
Moonlight Jitters / 41
In the Owl's Eye / 54
Haunted Day / 62
The Bell-Ringer / 66
Fifty Cent Tip / 67
The Fair / 91
Of Birds and Time / 96
Cactus Flower / 100
Beneath the Cedars / 105
Winter Memory / 113
The Shark's Tooth / 115
The Is of Things / 129
Prospects / 132
Seeds of Hate / 137
Jack Straw Says / 142
Weeds / 146
Bob's Café / 155
Black Moon / 162
Cold Shower / 172
Snakes! / 173
The Ever Pond / 200
Thirty Year Summer / 203

SON OF EVE AND OTHER TALES

SON OF EVE

Rained the day...evening sighs through the gutter down the river to the sea. Night darkens to a medieval sky, high-arched and domed, revealing stalactite drippings above the city's tall phallic forms. The silence monastic, damp and chilling, like the seepage of rainwaters rushing to the sewers. A brief lull and again clouds thicken and lower like a giant maw threatening to consume all to a cavernous depth as earth, wind, fire, and rain join in virulent swirl towards an unmitigated hour of finality. Lightning fissures the night in blind maniacal reach while a random bolt strikes down rousing a fetal breath from the mud...a lapsed breath of dream and terror, not quite flesh or heartbeat, faint, emergent, a lone shadow of growing intent and will.

A high slithered moon glints dimly as burly clouds shoulder across the sky while gargoyles crouched in stone spew water from roof gutters into the street below. An old city for it holds the bones of dead long forgotten; and large for it contains those unknown to any. A harbor in an upper bay held by a strip of land from a broad cold ocean throbs and sloshes with refuse, sewage, and other wastes flooding from infernos of industry and inland regions stretching through a continent of numbing toil and fervent greed. An old city, leave it nameless as the street in a quarter largely forgotten, intersected by a series of railroad tracks west, warehouses and harbor to the east.

As the storm ebbs a man steps down from a warehouse, another leaves his labor by the docks, yet another stands in wait, walks a few paces then turns, observes a cat in slant prowl, a skiff of wind.

A fog of distant time and doings rolls in beneath lamps lit here and there, many then few, as a chorus to a whisper. Whether of tallow or gas-touched flame or electrons streaming to a glowing filament trapped in glass, the light-born sediment filters down over the damp brick street trailing off through the mortared rubble. And where it leads matters little to what pends and waits. And when, whether at the end or the beginning of a decade or century, matters even less.

A shadow evolves, undulant, briefly taking edge and shape...there in the periphery... no, closer yet... then nothing. The man that paused to note the cat now turns his collar and hunches his neck to the chill behind, peers another moment then continues on. But the shadow stands with the sudden force of mud, blood, tallow, and electron to seize and suck his breath, absorb his flesh and form then drop his skin like an empty sack to the curb. A skin-sack the cat flits past...at which a skinny dog sniffs and howls.

Now it walks, the shadow, the cat following at a grainy distance, instinctual, somehow tandem to this dark figure of indeterminate guise, bearing his mark as ever. Call him Cain. He rounds a corner, down another ruined street towards a haze of bluish light humming between violet and red. Drawing near, he pauses by the arched alcove of a boarded building, the entrance strewn with glass shards and empty bottles – he grasps one up, fondly, as if beholding a lost soul. In the grottoed depths another dark figure huddles, slowly unwinds its limbs and extends a grimy hand, nails jagged, palms rough and calloused. The whole of him as if sinewed of jerked meat and dry tendon, rank of urine and filth, his clothes crusted to his skin like burlap rotted to the ground. A croaked laugh reveals two yellow teeth decaying in the spittle next his gray tongue.

"Har-ack! Haw...!" Throat cleared, finding voice, "D'I know ye?" he asks of the one standing, wormy eyes rolling up in squint of the dim figure, peering in question, as if only just risen, unearthed in rude awakening to light and air.

"Yes, old Laz. Known...but not remembered."

"Laz?"

"Lazarus you are."

"And you?"

"Cain. I have come...from the mud."

The wormy eyes widen in wonder – "But...why? How is this?"

"That I leave you to ponder...as the stem does the seed...as the bottle, to the last tincture." He stands motionless, silent, then asks, "Have you no words? You once had words, profound words to share."

The other closes his eyes and groans, "No, no...I have only profound thirst."

"If watered, would it flower?"

A sly grin spreads the withered lips, "Nay, only thirst anew."

"Then ponder this" – offering him the bottle filled in the instant.

"Ah..." Laz takes it reverently in both hands, one in support, the other at the neck, then pops the cork and tips to savor, his lips moist, supple, his eyes clear in recognition. "This I know...brew of the wine-dark sea...where gods might play and all enchanted things hatch out, pearly shells and mermaid visions..." He takes a long lusty drink then asks, "Like a pull?"

"Perhaps later."

"Later will be too late."

"Then drink less and savor more."

"No, I drink too little as is. Too much time to think. Dry day and night, through slip time and deep gone. Moon in cycle, earth in spin. Too much time to think..." He rests the bottle and casts his eyes, once more confused. "Too many multiples, you, me, this..." He looks to his hand, "Nothing here, really...nothing specific. Just ailing flesh that sustains thirst. When young and mostly sober, I read many things. There's a space opposite, under, in between...beyond what we sense and see. Yet is here...here, in the cup of my hand..." Again he shows his hapless grin and repeats, "Here, in the cup of my hand. And in that space, a tiny speck, a mere mote in the cosmic blizzard. It exists here, there, enters and exits in a blink. Yet far away to China...even to the last star...its exact twin, another wee atom, dances the same and dies. Not one, not two, all multiples of the very thing. The first thing."

"Which is?"

"Thirst, always thirst. Lust, hunger, greed...*pride*...the everlasting me. All are thirst. When I thirst, every throat in every city thirsts. And when I drink all the wine stomped in vintage goes down the ol' gullet. *Heh-heh-heh!*" He chugs fully and gasps, slurring his words. "See? All mul'ples, frien' Cain."

"No, old Laz, there's only one of you."

The other squints again in question, "Frien' Cain, I see thee...but don' recall?"

"No, of me memory has no claim..."

Leave mind, wine, and breath to ponder the is, was, and yet to be, like the many layers beneath the pavement walked and the walls and supporting structures on either side to the far corner down alley and street...the maze of all the lives lost, taken, tossed away amid the grim chiaroscuro, the charcoaled gradations of hope and despair.

This once a thriving row of gin joints, jazz, and festive girls in flapper skirts and bobbed hair, their painted lips thrilling flesh and eye. All long past and gone, quiet, hardly sang of, only remnants like posters torn and faded in the wind and rain, here and there an all-night diner or strip-joint featuring ill-formed flesh in rude parody of the high burlesque once matching dance and Eros like faint perfume and fine wine sipped and savored, not spit into or gulped down. Now the haunt of shiftless fools, laborers, and thieves, where they and others, mostly sailors, port their weary lust and fatigue. The timeless sailor, furloughed a week, hear him now, conjured by Cain stirring air and time, gathering elements to forge a task, drawing the sailor from the sea, her hypnotic cresting and fathomless depths, to swill each cup and down each bottle, ship-wrecked, marooned night after night, from bar to bar, in myth and song, his voice booming out a side-street tavern, smoke and raucous laughter lacing to the sultry air:

"There be no time gone from shore, all ticking ceased, all centuries one to the watery waste, the night 'n storm. I've hoist sails...canvas cracking like cannon shot in a black wind, seas roaring o'er the deck, all submerged then up again, I roped to the wheel, sucking ocean through me pores, spewing sea-foam till my teeth glint scales, my ears shrink to gills and my limbs form tail 'n fin to steer us back on course, breasting wave on wave, buoyant in the palm o' the Lord...!"

Buoyant like the street on which the passer walks, Cain, shadow now man, to most eyes hardly seen, merging with varying forms over strata and ravage of time. The cat, an old tom, dull yellow, trails at his heels, fur hung loose like a torn sweater, large as the woods breed, only this an alley kind with tuft ears gnarled like a fighter's, left eye milky-white, blinded by a claw, the right clear and golden, prescient as glass, keen to every footfall and where. They continue on as harbor waters lap nearby, as coal cars couple and de-latch in bullish clang and rut, in search of another to conjure, an innocent, yet filled with need. Through a weave of streets trafficked over, trod upon, here a footprint stamped alongside thousands of others who have passed, ghosts of tragedy and passion, where nearly three centuries have been woven, are frayed and rewoven, blood dried and aged, eroding like rust in the gutters. And here in a quarter once genteel, a memory ghost replays like old film fragments starkly etched and voiced...

At an upper window in amber light stands a young girl clutching a lace drape. Breathing in the night air, drawn by far sounds and mysteries, she probes the ruffles of her nightgown in yearning for the taut flesh to tear her maiden velum and burn into her thighs. But her father notices, places a subtle hand to her shoulder and speaks:

"My daughter...the night offers brief repast, snare of common fools. Leave it, for there is blood and 'the' blood...the promise of an eternal feast. Leave said darkness to the animals, for they are innocent of sin, and we are not."

There's a flush to her cheeks as she lowers her eyes in shy waver between pleasure and guilt. Her father's whiskers softly brush her flesh as he whispers to her ear:

"To bed with you, my darling. Sweet dreams..." They exchange endearing smiles, a kiss, and she passes to her bedroom followed by his gaze. The window darkens, again boarded over as the memory dissolves though the cluttered night...

Below, Cain walks on while the cat lingers by.

A tired little man trips off the curb and crosses the street where raspy jazz and coarse burlesque play to the eye and ear. With each step the little man stumbles like one continually stepping off an unexpected stair, his left leg crimped shorter than his right. Passing beneath a lamp, he staggers, his shadow leaps to the far wall, flushing a rat down the alley as a car idles past in rivulets of color fading in the dark.

Further on, from a gauzy depth, neon flashes "Dancing Girls" and "Drinks" to draw the numb flesh to tempting promise and sensation. There the yellow cat awaits the tired little man, sits in watch as if guarding a portal where by its subtle glance one gains entrance, or mute as the Sphinx, indifferent, it bids them pass. A place of no address that appears intermittently depending on the wayfarer's tread and the old tom's whim: if the cat so chooses the sidewalk opens and a stair descends to the *Under Cave,* named by a neon sign in blue glow upon a brick wall bearing coal tar and grout from a prior century. At the cat's exit it closes; when the cat reappears, it opens. Ghostly, erratic, yet real as a heartbeat in pause, whether to enter or pass. Like the little man now enlarged below the neon letters spelling "Under Cave" and "Girls Wanted" – enlarged like his shadow cast to the near wall, and no longer in limp, but striding full fleshed and lusty as his laugh as he throws back his head in jaunt down the stairs after the yellow cat to the sublevel hold, entering a whale's belly of din and pleasure. No longer a tired little clerk or scrivener, but bold and gutsy, mug in hand.

Gas-flamed wall torches throw phantasms over the low-vaulted ceiling, crudely bricked, an old sewer walled-off and filled with froth and voice of human kin. Already scent-clad flesh struts the bar top, though hardly a girl, broad and fat as the bass notes thumping from a torn tweed amp, strings plucked indifferently by a mute black man who smiles nonetheless bemused as she snaps her G-string and tosses a black-rose pastie to the boisterous crowd of bulged eyes and bared teeth, hands reaching anxious to stuff wadded bills in the privy folds of her flesh. She ignores all, fixing her want on the wiry old sax player stepping onto the bar, bent over his instrument, blaring his soul into its brassy depths, its surface pitted, scared like the player's sweaty face, but the notes play like his heart, vital and erotic, thrusting his orifice to hers as she spreads her tattooed thighs, dripping musk honey to the throaty depth in ecstatic moan to the throng that cheers her on…while beyond the garish chorus beat the drums – snare, hi-hat, and kick, their once black satin finish, dulled, chipped, and cracked like the dark smile of the hulking player seated next the bass-man, his sticks a blur of air one moment, then sharp on rim, skins dimpled by pulsing rhythms played through countless nights, his expression jaded and sullen as if he sets the tempo that marks each tide.

And now a lull in rhythm as the tall, dark-suited patron, Maître d', quiets all with raised hand and asks, "What will you have…?" – slender, ceremonious, like a priest sans collar, his white-blonde hair fluffed back on top and sides, brows thinly etched, grey-blue eyes sharply focused, teeth barely hidden by a slight constant smile, insidious, cunning, insightful. Three jewels ring his fingers: turquoise for the earth, pearl for the moon, and a gold band set with diamonds for the sun and stars. His coat black as night; his skin so pale it shines tight against his skull as if he hatched from ice. And pendant from his neck on a thin silver chain, all but imperceptible, the withered grip of a fetal hand.

Again he asks, "What will you have…more dance or feast?"

"Dance! Feast! More…MORE!" – the crowd wildly divided in delirious shout.

"Then it is for the dancer to choose…our initiate queen…" turning to regard her ample flesh posed in pout at his interruption, sensual, sweating, yet admired as he nods his approval. "Yes, and chance will decide…" he adds with a flick of his hand and a coin appears as if grasped from air, a golden coin of crude, ancient mint. "Chance, I say, and the dancer must choose by toss of this coin forged in fire from before the flood…in the age of Noname and the time of Nolove. So…by head of the beast or tail of the serpent, chance will decide as chance brings each to this moment and takes each away…whether in dance or in feast. Now then, you must choose…heads or tails."

She bites her lip, somewhat tentative, perplexed, and says, "I…I do like a party."

"Of course you do, my dear. Now you must choose…heads or tails, whether you dance…or whether we feast…"

At toss of the coin she calls *"Heads!"* anxious to continue her dance, her flesh tempting each eye and hand towards ecstatic applause, climatic, like a phallic thrust through her stranded soul. All watching, waiting, in lapse time as motion slows and the coin flips, catching light and shadow, then abruptly drops to the open palm.

Maître d' casts his eyes and grins: "It's the serpent's tail! We feast!" – echoed by their immediate chorus and roar: *"Feast! FEAST!"* Again he silences them with raised hand as if in blessing to all and announces: "Let the bidding begin!" asking, "What will you have?" He gestures to the dancer and repeats, "What will you have?"

"I'll have her ass for a hundred!"
"Bah, you skin-flint...two hundred!
SOLD!
"I want her breasts, twenty each!"
"Nay, they're worth forty...like they measure! Ah-hah-hah!"
SOLD!
"I want her tongue stuffed deep in my gullet!"
"Me too..."
"And I...the catty patch below her belly!"
"Her pussy, you mean!"
"PUSSY! PUSSY! PUSSY...!"

Amidst their clamor the woman stands shaken, puzzlement turning to horror as she is seized and dragged to a large oak table, its surface knife-hacked and stained, where she is promptly stunned by a wooden mallet, spread and slaughtered, Maître d' providing the initial slice to gain the heart while full butchery ensues, blood and viscera hosed down a grated floor drain and prized flesh passed to respective owners to season and filet, to fry, boil, or bake to their preference and taste – thus the sign flashes "Girls Wanted" above the stair. Witnessing this, the little man shrinks back in revulsion, no longer enlarged, emboldened, again limp, his abhorrence drawing the eye of Maître d' who stares at him and says, "None who enter here may exit...unless they feed. If not..." he points to the bloody table. At which gesture the little man accepts a proffered morsel and slinks to a far corner to nibble like a frightened rat.

No! It cannot be! But is, has happened, already was. And as the ritual plays we go without, up the stair with the yellow tom, joining the cat's eye as the sidewalk closes over and the neon fades, and the cat rushes on, its eye a roving lens zooming here and there between the harbor and the scene in search of the man-shadow, Cain, who stands beyond in search of the fallen one.

But where? Not here, not there...on that corner, down that alley, again no one, nothing but other shadows, formless, natural as light and shade. Yet further on a figure comes into focus, forlorn and withered as if crawled from an ash barrel, a skin-clothed skeleton of splintered staves held together by a tattered coat, her hair a snarl of grayish threads and spider strands. An old woman pushing a grocery cart, the frame bent askew, wheels wobbling over paver bricks and curb. Breathless, of human salt, the air is hard, grating, and full of pain, the overcast so gravid and heavy the streetlamp barely shows itself or her as she halts by a trash barrel reeking of garbage to paw through and glean, delicate of hand, eye, and touch. Once a beauty who danced for a price, enthralled and was bedded for furs, jewels, and more, then aged and was cast aside like the refuse she meanders through on these side-streets in shadow.

And the shadow-formed Cain finds her now and calls, "Old mother, I have come..."

She answers, "Come?" waiting in question of his approach.

"Do you not know me?"

She gazes from him to her hands shriveled like relic bones, sees a swaddled babe once held that she holds again, its rags torn in haste and soiled by afterbirth and the blood-cough that claims him...she tastes the harbor air and sees the black water at her feet as his bundled body slowly sinks away. Tears of recognition stream from her eyes down her wrinkled cheeks as his arms enfold her shoulders in draping shadow that turns her coat to black cashmere lined in purple silk next skin cleansed of filth and age, grown creamy young next the warmth of him. A radiant warmth that holds her in a glow, a yearning in her heart and blood that races to her skin and colors her hair lustrous red in a long fall of curls, and her face a vision of beauty as she raises her chin from his chest and opens enlivened green eyes to find him gone, vanished, as if she embraces only damp night air. But there her image shines in a puddle, and there reflected in a window, and she is beautiful and young, 19 or 20...Magdalena Eve, reigning queen of burlesque, from lamplight to limelight, night after night, raved for and paid for by lines of men, celebrated in song and verse.

Now where? But to the shadow that reclaimed her.

Cain waits a few paces on, the yellow cat at his heel. She leaves her cart and follows as the cat scurries off, leaping across pavement, concrete, and gravel rubble, down a brick path to descending stairs, a door sprung ajar wide enough to enter and exit. Yet the cat remains street level, guarding the entrance. Where else? Beneath the blue light that blinks "Girls Wanted" above the stair to the Under Cave.

Along the way, crouched in his niche, another sees her pass, rises like an old dog catching scent and follows, Lazarus, benumbed in ache, uncertain why he's drawn, but memory paints her there in name, place, and time ...Eve, once his to love and hold. He the singer, she the song...

She enters down through the sprung door and glances at the worn stoop where a drunken whore once fell and nearly strangled on a snagged necklace, no one caring or stopping to lend a hand as she gasped in struggle till...who was it? She never knew or much cares, remembers little of past time, younger now than then as she answers to the nod of Cain and skirts to the shadows to remain there hidden.

Beyond the shout and smoke the yellow cat slips through the cracked door to curl from leg to leg, feeding on scraps till kicked then turns in squall to vanish out the door. Meanwhile Cain quietly merges with the host of revelers. To most eyes a mere shadow, unnoticed, but to one engaged, spoken to, he offers a vague transparency, his face and figure partly focused and partly blurred as if seeing double, as if the spirit had not quite confirmed the flesh. This question posed within each he encounters, but only in the initial moment, for at a blink his form and image steadies, apparently real, natural, while the doubt lingers, nagging at the senses, something askew...yes, as if this transient one was not committed wholly to his flesh.

"And who...? Have I seen you here before?" the tall patron asks the dark form next his own, unobserved till his present glance and scrutiny.

"Where but here? When but now?" the other answers like a cat in wait.

Hearing this, the patron's thoughts drift uncertain in the curl of smoke.

"Once more I ask, who are you?"

"I am but seldom. Better to ask who I am not. Not you, nor her, nor she that was. And when I am, another soon is not."

To this the tall patron creases his eyes, a glint of premonition.

"Then perhaps I should introduce myself," his eyes widen in imperious gaze. "I am Maître d'… d'Viande… d'Charnel… Dieu, Dios, death, desire…here I am God and all devolves from me."

"*Nullus Deus*," the dark one replies. "I see a deuced pair, a dicey play of chance, nothing more…" He glances to a black fop with ringlet hair poised back of the patron. "Who is snake eyes?" At this the black shifts slightly, clad in a leather suit of emerald green worn like a snake skin on his lithe limb and frame, sleek, supple, alert as a snake set to strike, as if a lizard tail twitches back of his legs.

"This is Miguel, my dark angel, my right hand…" Maître d' pauses in thought. "So, in our game of chance…what do you wager?"

"Each numbered day."

"But it is night."

"An eternal night for many," the dark one vouches and draws a silver flask.

"I see you bring your own. What…and why is that?"

"*Sangre del Sol*…because you serve sow's blood." At this the patron blanches as though accused. "The foulness is on your breath, in the air. I know without seeing…by the smell. But this," raising the flask, "is distilled of the sun. Sangre del Sol…blood of the blood, pure and flavored to please any tongue. Let you see and hear what the ocean holds, what time may tell. Life to some…" he tips it and drinks, "and poison to others. Would you sip?"

Maître d' smiles thinly and says, "Keep your Gypsy brew, we prefer our own."

"Here now, I'm not too proud for a nip!" A giant sailor strides forth and grabs the flask for a long draught then grins amazed it's still full.

"Go ahead, take another and pass it on. Have no fear," speaking to all, "sip or quaff. You cannot empty this flask. Call it mystery, magic, miracle…call it what you will. Sip and feel the floor begin to surge, the ceiling open to the sky, the stars, to your dreams. You have never seen beauty, never seen her dance. Soon you will…"

Another score partake in cheer and jostle, passing the flask through the crowd until it returns to the giver's hand, each tongue in savor, each eye in gleam, seeing in the dark man a familiar specific to themselves – a lost friend, a brother, a cousin, a pal.

Licking his lips, old Laz sidles forth and asks, "May I too sip?"

"Earlier you had a bottle. Was it not good?"

"Yea, good, but not so fine as from a silver flash?"

"Sip then, have your fill…"

Laz tips it delicately to his lips for a modest taste then smiles, "Ah, this is the true blood. Now I remember why I was and who I am. Once a man who longed to touch the sky and walk within the clouds."

"You old fool," mocks Maître d', "I warned you never step foot in here. Touch the sky. Hah! Return to your doorway, to your slump and filth."

"That is my watchtower…and I…the sentinel. I see what comes…and wait to see you gone!" Old Laz stands defiant and takes another sip. "My friend bids me drink…I drink. And foolish, yea…are most who mistake the skyline for the sky. These towers of rubble, like craven claws, scar the heavens. But where I stand…no, not down here, but upside, mindful where my feet touch the earth, there begins the sky. And come morning, when the fog rolls in from the bay, I walk on clouds."

"Enough! Crawl back to your cubbyhole and cloud your mind. Stop filching drinks and crowding our guest with droning lies."

"Guest? Then old Laz is my guest as well. Let him descend and stay."

Maître d' purses his lips and nods, "Very well, if his stay is brief…have the old monkey for your medicine show. But I will have your name."

"Then call me Cain."

"Cain? Who killed his brother?"

"I have many brothers, all deep gone, of no matter or name."

"But what of your brother, Abel?"

"Conceived and lost…you should know…you ate him," noting the necklaced hand. "And in your feast and infernal barter…your daughter clasped her first-born and fled."

"But it…died…and you? How this? Who sent you?"

"Chance…and I…a brief presence of deep knowing. But of names, better you ask of hers…" He turns to the near shadows and calls her forth, "Magdalena Eve…lover, mother, daughter to us all…"

She moves from the shadows into the light like a shadow shedding her coat, her flesh a glow of wonder as she ascends the steps from floor to bar with graceful ease, her gaze keen and unnerving as she looks to and through each eye. Utterly naked, even her dainty feet as she arches to her toe in twirl then leans in bow, an arabesque. They share one breath of awe in wait. Then the music begins, music transformed as are the players, each a bare-chested, cloven-hoofed beast – feral Pan, Faun, and Satyr of the dark woods and bacchanal – one with flute, one a harp, and the last, his head wreathed in lion's mane, beats a thigh bone on a skin drum to frenzied melodies of raptor cries and roiling brooks, wild and dissonant yet hypnotically pure as her nymph dance, erotic, enticing, her hair flowing past her shoulders as she leaps across the bar, fawn-like, to rhythms old and fresh as day…flawless, captivating, drawing each breath to her. To some she is a sacred vision to which to kneel and pray; to more a lover to have and hold; to others the virgin mother who bore them innocent, bathed, caressed, and supped them; or a sister or daughter to protect. A matchless beauty undreamt of, a spirit possessed of flesh and motion, her eyes a mix of jade set in pearl and sparkle of morning dew; her skin a perfect contour, smooth as marble, soft as a lamb; her lips parted, moist as tangerines, sweetly voicing each man's name, Madonna hands fanning the air, divining their want, her nose and ears small and precious as a child's, her breasts erect and budding with the nectar and tension of tulips in bloom. Her legs and arms like ivory, slender, delicately fluid in rhythmic writhe, firing the loins of her admirers. Slave women also ache and shudder, but reaching cannot touch and so shriek in desire, each hand checked by a stern will short of her flesh.

Men in frustration begin to pant and howl, stomping the floor in sync to the skin drum. Yet only one does she lean to and touch, cupping old Laz's face with soft hand and breath. And in one breath he is again the handsome young poet she so adored, who sang her songs of beauty and truth when their love was whole and full of mystery. And what was his song? That the purest beauty is frail and transient as a snowflake, a singular creation destroyed at a touch...the warmth a finger may alter, subtleties present when the golden pollen strikes the sonnet chord in the pistol of a flower, or taps the tense sinew of veined marble...all beauty the spawn of a precisely balanced conception when placed in man's reach is inevitably reduced, made ugly in give and take, the exchange of goods and money. His disdain for such led to cynical drink, to sloth and failure, to visions of the damned, his final song that left her without child or hope. But not now, now he holds his first song, his initial song when their love was fresh...a mystery still.

And he sings her name, "*Magdalena Eve...*" and sends his breath as she dances on, each hand in reach for her flesh, her beauty, but none can touch except by her will. And again she chooses, selects the giant sailor, first to sip from the flask, the stalwart seaman who roves every port – tall, robust, with tattoos of anchor, mermaid, and heart branding his arms. He wears a gray sea-sweater of Irish wool, a dark watch-cap, red curls bursting forth, the same on his bristly brow and whiskered chin. Eyes pale blue, his jowls ruddy with ready laugh bellowing in jest and howl till night waxes to dawn then back again for hair o' the dog and further *HOWL!* Insatiate, untiring, never done till dumped stone cold sober into the sea. Call him Jonah as her lips form his name, as her hands beckon to and grasp his palms and she leaps seated on his right shoulder, her legs sedately crossed, one arm around his neck, the other held high like a circus girl on a grand tall horse.

Now they cheer instead of curse, cheer her triumph and Jonah's as well, the most favored in their midst. All except for two, Maître d' and his squire Miguel who seethes in jealous craze and envy. But the master merely stares, cloaks his hate, an ancient grudge against this daughter groomed and urged to share her fruit, bid men eat...then escaped and gave herself to this foul poet, this fool who thinks he knows a thing! Faithless, willful wench, he should seize her throat and drag her to the chopping block, piece her out to all. Should and would, but can't, his hand too held in check. Just how, he cannot say. By who? This dark one, this no-name Cain who stands looking on as the giant Jonah commands the stage and hoists the beauty.

"Come now, Lass, lock yer heels to me chest...rise up 'n rule the waves as I grip yer arms like a boom what holds the sail. Aye, now lean forth, let all admire yer feathery limbs and blessed ass, deep curving spine, yer nippled breasts, our prowl above the sea, and I yer mast, hull, keel 'n stern..." He hurls her high above the mass of all elbowing round. "*Back ya sotted fools!*" he shouts. "Make way ya land-lubbin' clods! She's me honored queen, I her captain coursing wind 'n sea! *Back, I say...!*"

They give way in a chorus of lusty cheers, a surge of flesh and music till floor and walls seem to billow and sway, making a path before the rare beauty and her champion. Jonah beams, his broad face red from drink and laughter as he tacks and turns hither and yon, presenting her matchless form to their senses like cresting waves in spew and want. Wanting more the more they see. Maître d' most of all, haunted, plagued by want. Ache and knowing steels his deep flesh, dripping semen to his thighs while his eyes lose their human glint and shrink into the sockets, a vacant skull stare of vengeance, lust and hate. She who he'd tutored in all exquisite pleasure only to forswear her promise and refuse the blood that would make her his, spat into his face and rushed toward the sun that withers all and leaves them dust. All for that fool and now this giant striding clown. His skin tightens on his skull, showing more and more his teeth as he hisses to his man Miguel, "Snatch her back when you see a chance...seize her."

"I will if I have her flesh to gnaw," the demon grins, his hunger hot and sharp-edged as his knife, his lizard tail in active twitch back of his thighs while urinous stench oozes through his viscid skin, his eyes and lips drawn to keen reptilian focus as he attends his lord's reply.

"She's yours...but first her heart is mine. Understand?"

The black lizard tongue flicks in rapt delight, waiting his moment as her flesh and form beckons to his sleek hunger, thirst, desire...for this he crawled from beneath a rock and feigns himself a man.

Presently Lazarus hails the goodly giant and Jonah gives a jaunty "Heave ho!" and eases her to the floor then stands in anchor before the poet's praise:

"You are Odysseus, slayer of the Cyclops, staunch sailor of the far blown sea, bearing our fair Penelope. You the doer, I singer of the song..." With his words the music softens and slows, muted like the rough voices hushed to solemn whisper. "And she is a siren, our Calypso, now our Helen who we fall before like fool Paris drawn to her light. But no, she is Beatrice, and I Dante...my love, my faith. Were she Magdalene, I would suffer crucifixion to hold her but once and shield her from the stones..."

"Then I am Judas!" the demon interjects, shrill and biting, his lizard tail erect in full whip – "And this knife will be my kiss!"

Jonah shouts "NO!" and shoves him back.

The demon recoils, containing his urge, feinting left then right in breathy snarl, "Hand her to me...! Or I will bleed you out like a wineskin!"

"NO! Not to you, *never*..."

Yet before his breath closes on his words, the demon strikes, quick as light to shadow, driving his knife into the great chest, sheathing the darted blade in the heart, deeply quilled then plucked, blood inking through as Jonah lurches back before three successive thrusts stitching his belly, blood reddens his gray sweater, filling his cupped hands, his eyes wide to the fading light as he sinks slowly to the floor, there capsized, staring up, hands flapping briefly like a foresail in a breeze, then folding to cease all motion. Music and voices cease as well while gas flames flare and hiss and all gaze down on the mound of man so brusque, buoyant and alive, now stilled.

The fair one kneels by and lays her hand to the dauntless brow.

In the silence colors dim, the flesh pales while blood drips from the killing blade. The lizard man extends a hand in strangely formal behest and says, "Come now...*a moi, ma Charnelle.* I prepare a table and serve you neat..." his lidless eyes intent and deadly, his voice smooth and certain as fate.

"*Damn you fiend!* Try the blade on me!" Lazarus now stands before the precious one in challenge. "Can you stab a drunken storm, slay the raging sea...?" To which the fiend returns a scaly laugh with flicking tongue and coils again to strike.

But quicker still is the intercepting hand as Cain leaps forth, the blade piercing his left palm which though wounded closes around the murderous claw and crushes bone to mush. Fiercer yet his right hand wraps the ringlet hair and drags the demon through the parting crowd to the oaken slab. Their senses stir, smelling blood and meat. In slither and struggle the demon sheds his man mask, his leather suit and flesh now one black-green skin mottled yellow as his slit eyes flash side to side, held to the butcher block by many hands eager for the blood-spill as Cain slices the demon's throat to drain him to the last drop. Then they roll the slack carcass to reveal the three-foot tail, thick as a fat snake, tapering to a point and twitching still. But twitches no more as Cain severs it at the spine then whips the tail and drives them back.

"Leave him be! His flesh is poison, foul, not fit for beasts of the air or field. Now you three..." he points to a trio of red-eyed sots waiting like vultures keen for meat, "lift the grated drain and drop him to the sewer. There...done with and gone," he nods as they swiftly tend the deed. "But this!" holding up the tail, "this meat is choice. Slice it thin and deep fry in grease!" He tosses it to the three who cast the demon out. And the crowd, briefly stunned, now cheer and follow as the tail is flopped to the slicing board. Even the tired little man shuffles forth, all elbowing round in drool and howl, awaiting a tendered morsel.

Maître d' stands apart, at a loss amidst the drama that plays beyond his beck and call, remaining mute, though tempted, his mouth watering in savor as Cain proffers the delectable tip dipped in blood, rolled between thumb and finger as if considering whether to give or not, then closer and closer to the tensed mouth till the lips part and snap it from his hand...in rasp and bite chew it down. Lidded eyes held closed a moment...then open, calmly assured and sated. Once more *Maître de soi*, he sneers at the trifle shared:

"Call this a feast? It is but a taste, *un apéritif*..."

"A taste? Yes, but very special. You should know, flesh of thy flesh. A flesh corrupt as its host. Add foul to foul...and see it act on each as they falter and fall..." So saying, like tendrils of smoke settling to the floor the whole of those within begin to lose shape, color, and substance...soon mere shadows and stains on chair, stool, and floor as if they never were but stain and shadow. "But you...are immune. This flesh is thine, taken in it cannot kill or destroy what it shares...like snake to tail. But self-eating-self slows and dulls the will. Your will. As do I...and they..." he looks to Lazarus wrapping Eve in her coat, and to the dead sailor at their feet. Then he points to Pan, Faun, and Satyr – "And these as well, for they share music and take no meat and so sustained will play on until the first and last cause says enough."

"Let them pipe and drum. I'll have my feast...I'll have HER!"

"No, she is clothed, safe from your eye, hand, and teeth."

"Clothed? Covered? Still I smell her warm succulent flesh next the silk. Corn maiden of reddish tassel, ripe kernels neatly sheathed. And wrapped can be unwrapped!" he scoffs, forming his hands like claws.

"Mere words...chew on them and swallow. Watch now and see..."

Cain glances to the maned Satyr, "Beat you a heart song..."

To Pan he says, "Pipe the living breath..."

And to Faun, "Pluck the strings that stir the flesh..."

He kneels to the fallen sailor in silent pause then moves his hand over the body, leaving a shadow in its wake like a dark blanket enfolding all. Then slowly to play of drum, harp, and flute the blanket ravels and stirs as wool and blood knit and weave to a tawny-furred mass from which a large Mastiff heaves up and stands as if in one breath made. The great beast gently takes Eve's hand in his black-maw intent to lead her out.

Astonished but not yet done, Maître d' lashes out: "You wench, faithless bitch, Jezebel!" he cries. "Rip her arm, dog! Rip her to pieces, I command you! Leave not skull, hand, or foot!"

"Choke on your spittle, fool, you command nothing. Your words are like water cupped in sand..." Then to Lazarus Cain says, "Rise now, you and Jonah-dog, and take her up the stair."

"NO! None go but by my say. I seal the door!"

"Seal your lips. We come and go by the cat, by his say..." The cat sits staring in, subtle, inscrutable, stern warrant to the words.

"No, I am Maître d'...I hold the golden coin and only by chance can you go."

Cain regards the coin held before him and says, "So it is, and you...as headwater in this horrid crucible...may choose. But only if the coin is let fall to the floor once leaving your hand."

"Agreed!" His lucent eyes gleam in triumph as he flips the coin and calls, "*Heads!*" The coin arches briefly then slows at apex and drops to the floor in brief wobble to lie flat.

"It is tails...and the tail of the cat will lead us out."

"Then I will follow and stalk her till she is mine!"

"You forget the sun...it denies, destroys...turns flesh to dust."

"Bah! I have faced the sun...barely a blister. See? I am, have been...always!"

"So you claim. Then as you will...rise and follow."

"But this has played before ..." his protest weakens, giving way to doubt. "Lazarus has played...she has played. And you...your fate and flesh done with and finished."

"No, between you and I...and them, there is only one act and play, here and now. And by my coming it plays on..." At the door he raises his arm to the mythic trio and shouts: "Play on!" Then he hatches flame in hand and casts it to the walls and ceiling, fire taking root in the torch-lit shadows and ghastly stains, silhouettes dancing up amidst the frenzied howl and music, the savage swarm fed by Pan, Faun, and Satyr.

At the cat's yowl Lazarus and Eve ascend the stair led by Jonah-dog. They reach street level in a shaft of light as Cain emerges, followed by Maître d' who proclaims:

"See? I am! I face the sun and still I lust and hunger!"

So he stands, white flesh in shimmer, black heart wrapped in wormy hide.

"As you say," Cain answers, "you may defy the sun, but not

the sun-tipped blade..." Stabbing low and deep, he rips the fiend from bowel to sternum, jerks a coiled length and cuts it loose. Then grabs the vile throat and with flexed knee shoves the screaming husk back into the flames. In that dark descent the shaft seals over, the molecular dust rising, coalescing, leaving the prior surface of scaly concrete where cigarette butts and assorted litter float in oily pools of a late night rain. Then he grips the coiled bowel like a bloody rope and loops it from meter to post as if to mark a crime and warn the unwary – the whole left hanging, glistening in the morning light, soon to shrivel and dry like an evil worm caught in the sun.

    Finished, Cain looks to Lazarus and Eve and Jonah-dog, and to their questioning gaze says, "He is gone and will not return till your time is done. But by cycle of sun-moon-star and chance he will recur...as always, hunger emerging from the dust."
    "Where do you go?" they ask.
    "Back to the dark water, the deep gone and never was..."
    To this they simply stare in wait.
    "Old mother," he says, and speaking he sees her age – with each wrinkle her face winces and cruelly contorts, her legs lace with varicose veins fingering up her shins like old tree roots naked above the soil, her flesh darkens and dries like flacking bark, her glorious red hair dulls to tangled gray, her fine coat again hangs in tattered rags, still the faithful dog holds to her withered hand – "Go now, old mother," Cain points to her cart across the way. "And take this..." he gives her the tiny fetal hand snatched from Maître d' in fall, now held weightless in her palm, clinging like a cicada shell. "Keep it till your atoms mix with the mud and the far void. Now go," he urges, "Jonah-dog will lead..."
    She fumbles the relic into her breast pocket, numb, perhaps unknowing, her eyes nearly blind from all they've seen then follows as bid, crossing the street to reclaim her cart and there fend a garbage meal for herself and her guardian beast.
    Cain staggers briefly, blood still dripping from his hand, weakened by his task, by sun and time, by the will to take shape and act. He straightens and looks to Lazarus who has aged as

did Eve, his flesh shrunken, jaws toothless, his clothes filthy and torn.

"Go back to your doorway, old Laz. From time to time Jonah-dog will pass and lick your sores. Go now to your remaining days and final words..."

Lazarus squints his rheumy eyes at the blurry form speaking and can't quite name him or say why he talks of a dog, but does as he's told, returns to his doorway, his mind blurred as well, holds no memory of the night, only a vague notion that it was and is no more...whether dream or delirium, vanished and not recalled.

Crouched in his cave, cross-legged, he licks his whiskered jowls and rocks back with a gaping yawp, "Ah-hah! See!" he points to breaking clouds painted by the rising sun. "They've come. The four foretold. Not horsemen, nay...but the bear, owl, fox, and lizard. The bear rides a burrow, the owl clutches a lamb, the fox reins a pig. And back of all on hind legs and tail the great lizard stands...eating man. Hah! See it not...?"

"You see too much, old Laz."

"No, I drink too little," the crouched one laughs.

"Then swill on this..." Cain rolls a bottle clattering to his feet.

Lazarus takes it up to his eye a moment then scornfully tips it down.

"This holds no drink. Empty!"

"Breathe through the neck and it will fill. Drink and it will not empty."

Lazarus puffs his cheeks and blows a low whistle and the bottle fills with amber light, sun-distilled. He takes a mighty pull and holds it to his eye and sees it full.

"Ah!" he grins, "thank ye. This is good. But...?" he squints in wonder. "How is it...I know you? Yea...I know you are...and are not. And I...who am I? And why this day...you and me...?" He rolls his gauzy eyes at the dim figure drifting on, the yellow cat following at the heel as they round the far corner, gone, all else mere shadow along with memories he can't recall, of no form or substance...nor even her who danced upon the bar, of who he sang...all lost, forlorn and haggard, her beauty lapsed into a sad ugly presence clothed in rags barely distinguishable from her flesh as she and Jonah-dog pass by without a glance or word.

    Moving beyond around the corner, the yellow cat sees all, its lone eye inches above the pavement as the heels lift and fall, each tread marking a cursed fate unredeemed, never settled. The cat pauses in watch as the figure turns down a shaded alley, the sun at low azimuth, blocked by high-walled buildings. The figure stops by the skin sack sucked empty in the night, left sodden with other refuse along the curb. Now the figure quivers in flux like an image aflame or swirling leaves, losing form and density, dissolving into mist, while below the skin sack swells, taking sudden shape and person.
    The man slowly rolls to an elbow, draws a quick breath into his empty lungs and gasps, "What the...?" blinking his eyes at self and surroundings in wonder how he's slept the night in an alley, having labored the day before and walking home, stumbled. His left hand pierced through, still bleeding...like a freak stigmata. Damn! He crosses himself and hasn't done so in years, not since he was a boy...now awake to another day in bone-ache and hunger, yet sober, mind clear and certain, but no, not certain of his hand or what part he's played...the whole night lost.
    He watches a yellow cat passing by, and curious, he rises to his feet and follows.
    The alley leads to the harbor, a boardwalk peer, then to black water and the ebbing tide. Across the slough mud the morning fog steams smoky gray among stranded bottles and rubber tires. And the cat gazes on as if it sees something crawling through the muck and shallows, sprawled face down...half in, half out. But no, merely flotsam of river and bay, trash and weeds left strung like guts by the ebbing tide. Only that and the spew and slosh of the current like the hunger gnawing awake in his belly.

LION JACK (from *Banks of the River*)

It was hot, a biblical heat, like forty days in the desert. Hot enough to make a saint roll his eyes heavenward in supplication to the Lord for the deliverance of a cool autumn breeze. But it was mid-July and Jack Marshal was no saint. They'd thrown him in jail for a 48 hour cooling-off period and *Christ!* He had to laugh at the thought.

"Dammit all," he grumbled, trying to roll a cigarette with sweat-damp fingers only to tear the paper and lose the fixings to the floor. After wiping his hands on his shirt, he crimped another paper, added tobacco from the red tin can, and this time successfully completed the task. He wet its length with his tongue, placed the tapered end to his lips then struck a blue-tip match against the rough wooden frame of the lone cell window set about chest high in the wall. The sulfurous flame left a burnt streak as flecks of paint fell to the warped sill encrusted with layers of dust, cobwebs, and dead flies. A shortened broom handle wedged in the corner propped up the lower pane. With the first puff he tossed the match and leaned against the jamb. The smoke coiled lazily through the opening past the iron bars mortised into the outer sill and lintel.

The old three-story jail, built out of native limestone in 1903 as proclaimed on the arch above the main door, occupied a corner lot several blocks up from the town square. Its time-lashed walls were dappled by the meager shade of two malformed elms and the towering spire of a lone ragged cedar; the trees stood lank, indifferent, limbs and leaves motionless in the mid-summer heat. A sparse no-man's-land of a lawn, dormant brown from lack of rain, worn down by children's play, extended to the street. Lodger and local alike had long addressed the dilapidated structure as "The County Home."

But to the one now caged it was *a Goddamn stink-hole!* Yet strangely enough the smoke had a cooling effect, its mild narcotic soothing him as he gazed out and caught the colors of the day, the dry withered hues fading into dust. The air was as still outside as in, but standing there he could at least partly escape the urinous stench that hung like a fever in the fan-less cell and rose particularly strong from the stained tick mattress that only served to torture sleep.

The bedding was changed weekly and the cells swept out, clearing away discarded cigarettes, matches, playing cards, and newspapers, yet it could never be said the place was truly cleaned. No one ever witnessed a floor being mopped, a wall washed down, or a stool or urinal disinfected. But the jail served mostly as a holding pen for local winos, and they lodged no complaint. The food passed regularly through the sliding metal opening set in the wall between the kitchen and the area where the prisoners fed, fried spam, scrambled eggs, beans, cornbread, and black coffee, tea, or cool-aid morning, noon, and night, served up with frank good humor by the broad plump wife of the wiry under-sheriff amidst the general cacophony of their boisterous young family. Kids were forever poking their laughing faces through the food door and calling out to one prisoner or another in the familiar "Hey Jonesy!" "Crazy Bill!" or "Uncle Alf!" And aside from the occasional antisocial miscreant, most viewed their incarceration as an unplanned layover in the home of a caring family, wholesome and festive, spent in the confines of a quaint, albeit filthy, rural county jail.

However, the large man now standing at his cell window the kids all respectfully addressed as "Mr. Marshal." He was not a regular, in fact had never spent a night in jail. But law of fate-logic-and common sense would dictate that he who'd long ago gained the moniker "Lion Jack" should one day be caged. Whose exploits, formed of vague rumor and vivid fact, all confirmed that here was one born to test the bounds and perimeters of the human soul at play. A prowling intensity that suggested to all that there was yet a great deal of animal left in man. His reputation in his hometown and through realms beyond was legendary, and no child—*instinctively*—would use the familiar with Jack Marshal without his say-so. Not Lion Jack, his voice a low melodic growl; not Jack of powerful suppleness, the once great athlete still lithe in spite of his growing girth; not he whose human form never quite contained the aura of his impulse.

His face matched his habitual expression – *Dammit all!* – massive, hard-bitten, weathered and sardonic, but which, when amused, fed a lie to this menacing veneer with a wink and a smile that any woman or child who dared notice read as genuine, and those laughing black eyes that sang to their deepest longing and thirst. But gentleness he saved for quiet appropriate moments and pounded through most doors as if it were his duty to test the strength of the hinges, the station of the frames, the resolve of creation. If gravity had loosed its hold one instant he would have bounded through the sky and brought the moon back to earth just for a laugh. Or so it seemed to the boys who watched him cuss, drink and smoke, race his car, and heard rumors of him chasing after women and wanted to grow up and be just like him. Jack Marshal, his own man.

These were the boys he coached in little league each summer. And Jack's boys played ball for keeps, down 'n dirty, hardball certain. They fielded hungry, like young coyotes running a rabbit. They hit like swordsmen, slashing the leather from the ball. Others stole a base, Jack's boys tore 'em from their moorings – ate up home plate like a platter of fried chicken. At the grand watermelon feed following the championship game, it was seeds 'n all. You betcha, a can-do scruffy bunch molded by the master.

Even the white-haired priest looked forward to manning the confessional on the rare occasion when Jack, goaded by his wife's prodding and a tinge of conscience, decided to unload. Therein the priest witnessed the most intriguing revelations in his 50 years of wearing the cloth. Jack simply possessed too much vitality, too great a thirst to be satisfied by any one woman, song, meal, feast, what-have-you that provided other men's satiation. In the proverbial phrase he was "Full of it!" Possessed of a joyous hunger to grasp each pleasure offered and take it in. Full of it – the devil. He simply loved too deeply for faith to cure, loved too deeply the marrow of life. Faithfulness did not become him, it would not fit, like a clean white shirt would rumple and soil within minutes of his dressing. He was the goat-god's own emissary to the times, the beast that is set in us. Arrest his passion? Throw up your hands. He danced the hunt and left his lion print at dawn to frighten the timid. The hints of gray in his black unruly hair only served to incite his vigor and further weaken a woman's resolve.

"Y-yes," Father Horabet stammered, his voice betraying heightened interest as Jack Marshal, ever reluctant to begin the

Father/Son charade for he had been fatherless from an early age and viewed the exchange as bad form if not a sacrilege, cleared his throat in low growl and leaned toward the veiled confessional.

"Bless me, Father...I have sinned. And it's been awhile since..."

"Speak up, my son. T-tell me your sin," the priest urged like darkness longing for light, breathing in the rich whiskey scent.

Shifting uncomfortably in his chair, Jack glanced back over the congregation to insure that the jackals and gossips were keeping a proper distance. Such affirmed, he warmed to his tale.

"My trouble concerns a mother and daughter. You see, I knew the daughter, let's say...in the biblical sense. Now the girl, actually young lady, Father, is of legal age. Out of school, all of eighteen, I swear. An innocent I had the honor in helping become a woman. A duty, I believe" – his eyes riveted on the listening shadow – "once performed by the priests of old." The listener squirmed as if accused, awkward in the brief silence before Jack took pity and continued.

"Of course the mother was quick to note the change, that womanly swagger..."

And as quickly she guessed the hand in her daughter's initiation. Which was none too difficult as Jack had been working nearby laying up a stone wall. The young lady often stopped to chat, and one thing led to another. She worked at the local bakery, had just graduated and was hoping to attend business school in Salina, the regional hub sixty miles due south, come fall. She shared her plans, her longing to escape the small town, her mother. Jack listened, cordial, attentive, treated her like an equal.

"You 'n me, we're a bit different," he observed, "antsy...not cut out for the slow go." He set another stone in place, tapped it with his trowel, caught her eye. She smiled, swaying expectantly. Her flesh carried the sweet scent of flour, cream, and fresh dough. What a lamb. "Life is right here, Macie," he said, "right here and right now. Not down yonder somewhere, someday, waiting. You gotta reach out and take it."

Pluck it like an apple he might have added. Instead, he suggested they meet, to which she was willing. So that evening, after sundown, Jack picked her up a couple blocks from her home and drove west out of town, pulled into a freshly cut wheat field and parked. He spread a blanket on a bed of straw, the stars looking on like ripened grain suspended in a sea of black, air perfumed by the harvest wind wafting in the warm June night. He took her gently considering her virgin need and his quickened desire, put his flesh to hers in a most practiced, certain manner. *Right here...right now.* And the lion lay down with the lamb.

Though he related little of this, the confession focused mainly on the consequence.

"Anyhow, couple days later she cornered the girl, got her to fess up. Then sent word demanding a parley...next day...her house. All happened last week. I obliged. When I got there she was in one helluva temper. You know women, Father, way beyond reason. Called me this, called me that. I tried to stay calm, be polite...adult to adult. Soon she was throwing punches. I took some, ducked a few, then caught her wrists. Held 'em tight. That's when it happened..."

"What?" The priest edged closer. "What happened?"

"Like night 'n day, her black rage gave way to pure heat. I'd dated her a time or two back in high school and what I wanted then...well, she gave. Fact is, demanded I take. Shucked her dress and commenced instructing *me* in matters concerning man and woman that I'd never quite guessed. And I've seen something of this world, Father, but swear I never had a woman present herself like a—" Jack caught himself before making an off-color remark, again shocked to silence by the woman's frank display while no doubt savoring the memory as he had the act.

"Like a...what, my son?" Father Horabet wet his lips, his tongue thickened.

"Forgive me, Father," Jack said in sly deference, "but I'm afraid that's too ripe to mention here. It's just a mite messy is all...you know, a mother and daughter. Thought I best get it off my chest."

"I see. Certainly..." The priest's diminished tone betrayed his disappointment, his flesh numb beyond redemption, cast down, dreadfully fallen. The world receded so rapidly these days. He recalled his lone lapse from his vow like it had been an epiphany. She a widow, he of middle years and failing faith. They had comforted one another for a time. Had it really happened? All so brief and long ago. Or was it merely a dream? He pursed his lips and sighed. "And the woman's name?" he asked absently.

"Name? Why..." Jack growled in slow surprise, "she's a good wife and mother. I can't name her."

"Do not compound your sin by lying in confession!"

"But Father, I don't lie. I just don't name her. After all, if I coughed up every speck of dirt there wouldn't be time enough this day to get through half my tale. Would that be fair to the others waiting to unload? God knows all anyway. Right, Father?"

"Perhaps so...if you stay with the truth, my son."

And the truth was what made Jack so charming. Though highly selective, he generally told the truth. He engaged each man on that point of truth that blood and instinct rush forth to hold. In young boys he unleashed the demonic will needed to seize the glory they dreamed. And every woman he ever coaxed and fondled to their mutual pleasure possessed a spot of beauty he could truly praise—the turn of her ankle, her slender hands, the deep curve of her lower back, not to mention his stallion urge for the musk-scented pelt shared by all.

"That's about it, Father...the gist of my sin." Jack rubbed his powerful hand over his jaw, looking thoughtful. "As you know, the flesh is weak. And my weakness for the flesh is greater than most. But this time, well, I gotta admit...it's six one 'n half a dozen the other. You see," he said, leaning closer in play of confidence, "I'm strongly tempted by both...mother and daughter."

With this last statement the old priest's eyes glazed in utter confusion, his mind blurred searching for a glint of clarity amidst the oddly shaded situation – a debauch so bountiful and bold. To firm up his faith and cast out the demons of doubt and dormant lust he shook his head with devout severity, swiftly calculated and declared:

"For penance, p-pray the rosary for one week."

"Pray the…" – Jack winced like the very beads had caught in his throat at the thought of losing a week's labor bawling like a sick calf over spilt milk. "Come Father, pray the…have mercy. I'm a hard working mason, a stone cutter. I've got a family to feed, the Church to tithe. I can't be losing a day's work, let alone a week. How 'bout five…five Hail Marys, Father? Now I don't aim to be bargaining with the good Lord for my soul, but I could use the Holy Mother's aid in this matter. And seems to me five is a righteous number. Natural, God-given, rooted in a man like the fingers of his hand. Complete like a fist. The firm fist of repentance! A number God would favor, don't ya think, Father? Five Hail Marys I swear I'll perform. There!" – Jack struck his right fist to his left palm as he rose to take his exit – "I feel better already. Like lava soap to cleanse the soul," he beamed. "Thank you, Father."

So Father Horabet remained silent and swallowed his protest, grateful the sinner would commit to something, had known the prodigal since he was a youth and secretly admired his wayward ways. A brief wan smile graced his lips as he allowed himself a moment's pride. Shepherd even of this black sheep.

Finished with the cigarette, Jack remained standing at the cell window, his mood reflective but in no way repentant as he deftly worked a nude-Venus quarter through the fingers of his right hand. He caught the coin between his thumb and forefinger and briefly examined the brazen image: a woman's head thrown back exposing the subtle line of her neck and shapely breasts; turning the coin revealed her backside in full relief, long legs supporting a fine shaped ass. With a wry smile he snatched up the prize he'd won in last night's game.

Jack usually took no pleasure in poker, too sedentary for a sportsman, none of the rush to action he felt while loading for the hunt, uncorking a bottle, or warming up a woman. Good hand or bad, the big numbers and face cards reminded him of the drear tedium of grade school – *"Sit still…wait your turn…don't speak"* – the jack overruled by the queen, the king, and the omnipotent Ace. But locked up on a Saturday night, it was either climb the walls or play cards. So faced with the choice of remaining in his cell or joining the others out in the dining area for gossip and jailhouse poker, he accepted, albeit grudgingly.

In the smoky haze beneath the unsheathed bulb, the garrulous pack of old fools made room at the table, cut the deck and dealt him in. And Jack, disdainful of odds and headlong as ever, forced them to fold or call on every hand. The archseducer could easily bluff a bunch of winos who collectively regarded him as god of feast, passion, debauch, and chance, in fact counted it lucky to occupy space proximate to said deity, eager even to lose for losing in a sense was a form of offering, a sacrifice, a guarantor of future favor, because all knew that the Lion was lucky, and those gathered around that table longed for his luck to flow to them like cream to a kitten. And though he lost a time or two, he mostly won, confirming their faith. Won a pile of matchsticks later redeemed for tobacco, pocket change, and the nude-Venus quarter – symbol of that which he was seldom without on a Saturday night. A woman.

Jack scraped his stubble growth with the edge of the coin. Now mid-Sunday afternoon and his once festering rage, lanced by slow-passing time, had nearly drained. Somehow, in spite of his lion-will, his temper cooled, even in this sweltering stink-hole. Another few hours and he'd be free, perhaps to finish the one deed his whole being still begged to perform. But the moment had passed and he felt it gone forever, the act that would have confirmed for him that justice could be had, seized, taken like a woman, that man was no mere leaf buffeted by the wind, but a force in his own right. He gripped the bars with a cold certainty that the ache for vengeance would never leave him. If only he'd pulled the trigger.

He had no inkling of the events to come that previous Friday as he laid up the capstone on a retaining wall he was building for Mr. Chesline, a retired farmer recently moved to town. Jack, anxious to be done and have his money – for the old man was fussy, humorless, impossible to please – had worked through lunch, while Johnny, his ten-year-old son and apprentice hod boy, had run home to fetch more water from the cistern. Johnny was eager to learn the trade, and Jack had every reason to be proud of his son's effort, only his first job and already Johnny showed signs of filling a man's shoes. A demanding father, though never one to hide his pleasure, Jack kept a keen eye out, firm but fair. So as he turned to heft another stone from the dwindling pile and noted Johnny's wavering approach across the way, he knew immediately something was troubling the boy – the downcast eyes, the rag from the crock-jar dragging the ground. Jack wiped the trowel on his pant-leg and waited. Johnny soon stood silent before him.

"What's up, son? Tell me, John." Patience lost to concern, he barked, "Johnny!"

"Mom says you maybe oughta know" – words rushed, chin quivering.

"Huh?" – growing apprehensive, for it always seemed to Jack, one accustomed to a free rein, that when Anna expressly wished to inform him of something, that something usually entailed the tightening of the cinch about the heart.

"Bonny's pregnant..."

"Pregnant?"

"By ol' man Thurman..."

"*Thurman!*" Jack's eyes blazed red, while Johnny, stricken by his sister's shame and fearful of his father's rage, began to whimper. The pitiful wail no doubt fueled Jack's anger as he, in a series of maddened kicks and blows, torn down half the wall they'd built, upset the slue box, dashed for the car and roared off down the street, tires screaming as burnt rubber left its dark stench hanging in the heat waves drifting up from the tarred surface.

A minute later he stormed through the yard, banged open the front door, bounded up the stairs, ripped a drawer from the bureau and grabbed the nickel-plated snub-nosed .38 he'd wrestled off a railroad "dick" down in Kansas City during the wild tempests of his youth. By now his wife and daughter, reacting from their numb shock, were running after him, pleading, "No...Jack...don't?" But he gave each a chilling stare, shoved on past and was gone. In an instant the dark-green '49 Ford V-8 lost in a cloud of dust. Streets still not paved in the part of town where they lived.

He drove slowly past Thurman's farm, carefully scanning the fields, pastures, hedge-rows, and fences. Saw the hapless gelding, a palomino, standing in the shade of the barn, swishing its matted tail, stomping at flies with spavined legs. No sign of its master. At the farm house, again, no one except Thurman's gangly teenage son Riley, sipping ice tea on the front porch, listening to the A's game over the radio. And the boy, himself a year younger than Bonny, had no idea what was afoot or why Mr. Marshal was glaring hard out the car window, asking after his father.

Jack spun the car around and tore up the drive...in his mind's eye he could see the sweaty bulk of filth pressing down on his blue-eyed Bonny. *Christ! a fifteen-year-old girl, the Bastard!* Where could he be hiding? Jack jammed the pedal to the floor, fish-tailed onto the road and sped for town. Find a coward in a crowd every time.

In hindsight it all came so clear, the result inevitable, really. His own damn fault. Willis Thurman, a widower the past winter, had been declaiming one evening in late spring over the harsh burden of grief and keeping up a house while looking after a farm and a boy to boot. And Jack had volunteered Bonny to cook and clean for the summer; the girl needed work, a chance to earn some money. Dumb...spoke right up and in-as-much-as said, "Take her!" Put the beauty in the clutches of the beast. And the beast had acted wholly on his nature. Jack and Willis had buddied some in their youth, and though they were more casual friends than pals, he knew the man well enough. Could see the giant, for Willis stood 6' 9 and weighed over 300 pounds, reach out and snatch the plum. Could see too, and felt himself condemned by the thought, why a man would be tempted, want her madly, for she was ripe. But dammit all! Not for the picking. Not at fifteen. Young, so young, still filled with that unwarranted trust. And how easily the cunning hand could insinuate and overwhelm an innocent. She hadn't stood a chance, not tender, trusting Bonny. Not against that giant's swollen need.

And Jack packed the gun along not because he had any fear of Thurman – he could've ripped him limb from limb with his bare hands because Willis was only a weak bluff of a man hidden in a great mass, a four-flusher – no, Jack had no desire to whip or in any way punish Willis. Precisely, he wanted to execute...*Murder the Bastard!*

The Ford, tinted ghostly gray from the feverish hunt down country roads, prowled past assorted stock-trucks and pickups parked outside the sale barn at the south edge of town. Nothing. Then on to the business district, past several bars and restaurants that Thurman was known to frequent. The lengthening shadows of sunset angled down the alley back of "Pete's Smoker" as the stalking Ford crept to a stop before the fire escape. Beyond a trove of empty bottles and lidless trashcans oozing ferment to the paved brick sat the prey, reeking of guilt, parked in a niche between two buildings and hidden about as well as a bare-assed whore in a barracks – Thurman's spanking new '59 Chevy pickup. Washed and waxed! Bright ass-hole orange, thought Jack, like the unwelcome brightness of a sunup following a binge, or the bright-orange of hot shit, a color to draw flies. Jack got out and strode around the building to enter from the front.

This would be a public execution.

The main door of weathered oak, its varnish lost to the wind and rains of half a century, was wedged open at the stoop. Man-ripe scents of tobacco, beer, and sweat mixed with the evening's muffled laughter and wafted out through the screen that veiled the shadowy interior. The screen door shot back with sudden force, freezing the action within. Flash! – all eyes front and center as in a faded-brown tintype. Silence, not even a jukebox, because the owner and barkeep, Pete Charbowski, reckoned music only drew women and women caused fights and he wanted his place kept a refuge for men to spit-cuss-drink 'n talk, play cards and shoot pool.

A cue ball softly tapped "the eight"; a hush of smoke drifted above the green velvet surface. Ceiling fans hummed indifferently.

From the far back corner came a gasp like steam escaping a pressure valve as Willis Thurman spied Jack Marshal standing at the entrance, searching the room with feverish eyes and that nickel-plated pistol held ready. Then aimed and fired! The bullet grazed a whisker's breadth past the intended's head and exploded into the plaster wall, splintering the lath. Thurman lunged to his feet, upsetting the table, card players, and chairs. And if a big man could ever be called quick, in that instant Willis quick-stepped like a water spider past several more tables out through the back exit, weightless with terror and bad conscience close behind. Not to mention Nemesis.

"*Thurman!*" Jack's roar sounded more frightening than the pistol shot as men gave way, hugging floor and walls like shadows before the Lion's swift pursuit.

Out the door, over the rail, down the alley – Willis made a dozen vain strides to escape before hitting the front fender of Jack's Ford, tumbling head-over-heels, ending in a pathetic sprawl across the brick pavement. Jack closed on his prey just as the sheriff's white '55 Chevy screeched to a halt five feet beyond, lights flashing.

Deputy Guy Craig jumped out, followed slowly by the expansive bulk of Sheriff Charlie Simms, whose only distinguishing feature aside from a capacious mouth, pug nose, and tiny slit-eyes was his utter roundness. Each wore workmen's khaki in lieu of uniforms: the sheriff's neatly pressed, though it needn't have been as it fit him snug as a second skin; the deputy's shirt and trousers hung loose, indifferently tucked, worn casual as the sweat-stained felt hat tipped slightly back on his head. The sheriff wore a crisp straw Stetson low to his eyes.

"Dammit all Guy, Charlie...*Stay back!*"

"Now easy, Jack." Guy chambered a shell and held the shotgun ready, though not aimed. "Don't do anything we'll all regret."

As usual, Sheriff Simms, neither fearless nor a fool, stood back of his deputy, left his pistol holstered and let Guy do the talking, the immovable will behind the intrepid force. While the sheriff was pleased to mind the political store, he gladly left Guy a free hand to manage the rough and tumble of maintaining law and order in the community of people they both served and loved. And for Jack, at this moment, Deputy Craig was the worst possible variable that could enter the equation, because Jack liked Guy, always had, and respected him. The flint-hard little man had guts; they were friends, good friends. Co-captains of their high school football team, state champs, Guy took the snap and handed off while Jack ate up the yards and gathered glory. They still bowled together and ran bank lines, taking big cats from the river. The past spring they'd pulled in a 90 pounder; each family's icebox fixed for catfish through the next winter.

Willis crouched, trembling on all fours in a puddle of fear, having wet himself. Begging as Jack pressed the barrel to his temple – big, freckle-faced, red-haired Willis pleading for his life in a tiny choked voice:

"Please don't, Jack. I'll marry her...Bonny. Honest, Jack. God, please don't...?"

Jack cocked the hammer and snarled his intent:

"Know what this bastard did?"

"Whole town knows," Guy said, calm and steady. "Knew 'bout the same time as you, I 'spect. Word travels fast from the phone office. Anna called us. Said you were out after Willis and why. Said you likely meant to kill. Now I ain't gonna shoot ya down, Jack. Not 'less you shoot ol' Willis there…" He paused briefly, considering the prostrate form reduced to blubbering incoherence before them. "Might be Willis deserves shooting. But you don't. You pull that trigger you're either dead or in prison. No other way. I'll do the job I swore to. So be mindful of your boy, Johnny's a fine boy. And Bonny...Anna. With you gone there'll be no end to their troubles. Think it over, Jack. Hell, if you're gonna shoot...you can't miss."

Cool even-tempered Guy, never forced a man's hand, left Jack free to choose and waited. Jack itched to pull the trigger, longed to see Thurman's head explode like a fat pumpkin. Perfect...like a grand slam or sinking a 40 foot jump shot at the buzzer, like a 99 yard run or breaking the tape three strides ahead of the nearest sprinter—the pure freedom of the perfect act. Victory! And no doubt he would have killed Willis had they remained alone in that alley. But Guy's calm, reasoned cadence blurred the murderous will, and Jack, bewildered, confused, having sensed the folly of his own lust mirrored before him, finally lowered the gun and stood down. Like a common Joe, Lion Jack let the deputy and sheriff lead him away.

And now, 44 hours through the 48, well...dammit all. Jack

eased his grip on the bars. He could have killed in a rage, a fury, the white heat turning the spittle to foam in his mouth, but in cold blood, the carrion stink of culpability filling his nostrils, probably not. No, Jack was a sportsman, a fair dealer. When he stood down, he meant it. Still, the thought of that cringing bastard siring his grandchild sickened him to no end. But the matter had grown beyond fixing, sadly, as with all else, accept it or not, he'd have to live with the imperfection. Disgust rumbled in his throat, the one perfect act of his life had slipped irretrievably from his grasp. And though it never formed clearly as a thought in his mind, the fear gnawed at his gut, stirred through the depths of his being, that his progeny would pay with bad luck forever, somehow carry the stain of that unavenged wrong: The brute's invasion of the fair one.

CIBOLA CITY was writ large on the water tower that stood just north of the jail where Jack now cast his eyes, where each and all looked from time to time as if it were a beacon by which to fasten and fix a path through circumstance. Somehow its presence and name marked the crucible of his life – he'd gazed there since childhood, played in its shadow, climbed it in high school to paint he and Annie's initials, announced his love to the world – all the events and thoughts including those current contained in that presence and name, the history and myth of Cibola City.

People commonly thought it had been named for Coronado's fabled lost cities of gold. But "cibola" also meant "bison" in Spanish, so the founder may have dreamt of attracting the hide trade along with the railroads. But whatever, his dreams and reasons died with him, killed by marauding Cheyenne a year after establishing the trading post. Others found his scalped remains a day or so later, spoke due words and buried him. His name and grave long since vanished to the Kansas prairie. Only thing known of the man was that he hailed from somewhere east of the Missouri and founded Cibola City on the north fork of the Solomon in 1864. People liked the irony of the name, the only gold in them parts was the wheat that covered the surrounding plains like a golden sea in June, the price devilishly low again that year.

"It ain't a City of Gold," they'd joke, "it's just Cibola."

And Jack wondered at that irony, that history and name. So many lost promises, faded dreams, faded lives. He felt his own fading, his youth and promise. The moment lost. With vague resignation he turned his gaze to the street and immediate foreground. Presently, from around the corner yard ran a lively trio of boys led by Deputy Craig's son, Ross. Seeing Jack at the window, they stopped abruptly and sang out:

"Hey, Mr. Marshal!" "Hello!" "Hiya, Mr. Marshal!"

"Boys," Jack answered in laughing growl, "What devilment are you three up to on a hot Sunday afternoon?"

The boys – Ross, Michael, and Arran – their ball caps shaped and fit to their heads in the manner of favorite pros, were Johnny's friends, same age, all chewing gum, all under five feet and prone to swagger, but still boys, socially awkward, coached by Jack in little league, and all drilled to speak up when spoken to.

"To a movie!" "Yip, downtown..." "A picture show!"

"Well, I'll be. Three Musketeers off to the movies. So what's showing?"

"Cartoons, Mr. Marshal...whole carnival!" "And a Western! "With Randolph Scott!"

"Say now, that sounds great. You boys have a good time. Just don't be forgetting tomorrow night's game."

"Oh no..." "No way, Mr. Marshal..." "Won't forget..."

"And you tadpoles stay out of that swimming pool. Hear? Damn chlorine burns your eyes and leaves ya half blind. I want you all well rested. Remember! You're the Wolves! Them Badgers can't hide in their holes forever. We'll dig 'em out, rip 'em up 'n bury 'em. Right?!"

"You bet!" "Yessir!" "We'll get 'em, Mr. Marshal!"

"Right, now here..." He tossed them the nude-Venus quarter, adding a strict injunction with furrowed brow and upraised finger. "That there's secret knowledge," glancing up and down the street as he leaned to the bars in a conspiratorial tone, "not for show 'n tell, the church offering plate, or Mom's supper table. Keep it to yourselves or out behind the barn. Understand?" The boys, earnest and big-eyed, nodded. "And here...here's another four bits, the spending kind. Buy you each a cold pop at the movie. Now dammit all, run along. Cell window's no place for boys to be."

"Thanks!" "Alright!" "Sure thing, Mr. Marshal!" And with that crisp reply, and suddenly taller, the boys ran on down the street, proud to be the object of Mr. Marshal's gruff good humor.

Mr. Marshal...Jack grimaced at the thought, grabbed the bars and roared:

"Call me *Jack!* Or I'll kick your tails!"

"Yessir Jack!" "Jack!" "Jack..."

His blood raced with the echo of their eager chorus. Yeah, he had cooled, but there was still fire in the blood of Jack Marshal. Baring his teeth, he unsnapped the brass buckle from his belt and began chipping away the loose mortar at the base of the bars. Damned if he'd stay caged the full 48.

THE PLAYER

The player was a decadent man, not in any grand way, but caustic, aloof, of anomalous dress and manner. Tall, of grayish-blonde hair, with pallid flesh and silky hands, still sported a formal black coat and tie in the age of shoddy denim. Kept a silver flask in his breast pocket, let others swill their beer while he took a sip of brandy to savor then slowly lick his lips. No longer young, yet wide awake, out carousing well past midnight, shrewd and cynically aware of his surroundings and his odd placement there – a tawdry country bar off a back street in Music City, and he a philharmonic musician. But he and the owner are old friends, both twice divorced, so he drops in on occasion for a post-concert drink, to savor the contrast, the hoot and laughter and flip swagger of the current crowd.

A young Cajun of shaggy black mane and grimy clothes brushes past, rude, insolent, a new star on the scene – "A fiddler," the player's owner-friend by faint apology explains; "Y'know, in high demand. Does session work most every day."

The player's eyes harden as he juts out a jeweled hand, catches the Cajun by the sleeve and says, "Hey buddy, I'm a player too. Hear me? I play too, dammit!" The Cajun scowls and jerks his arm away. The player laughs it off, "Oh yeah, you bet...thinks he's hot stuff alright. Struttin', young, cocky. Hell, let 'im have his day. Every swinging dick has his day. But he'll learn. Fiddlers in this town are thick as thieves in hell. *Fiddlers!*" Again he laughs.

Trombone was his ax. Brass. The blast of horns above a sea of strings. The horn, a manly instrument, like an erection, stiff and proud. Or a weapon, ever dominant. And playing got him off, like killing.

"I played machine gun in Korea," he notes with a grin, if you can imagine a wolf speaking, muzzle shaved, teeth sharp and clean. "Killed 'em by the score, the Chinks, as they ran and fell, wave after wave, bodies piling up to form a wall. And still they came, yeah...a screaming horde, night after night..."

There he gazed, bullets like notes being played. Black

notes. And he saw it all again each night he played. The massed audience, the hush, the applause. The agon and crescendo...lost in the thrall of death and music. The vast darkened hall, the dimming lights, the amorphous silhouettes, like a low brumal sky hanging over that far frozen land, alien and forlorn, ghostly, a crumpled shroud covering slopes and valleys, shell-blasted and bombed, the snow soiled and bloody, desolate, over trodden, defeated on. Blackened trees, de-limbed, twisted, like mangled bodies littering the landscape, shards of their former selves as his machine gun waits still and quiet, anxious to play its ratty-tat-tat amidst the acrid scent of shell casings and cordite, the sharp metallic cold, the reek of human waste the only warmth, the fog of breath the only movement awaiting dawn or death. And each night out of that great silent space, they arose, a charging mass, thousands made one in menace like an angry mammoth raising its tusks to pierce the sky till the shriek of battle grew indistinguishable from the muted wind hurling snow to blind the gunner's aim, but the machine gun played its notes by the thousands, inerrant and true, brilliant brass casings sent spinning above the flashing barrel, ejected as the nickel bolt ratchets home in rapid staccato bursts, tap-tap-tapping in manic fury a death waltz in triple time. And his enemy falls before him like supplicants in a dark massed heap that slowly turns white beneath the blanketing snow...

Likewise the music ends, the curtain falls, another audience left massed and silent as the player recedes into the seamless drift of haunted memories that drone into hours until he plays again and the music once more lifts the veil and fills the silence like a pure white opiate to sweeten the moment and ease the pain.

"Yeah, I'm a player. I play..." he says to no one in particular. By now weary, drunk, sullen. Losing his edge. That crystalline edge that could play or kill. Aging, tired, spent. Like a brass casing, a last note, awaiting the cold, the silence, the dead beneath the snow.

MOONLIGHT JITTERS (from *King Harvest*)

Early evening, about an hour past sundown, the crickets and locusts ratcheted like air wrenches on lug nuts in a frenzied *click, click, clatter,* sounding out a brisk cacophony in the fluid night air. A warm wind blew gently from the south and several clouds skiffed low beneath the moon as Will, Ry, and Lee crossed the fence and headed into the pasture. Ry's younger brother Rowdy had dropped them off and was not the least tempted when Ry ribbed him about joining in.

"I mean it, Rowdy. Ya really oughta try hemp-picking sometime. We'll start you off right. Make you water boy."

"Bullshit!" he said. "Got better things to do –"

Tires spun out gravel and dust as he roared off. Eighteen years old, had worked hard plowing in the hot sun all day. Maybe there wasn't a war on, but there were plenty of wild times and hot women to be had. They didn't call him "Rowdy" for nothing. Off to town, ready to paint it red if so dared.

They stood at the rise and watched him go, headlights bearing south towards the lights of Cibola City. They waited briefly to let their eyes adjust then moved on. Each wore dark clothing and a web belt with machete, canteen, and running pack. Ry carried the stripping tarp and gunny sacks rolled over his shoulder like a Civil War ruck. Will brought up the rear and kept an eye to the road while Lee took the lead, having covered the ground earlier that day.

The moon lit the way with fair clarity, but there were always badger holes and barbed wire to watch for. Badger holes, edged by telltale mounds, were easily spotted; wire, on the other hand, left to tangle in the grass, gave little warning and had lamed many a horse and man. So they each scanned the ground, noting any obstacle, the least rise and fall in terrain.

While their vision was more broadly focused than during the day, once their eyes fully adjusted it was amazing what they could sense and see. Each blade of grass cast its shadow to another and all wore the tawny color of late August, except for the scattered bluestem spiked with red, or the blossomed milkweed so freshly white it glistened, and in clusters it earned its more poetic designation, Snow on the Mountain. Bull thistles, which the boys gave a wide berth, stood lone and tall as a man, aggressive and lean, showing a bluish tint on their spiny leaves.

On ahead loomed a darker presence, like a blacked out cityscape of towering spires with all the crenelated variance of a gothic skyline – closer up it resembled a regiment of black knights, some afoot, others mounted, grouped in wait, lances held ready, their helmet crests and pennants aflutter in the wind. Closer still the boys discerned the deep green hemp shooting up like a miniature forest from the surrounding grass. Female plants stood dominant, full-leafed and hearty, next to which the males leaned frail and withered, having shared their pollen – in another week they'd be nothing but stalk and stem. But it was the females and their lusty limbs laced with five-fingered foliage that beckoned. The boys spread out the tarp, dropped their web belts and waded in, gripping their machetes with gloved hands.

To select a plant they gauged it against the sky, careful to avoid any males still showing a latent vigor. Choice made, they bent it over and made a crisp down-stroke near the base, then cradling the plant in their free arm, they moved on to select another and continued in like fashion till they'd gathered a good bundle to shoulder back to the tarp. There they began stripping the leaves from the stem, tedious work requiring a strong grip and constant arm motion. It was usually best to strip against the direction of growth, from stem to stalk, what they called "back-stripping," though later in the season, after the first frost, when the leaves loosened and the seeds budded full, dropping to the tarp with a dull *thump*, it worked easily either way. But it was still early, the seeds barely on. Once stripped, stalks and stems were tossed to an outer pile to be later hidden in a gully or in the middle of the patch to make the harvest less evident. Likewise each man worked here and there through the patch, never clear-cutting like a sickle, but moving constantly about, culling the best, leaving a number of plants standing visible to the eye. In truth many plants were too scraggly to bother with, and morning glories grew so thick through the entire northwest corner that it wasn't worth hacking your way in.

On they worked, alone or in tandem, either cutting or stripping, depending on their mood, hardly saying a word, each lost in the fever and prospect of the task, breathing hard, finding the rhythm, listening to the night sounds, the wind, the hum of the traffic along the distant highway, and near at hand the swish and rip of stripped leaves and the intermittent *thwing* and *thwack* of a machete slicing through a bent stalk. Every few minutes one or the other would stop and blow a green wad from their nose, wipe it on their jeans and press on. For each rustled stem dropped a mist of green pollen in the moonlight, a pungent dust that made you sneeze, but magical as well. Part of the allure of hemp-picking aside from the money was its more fanciful and elemental aspects: the night, the moon, a machete, working simply with your hands alongside your friends to turn a mere weed into hard cash. The irony, of course, made it all the more fun.

The stars blinked in mute witness. The moon drifted west. From time to time the boys glanced towards town, noting the lights of the carnival camped at the northeast edge. The Ferris wheel spun like a crowned jewel surrounded by the lesser lights of lesser rides – the octopus, tilt-o-whirl, rocket plane, and such. And no one could miss the searchlight that beamed on its axis, sweeping the sky throughout the horizon, calling all to the fair. On past midnight the great color and swirl ceased as the carnival shut down and the town dimmed in the distance like a lamp turned low. The boys kept on working, soaked in sweat, didn't take a break till 1:30.

"Let's bag this stuff," Will said, wiping his brow. "Then let's have a smoke."

Lee snatched up a gunny sack which he and Ry held open while Will stuffed in the leaves, bearing down with the press of his knee after every few handfuls till it was packed full, leaving only enough slack at the top to twist shut and duct tape a handle to grip it by. They bagged four more to add to the three bagged earlier then squatted Indian style in the belly of the old buffalo wallow where the tarp lay, all in all making for a nice nest down out of the wind.

Will tossed Ry a ready-made and they lit up, careful to cup the flare of the match and the glow of their cigarettes – tricks Ry had learned in the war which came in handy in the patch. Lee had quit smoking and no one smoked while cutting, they chewed, mostly "Red Man," adding its *splat!* and slaver to the leaves as they stripped, laughing about what a fine kick it would give the hemp.

"Make some hippy see green," Lee said, pretending to take a toke. "Wow! What's in this shit, man? Tincture of swamp lizzard?"

All laughing at the thought, the antic, when Will suddenly hushed, "*Quiet –!*"

They listened for a minute and heard nothing but their own breathing and the tall sheaves of hemp rustling in the wind.

"Guess it's nothing," Will said, squinting hard, still alert. "Thought I heard a limb snap. A little edgy, I guess, first night and all. Gotta work out the kinks."

Will was prone to caution, at times overly cautious. But it was always wise to attend the senses because the boys had been surprised on several occasions in the past by sheriff and deputies and had to scatter like coyotes to make their escape. That's why they each carried a running pack with a change of clothes and some spare ration. Will's idea. And only a fool parked a vehicle in a patch, like waving a red flag at a bull, a sure way to draw heat. Whereas a determined man afoot at night was hard to catch no matter what hounds they sent.

Ry sat across the way, bouncing on his haunches, at ease but ready.

"Doubt if there's anyone out here besides us, Will. Probably just a tree limb."

"Yeah, you're probably right."

When they finished smoking their cigarettes, Will poured a cup of honey-laced coffee into the lid of his thermos and passed it around to give each a boast before going back to work.

"You sure it's okay to keep the stuff at your place?" he asked as Lee took a sip and handed back the cup. Lee had agreed to dry the hemp and sit on it at least until Frankie's plan came into play. Will couldn't keep it, his place too open, though Ned was tolerant, he didn't care to push his luck. Nor did Ry, not with his father poking his nose into every corner of the farm every waking minute, constantly in need of something to do.

Cole had been a hard drinker in his day, running buddy with Frankie's old man, the notorious Justin Sage. And while he hadn't touched a drop in over ten years, not since the day they buried Justin, he still had the fevered urge and knew it. So did Ry. Being the oldest, he'd taken the brunt of his father's rages in those darker times. Which partly explained Ry's calm concern.

"That's right, Lee, no need to risk it," he said. "We can dry it up some creek or pasture. Take turns checking."

"No, someone's more likely to see us. And I don't see any problem. Dry it under those cedars out back. No one can see in there. And ol' John doesn't snoop none. Heck, he's hoping I'll buy the place."

"You gonna buy it?" Ry asked. Will curious too.

"Might. He only wants twelve thousand for the house, barn, and that forty acre pasture. A good pond back there. Helluva buy, really."

For the house was truly a mansion, three stories high with wrap-around porch, a winding staircase, oak floors and bird's eye maple woodwork throughout, built in 1911 and still solid. All it needed was paint – *About a 1000 gallons worth!* was the standing joke. But given paint and set in any sizable town it would have easily fetched a hundred thousand or more. Lee liked it right where it was. It set back from the road with a huge front lawn and spacious corrals out by the barn, all in good repair and all empty, like the house before Lee moved in. Empty for three years. The old Tannis place, something of a legend. So big and so far out of the way that nobody wanted to live there. Yet only 13 miles from town.

"Not to worry you," Will said. "But some say it's haunted. Ned thinks so."

Lee laughed. "If it's haunted, so's my hat. Nothing in there except the damn mice. And those kittens you gave us made short work of them." The mice had enjoyed the run of the place, raiding at will, and the carnage had lasted a week or more with the skitter and chase through empty halls, the crunch of bones late in the night, now mostly quiet, the remaining few cowed and meek. Lee and his wife and son had been living there since wheat harvest, well over a month, and already felt at home.

Tempted to buy the place once he had cash in hand. Put a horse in the corral, cattle in the pasture. Tempted to put down roots. Though he had to admit, the house contained some odd spaces, strangely cold and distant, but he supposed any big house did.

"Oh, that's just people and their talk," Will shrugged as he cast out the dregs, "wouldn't lose any sleep over it." Then he stood and stretched, attempting to pop his back and relieve the ache. Suddenly he shot back to one knee.

"*Look –!*" he said in an urgent whisper, pointing towards the road. "There...in that low draw. *See?* Someone coming our way. See the cigarette? There again. *See...?*"

Ry and Lee crouched directly behind Will, eyes intent, nodding anxiously.

"Yeah...think so," Lee answered, noting the flicker of light and apparent movement. He flexed his knees like a halfback set to bolt at the signal. All three ready to scram like a wishbone on a sweep. Then another flicker appeared, and yet another, here, there, and all around. Scores, then hundreds of tiny lanterns flicking on and off.

"Fireflies, Will," Ry announced with a low chuckle. "Fireflies damn near ran us out of the patch."

The wind had died down and fireflies were out by the thousands, appearing through the pasture, the patch, down by the pond, like a galaxy of stars gently settling to earth in quiet play and motion. The boys gazed on, drawn by the rife magic and wonder.

"Jesus, have I got the jitters," Will confessed, breaking the spell, his senses a little punchy after being up all day and working half the night. "Bad as a damned rookie." But relieved and ready to get back to work. Though the relief didn't last, for they'd no more than reached for their machetes when a horde of mosquitoes struck, following the fireflies by mere minutes, as if the fireflies were scouts leading them to prey. No question they'd flown up from the pond – the shallow mossy water overgrown with rushes and cattails provided an ideal breeding ground.

Damn! Fuck the devils! Christ Almighty!!!

The boys cursed and slapped their arms and faces as the

mosquitoes swarmed, buzzing in their eyes and ears in relentless hunt and hunger, determined to feed.

"Lord, wouldn't you know," Ry groaned, all irony and no smile. "Left my *DEET* at the house. The one thing I should of packed." DEET was the insect repellent used in Vietnam, highly effective, and Ry swore by it, but didn't think he'd need any that night out in the open with a steady wind.

"I didn't pack anything either," Will said, thinking maybe they should call it a night, then quickly vetoed the thought. "Hate to quit now. Hell, we can cut another two hours. Got any ideas?"

"Might try smearing on mud," Lee suggested.

*Yeah, yeah...*they gave it a thought. Damn near ready to run down and roll in the stinking pond mud when Ry had another idea.

"Let's try tobacco juice. Stuff's pretty potent. They give it to horses and dogs for tapeworms. Kills about any stomach worms except the ones I've got. Maybe it'll scare these dang skeeters."

Worth a try, desperate by now, each took a big chaw and started chewing, soon smearing dark tobacco juice over their face, neck, and arms, and felt their skin tighten as the astringent took effect. Lo and Behold! the mosquitoes withdrew, still humming close, but loathe to land. Cheered by success the boys smeared on more, coated their stomachs, backs and chests, looked a savage sight and smelled worse, but felt great. Refreshed, even. They grabbed their machetes and went back to work. By 3:30 they had two more bags packed and ready.

"That makes ten in all," Will declared. "Time to saddle up and head out."

"Suppose we better," Ry said. "I need a good half hour to make it to the house 'n fetch the truck." Because Rowdy for damned sure wasn't going to pick them up, he'd made that clear when he dropped them off. Told his big brother in so many words that he planned to be waylaid by a woman or drunk on his ass by that hour, not running up and down country roads, checking his rear view mirror for sign of Sheriff Guy.

The Harling place lay less than two miles directly south. Ry would help make one tote to the road before heading on. That would give Will and Lee time to have all ready to load on his return. They clipped on their web belts and were preparing to shoulder a bag when they heard a loud snap. All three froze and listened, moving only their eyes. Definitely something out there this time. Something big and hunched, moving up the draw. And something else, further back, in the direction of the pond, lumbering through the hemp. Steady, unhurried. Then nothing.

"What the devil's that...?"

Each spoke in a bare whisper.

"I dunno..."

"Do you hear anything?"

"No, not now..."

Waiting, watching, listening.

Then an old cow mooed in lowing query as if to ask, *What are you boys doing out here this time of night wrecking our pasture? And why isn't the salt block back where I last licked it? When I's up here last it was down by the dam, now where's it got off to?* Cattle strung out towards the pond, all joining in, bellowing questions and complaints. *That's right, you tell 'em Bossy, where's it got off to? We want that salt block and how about a mineral block to go with it? Huh? How about some sweet hay? And whatever come of that handsome bull you dropped off last spring? My, he had good heft and thrust. My oh my, just the thought makes me MO-OAN!!!*

By now the cows were raising a righteous chorus of throaty moo's. A dog started barking in the near distance, threatening to wake the whole countryside.

"Shut the fuck up you old hussies!" Will threw a stick to silence the nearest one. She merely swished her tail and mooed again as if to say, *Why'd you do that for?*

"Christ, what a night," he said. "First off I jump at my own shadow. Then the fireflies, mosquitoes, and now these damned cows. If Sheriff Guy's waiting out by the road, I'm gonna bum a smoke and catch a ride to town."

The boys each shouldered two bags and marched off, putting tracks between themselves and the cattle left milling about the hemp, lowing back and forth like old women at a rummage sale, poking here and there, somewhat curious, somewhat critical, *Now where's that salt block? Where'd they put it? Is it over your way Martha? NO-O-O! Well then, MO-O-OVE on over, 'cause this ol' heifer wants to see for herself!*

The stars shone in greater multitude and clarity as the moon vanished in the west. The boys had no problem following the cowpath up through the pasture. Nor were they worried about meeting the sheriff out by the road, what with the carnival and fair and young bucks like Rowdy on the loose, he'd have his hands full. Nor was he a deep concern on any other night. Sheriff Guy Craig, who most people referred to simply as Sheriff Guy, was an older man in his mid-fifties, respected and well-liked. The boys liked him too. For one thing he didn't get too riled about hemp-picking, unlike some, didn't consider it a grave social menace. As long as you were discrete and took care not to harm person or property, he pretty much let things ride. You practically had to land in his lap before he'd take you in. But anything too obvious he'd step on.

He'd caught two bona fide hippies the year before. Rastafarians with wild braided hair and lit-up eyes that hit town in a psychedelic van with California plates and every *peace-love anti-this-that'n-the-other* sticker pasted to the back door and bumper. They got stuck in a plowed field trying to reach a creek bottom full of hemp. *What a bummer!* Then they had the bright idea to walk to the nearest farm house and ask the farmer to pull them out. They were polite enough, standing in the porch light, faces pressed up against the screen like two giant June bugs.

"*Hey man... Can you help us?*"

They offered twenty dollars.

The farmer said, "Sure, fellas. Be out directly. Just need to fetch a lantern and tell the wife." He told the wife to call the sheriff then went out and loaded self and the two lost causes on his old "Johnny Pop," a three cylinder John Deere used for row-cropping. They chugged off down the road, shooting black smoke with a loud *pop! pop! pop!* every third stroke as the Rastas tried to plug their ears and hold onto the fender wells to keep from falling, big tires spinning like paddle wheels on a river boat, threatening to suck them under and pave them to the road. The dark of night, no lights, clouds breaking up below a bright silver moon, and those ungainly silhouettes speeding past looked highly suspect to any coyote or raccoon that happened to gaze up and notice.

The tractor arrived at the field to find Sheriff Guy and the wrecker in wait. Sheriff cuffed the hippies; wrecker towed the van. Next day the judge sentenced each culprit to a haircut and a bath, levied a $50 fine for trespassing and sent them on their way, with a faintly sober cast to their eyes. Whole county had a good laugh over that one.

But it was an entirely different story in the neighboring county east. The Sky County Sheriff, Hoss Wayne, was an ex-marine and acted like Wyatt Earp taming a cowtown when it came to nailing hemp-pickers. The previous year he'd nailed 50 plus, practically stuffed the jail. Again, mostly out-of-staters coming in to feast on the wild hemp. But the easy pickings were all Sheriff Wayne's. And over there, if caught, you faced a $500 fine or 30 days and loss of vehicle. So after a few close scrapes the boys steered clear of Sky County, no matter how tempting. Besides, there was even better cutting to the north and west in Hill and Smith Counties. Tonight was more of practice run than anything; they simply wanted something close at hand, something to get their feet wet and their blood pumping.

They'd covered a quarter of a mile, still following the cowpath, breathing hard, leaning forward with the weight of the bags, straining to maintain their grip, when they reached the rise and stopped dead in their tracks. They let the bags slip to the ground. And it wasn't the weight of the bags that
stopped them. It was a light. Not a spotlight or searchlight of any kind. But a bright light in the eastern sky that shone
brighter than the most brilliant star, three times as bright as Venus.

And it moved! Zig-zagged up and down then zipped to the north horizon and stopped, stationary a moment before moving again by fits and starts like a luminous water spider – or the tip of an otherwise invisible sword wielded by a black-capped master feinting here and there as if toying with them as he slashed a brilliant "Z" through the northeast sector of the sky. Then it vanished to reappear, dimmed and vanished once more. Then as suddenly it reappeared, gaining in brilliance, drawing close, before returning east where it slowed to hover in a relatively fixed position.

It was certainly no lightning bug, unless of cosmic variety. And though fatigued, the boys were clear-eyed and lucid. And no hallucination could produce the same effect on three separate minds. What they observed was a visible fact, a phenomenon that lay outside the perceived order, utterly beyond their understanding. Yet what is perceived must somehow be reasoned with and commented on.

"Holy shit..." "You see that..." "I'll be damned..."

Each felt like a kid conned by some trick and speaking merely confirmed they weren't the only fool watching. Yet certain before asking that there lay no answer, no explanation to ease their puzzlement. For there was no swamp gas in Kansas. Nor was this a reflected light – not a cloud in the sky. Whatever its origin or intent, it clearly contained its own force and energy. And there was no jet, no rocket, no meteorite that could move like that. Not even a weather balloon hurled by a twister.

Ry turned to Will, raised his brows and grinned.

"Well Wolfer...? Is that what you'd call a U...F...O?"

"I'll be damned. I'll be goddamned," Will repeated like a skeptic who'd doubted Santa Claus made to witness the flying sleigh and the red-nosed reindeer. "Serves me right. Never thought I'd see such a thing."

Because they'd had an argument not a month before over the very thing – the notion of aliens, the mere possibility, most particularly Von Danikin's theory of ancient astronauts having visited the earth. Will scoffed absolutely, wouldn't buy it for a minute, sided with Frankie in pooh-poohing the whole idea of little green men. But given what they now saw, Will had to admit that the notion of aliens and ancient astronauts no longer seemed so farfetched. And his "I'll be damned" was offered by way of apology for being such a bonehead. Too bad Frankie wasn't there to eat crow as well.

Not that Ry was gloating as he chuckled and grinned like a kid having told you so, simply expressing his usual delight, perhaps a bit more than usual. Wholly amazed in fact. Most definitely the craziest thing he'd ever seen. Crazier than a foot-long cicada or those tank tracks left on the ridge above the jungle. He decided to check with Lee and see what he thought, knowing Lee had once aspired to be an astronaut.

"How about you, Lee? Got any ideas?"

"Not a one," he said as he slowly uncapped his canteen and wet his lips, trying to call reason into play. "Can't even guess, not really. A pocket of energy, I suppose. A ball of light that must have some form or mass. Every light has a source. A flashlight, a sky rocket, a lightning bug. The sun, the moon. And they say every star glows in its own ball of fusion. Now if that thing is a small ball of fusion...of pure energy and somehow self-contained, that might explain why it doesn't burn up at those speeds. Because at that rate anything we know of would flare into ash in the time it takes to blink —"

In the next instant they watched it flash from east to north and back again.

"What would you guess it...ten, twenty, thirty miles out?" Lee observed. "Or it might be above the atmosphere at ninety miles or more. Which would better explain why it doesn't burn up or leave a trail like a falling star..." He fell silent a moment as each thought begat another and all fell short like rocks thrown at the moon. "But Christ, if not weightless, the stress from those kind of G's, that kind of acceleration...anyone in there would have their flesh ripped from their bones like jerking a coat off a hanger."

"Think they've come to pay a visit?" Ry asked, convinced that anyone or thing that could fly that fast was smart enough to avoid turning to mush in the process and surely had something in mind.

"I don't know. And sooner not find out. "

"Me neither," Will said. "Whatever they have in mind I bet we don't want."

"Maybe not," Ry mused. "Kind of like the prey seeing a hunter, isn't it?"

"Yeah, something like that."

All felt a slight unease, somehow threatened, even as they gazed like star struck lovers who swear that all the stars in heaven blink just for them. Without question they felt singled out, in a sense honored by what they saw. But light travels in all directions and stars blink whether anyone is watching. And what they saw flying through the sky, whatever its motive, it lay completely beyond their scope. Perhaps inimical to their will and desire. For certain indifferent. That was the suspicion and fear. Yet their greater fear and the more likely outcome was their being called fools.

"One thing I know," Will said, voicing the collective concern, "if we tell anyone, they won't believe us. They'll just think we're nuts." Having experienced a dubious conversion, he wasn't about to go tell it on the mountain.

No, a thing so extraordinary could only be shared with those who witnessed it. And what they now witnessed was so extraordinary it could not even be named. Yet instinct told them that there had to be an intelligence involved, because it was so lively, erratic, and playful – whereas dead mute matter did not change course or accelerate unless made to do so. But what kind of intelligence, what possible reason or purpose had it for being there, hovering like a star in the east, like something being born?

The boys scratched their heads in wonder. Wise men they were not.

IN THE OWL'S EYE (from *King Harvest*)

Some things happen, bad things, beyond anyone's wish or will. At least anyone wishing otherwise. Such can only be witnessed, or told, no matter how much it turns the stomach or grieves the mind. The fact remains, bad things happen.

Joseph Conners was 18 years old, blonde hair, blue eyes, an all-league halfback just out of high school, working that summer at the Farmer's Co-op tire shop in Arcadia, the queen city of Sky County. He planned to attend K-State in Manhattan that fall on an Air Force scholarship, dreamed of flying. But lately he couldn't focus on his plans or his dreams. He had seen something bad. And what he'd seen could not be shared, dared not share it. He was so scared that the previous morning he'd stepped out behind the tire shop and vomited. The fellow he worked with, Chris Boswick, heard him retching and joked, "What's the matter, Joey? Too much beer last night?"

"No. I saw something," he said, still spitting, catching his breath. "Something I shouldn't have. It's got me so I can't keep my food down."

Chris sobered, sensing the boy's fear like the smell of vomit.

"Then go to the police –"

"*NO! I can't!*" His answer so sudden and final that it silenced them both.

Joey didn't say another word, already said too much. And he could judge the depth of his own fear by the other's reaction, because Chris Boswick's face paled as they went back to work and he didn't share any of his usual banter that day. They worked mostly in silence, either pointing to or reaching for a wrench or pry bar as if each sensed that words were now taboo and would only hasten bad luck. Chris was a veteran of Viet Nam and he'd seen many bad things, some of which he'd shared with Joey that summer, priming him like a kid brother to the dangers of war and life in general. "Afraid I've seen some bad shit," he'd say. Yet deep down Joey knew that what he'd seen was every bit as bad, all the more so because it was something he'd never imagined and involved someone he respected. But you can't compare bad things; they are all equally unimaginable till you see them, then you can imagine nothing else. He felt a wall form around him, looming like a shadowed cliff, closing him off as he dropped down a deep dark shaft, irrevocably drawn by the fear and consequence of what he'd seen. He no longer perceived a future, could not think of college or flying. He sensed his life coming to an abrupt end, a cold certainty gripping the pit of his stomach.

But he felt wholly alive that evening in the arms of his girlfriend Cathy as they danced to the music in the open air in front of the band stand. She was so pretty, warm, and vibrant. Beautiful to hold. They'd met at a Catholic youth camp the previous summer and had dated ever since. Even though she lived 40 miles south in Salina, they still managed to see one another two or three times a week. By now they were deeply in love, had eyes for no other. And her eyes were brown.

Her parents came from Mexico and her father worked on a hog farm at the old air base near Smolan, southwest of Salina. Her full name was Catalina Rosa Maria Torres. Though she insisted everyone call her Cathy, even chastised her mother till she relented. Only her father called her Catalina, and him she did not chastise, for he doted on her, his "Catalina bonita," saying it with such fondness that she could not refuse to answer. Still, she wished their last name was Terrel, Terrance, or Tillman. Anything but *Torres*. She'd grown up hating her brown skin, her black hair, and dark eyes. Longed to be blonde and fair. But lately she had blossomed and did not so much mind her color. Since meeting Joey and having his blue eyes gaze to her, she knew that she was pretty because he was so handsome and would not think her so if she were not.

Tonight, dancing before him like a butterfly fluttering in the moonlight, she was beyond pretty. Dazzling, seductive in her white dress which revealed the brief swell of her breasts and flared at mid-thigh with the shift and sway of her hips, her tapered legs prancing in perfect rhythm to the rapid rock beat which she loved and danced to with such abandon and grace that it made him want to catch her up and hold her. And he caught her now, took her in his arms and spun her around and around in dizzy swirl and laughter then set her free again.

Admiring her flesh and form and movement, biding his time till the music slowed. And she loved the slow songs too. Loved leaning to him, raising her face to his, brushing lips, sharing their breath and scent, letting her breasts heave freely against him, melting to his embrace with the press of her hips, feeling his flesh swell in want of her. And she wanted him so.

A half hour later parked in seclusion off a hillside road at the south edge of town, they nearly went all the way. She let him unzip her dress, remove her bra and panties. Her hair hung to her waist; her crucifix to her breasts. He nibbled at her ear, her neck, her nipples. She unbuckled his pants, freed his hardened flesh and gripped him in her hands. He felt so large that she could not imagine him in her, yet wanted him there. They groped and grasped, fingers exploring hidden recesses where juices flowed in want of further touch and friction, stroking one another till they grew faint, the urge so strong. She leaned back and spread her thighs as he shifted over and prepared to enter. Then she touched the crucifix at her breast. They stared, waiting, their eyes wild with want. With fear and doubt. She bit her lip; he drew back. They wanted her a virgin on their wedding night. And they planned to wed the following spring after her graduation. Attend college as man and wife.

"Is it so long to wait?" she asked, soothing his ache and need. Yet searching his eyes, she saw something else, something troubling him. Something wrong.

"What is it, Joey? Tell me." Then she panicked. "Is it another girl?"

"No, Cathy...no." He looked to her and shook his head. "There'll never be another girl, Cathy. Never. It's just..."

"Then tell me. Please?" She perched up beside him with her legs tucked under, brushing the hair from his eyes.

"Nothing really. It's just...sometimes life seems so short. Like it's about to end."

"Ah Joey, it's just beginning. We've got forever, you and me." Then she fluffed his hair, teasing him. "And soon enough, big boy, you'll have this chica all to yourself. Huh?" Which made him laugh. She could always cheer him up with some little antic or another. They teased and laughed as they readjusted their clothing, dreaming of the day when their love would be sanctioned and they could savor it free of guilt and constraint. And he tried to forget his fear of what he'd seen, the bloodied leg under the canvas and the voice on the phone that warned:

"Say one word, your little brown bitch is dead..."

He drove his parent's 1972 Ford LTD, royal blue with gray interior. A four-door with automatic transmission. A family car. Certainly no hot rod. But with a 396 V-8 and a four-barrel carburetor it could move, and he could drive. He often topped 120 down the long stretches of Highway 81 to and from Salina, and hadn't been caught yet. A month earlier he'd skidded off the highway onto a country road to lose a trooper in hot pursuit. He threw up a cloud of gravel as he fishtailed to the ditch, then straightened out and sped over a hill, turned into a field and cut the lights. Half a minute later the trooper roared past with full siren and red light flashing. At the next mile he slowed and cruised on around the section, finally reaching the highway and heading south.

Joey watched him go, waited a few minutes, then eased out and followed country roads back to Arcadia. Thrilled at his escape. And confident he could drive. He loved speed. Didn't smoke or drink, something of a straight arrow. And when his friends called him that, he'd say, "That's right, I'm a straight arrow. And I'll be flying jets some day while you're still poking along on a tractor."

Heading down the hill towards the main drag that ran north and south through town, he noticed headlights coming up fast in his rearview mirror and thought it might be a carload of friends out to razz the young lovers, honk their horn, stick their heads out the window and ogle. Like usual he'd play it cool, smile and wave them on.

But the black pickup that pulled abreast didn't belong to any friend. It crowded him to the curb as both vehicles came to a screeching halt. A spotlight glared, flooding the windshield. Joey shifted in reverse and burned rubber back up the hill, whipped around and took the only escape he saw — a gravel road heading south. He told Cathy to buckle up and hold on. She didn't need telling, having already bruised her lip against the dash in their abrupt stop. She glanced back and saw the pickup in pursuit.

"Are they some of your crazy friends?" she asked, hoping it was all in fun.

"No, Cathy. I'm not sure who they are. But they're not friends."

The speedometer hit 60, then 70. He had no fear of speed and knew the road, could anticipate each dip and turn. In fact he knew all the roads through the region and could map them in his mind, mark each blind curve and intersection, having hunted along them since he was a boy. Only now he felt like a rabbit trying to lose a hound. He checked in the mirror and saw the haze of headlights in the dust behind. He pushed harder, faster, trying to distance himself and her, racing beyond his headlights over the quick-shifting terrain as trees and fencerows flashed past like grainy film.

Cathy tensed with each rise in speed, growing ever more anxious.

"We're going awfully fast, Joey?" She looked to him in wonder of his haste.

"I know. You've got to trust me."

"What is it? Are you in trouble?"

"We're both in trouble. I'm sorry, Cathy. But I saw something. Something terrible. And I think they were part of it."

"What? What did you see?"

"I can't tell you. Can't tell anyone. I *can't. Can't* –!" He slammed the steering wheel with his fist, then caught himself and calmed. "Please, Cathy, trust me. Trust me and pray...pray for us both."

She said no more, gripped the crucifix pendant at her breasts and prayed. Prayed to the Virgin Mary, to baby Jesus, to Saint Christopher and to all the other saints for their timely intercession. For deliverance and mercy. Prayed in English, in Spanish. And she prayed that her mother and father would forgive her many tantrums.

Nearly five miles south of town they cleared a hill doing 80 and went airborne briefly before landing with successive bounce and jolt. Both gave a shout of laughter, giddy at the weightless moment and the wild thrill of holding the road. Then silent again as Joey quickly slowed, cut the lights, and turned onto a dirt road that dead-ended from the west – the intersection all but hidden by a hedgerow that overgrew the ditch. They sat, panting in fear and wait. Within seconds the trailing headlights rose upon the hill and descended their way, their pursuers traveling somewhat slower, steady and controlled. The pickup passed on down the hill then stopped. The spotlight speared through the darkness, sweeping up through the pasture and trees like a broadsword stabbing at the undergrowth, poking for prey. Then the spotlight dimmed and vanished while the red glow of back-up lights filled the view. In the next instant the pickup appeared in full profile like a dark menace as the spotlight shot through the back window, lighting the interior with Cathy's frightened scream.

Joey gunned the engine and raced on, cleared two more hills before taking the first turn south. Heading south in frantic flight as if instinct and duty drove him there. Heard Cathy crying. Had to get her home or her father would worry. Had to save her. There had to be a route of escape. *Had to be!*

But nothing and no one in this world has to be. The wind settled the dust of their chase within minutes of their passing as it would one day scatter the dust of all involved. Only love is immortal, and only in song.

Joey gripped the wheel, making ready for the curve up ahead, an "S" curve that rounded a hill and made a sharp descent down the far side. He skidded fine through the initial bend, but on the second he edged too close to the shoulder and the soft gravel left piled by a season of farm traffic caught his tires and pulled him to the ditch. He ramped a culvert at 50 miles an hour, took out a fence post, and swerved back onto the road, grinding to a halt on a broken drive shaft.

He only had time to grasp Cathy's hand before the pickup sped down...

A great horned owl lands on the upper limb of a hillside oak. Blinks its yellow eyes and scans the scene. Interrupts its flight to observe the rude approach of man, the rush of light and mass, like hounds in chase on the road below. Sees the first hound leap through the fence then kick and spin till it lies wounded, its lone eye shining off into the darkness. Soon the larger hound bears down, eyes beamed straight ahead, tracking with intent and vigor as it approaches the first and stops.

Doors kick open and three jagged shadows appear, ghastly in form and aspect like scarecrows blown in the wind, clothed in dread and hollow of heart and mind. They circle their prey. From the near side comes a brief cry silenced by a sudden flash and shot. The owl draws alert, knows the sound of gunfire as well as the scent of the hunter and of blood. From the opposite side emerges yet another shadow with a cry of rage and grief answered by a series of angry shouts as the scarecrows converge and drag him forth into the harsh glare of the beaming eyes that cast the struggle far into the night. Man shadows loom over the creek bed to the hill beyond, stretched like huge trees, limbs clashing in a hard storm. The very act staged in a wedge of light.

"Cathy? Why? Why did you...kill her, you –"

A pistol slams hard against his head as he staggers to his knees. Rough hands gripe him by the hair and smash his face against a headlight, pinning him there. Faces starkly etched in black and white hover at the periphery, screaming harsh taunts.

"Why you running, lover boy? Who'd you tell!? Cat got your tongue?"

"I didn't tell, I didn't...I swear!"

"Oh, listen to this, he swears. Got us a real boy scout here."

"You killed her, you bastard, you fucking –"

His words cut short by a bullet fired into his gut. He clutches and falls in fetal agony. A frightful pause as he grimaces at his murderer in the glare of lights, gasping through his bloody teeth: "Fuck you, fuck you, fuck you...!" *While the killer knells like a mock confessor, a harbinger of death, lingering a moment as if to savor his work.*

"No, fuck you, boy..." *Shoves the pistol between his legs and fires.*

Headlights suddenly appear to the north. The scarecrows glance in alarm.

They drag their victim aside and vanish as they came.

The owl again scans the scene. Blinks indifferent to the death and agony it has witnessed, but ever keen to the scent of man and his acts, wise to and wary of the road. The wind ruffles its feathers; it turns its head to the skitter of prey in the thickets below. Presently the owl spreads its wings and sweeps down over the creek in hunt, merging with shadows through the trees...

The bodies of the teenage lovers were found shortly after dawn by an old farmer and his wife on their way to church. The sheriff and deputy were called out, soon joined by other county and state officials. The investigation hotly pursued for a time and stoutly debated in following years, though nothing was ever gleaned beyond the notion that the boy had seen something bad, just what, or the who and why behind the crime was never known. People left vaguely haunted by the unnamed evil in their midst, till this too faded along with the dust and dried blood that settled along the road next morning. Still, the fact remains, bad things happen.

HAUNTED DAY (from *King Harvest*)

Diana had watched the sky mist over and thicken through the day, forming droplets on the windows in echo of those witnessed by Lee as she gazed out from time to time, hoping he might come home early due to the rain. The only man she wanted to see drive in was Lee. Feeling lonely and cold from the weather, she longed to be held, simply held, not seized, groped, or touched. Still wary. In part it was her violation, but that was merely the catalyst. The greater part was the uncertainty. Never knowing Lee's next mood or move. Not to mention his drinking. Sometimes he'd be off with a friend and not return till the next day. Though lately he'd stayed sober. Maybe he'd settle down and maybe not. Maybe she'd stay with him and maybe not. But such thinking filled her with disgust, reminding her of the school-girl game, "Love me, love me not..." and she didn't want to play any games with Lee and force him to be something he wasn't.

Over the past two days to suppress such questions she'd cleaned every room in the house, waxed the floors, polished the woodwork, including the entire grand staircase – rails, stiles, newel posts and all. At times she stood and straightened her back in wonder whether the house wasn't too big, too much for her, then instantly shunned the notion and bent to work, in fever to clean and caress its every surface, for she loved the house and was determined to stay. To possess and be possessed. There belong.

Diana even removed three old dresses she'd left hanging in Jessie's closet, having thought someone might return to claim them. Which was doubtful, for they were simply old summer dresses of flowery pattern with capped sleeves: two dark and one light, like those in style during the 20s that she'd seen her grandmother wear in old photos or like the one worn by the sweet old lady who'd asked to see the house. And there were photos as well dating from the same era, a dozen or so scattered in a dusty corner of the upper shelf – one of a young woman coyly posed in front of a Ford coup; another of a young man standing proudly before the same, his arms cocked to his hips; while the remainder were mostly group portraits from family gatherings and picnics.

To make a clean sweep of things Diana decided to burn the dresses and photos. This marked the day's big event for Jessie as he tagged along curious, watching her pour kerosene from the lamp into a tin can and grab the box of kitchen matches. He followed her outside to a low depression far back of the house where she burned all their trash. A good day for burning, damp and misty. Rue and Keeps slunk off towards the red shed east of the cedars, for they knew the routine and were wary of fire. Diana plopped the dresses down on the blackened bed of prior burnings and scattered the photos on top like fallen leaves. She doused all with the kerosene and warned Jessie to stay back.

"Careful, honey, it's hot," she said, striking a match and tossing it to the heap.

Blue and yellow flames leapt into the air to warm their faces. Jessie stood enrapt, watching the fire eat into the fabric as it burned bright-orange then a ghostly black and white – the pattern and weave bleeding through an instant before disintegrating. The photos caught like dried leaves, the images briefly given life in the hiss of flames while the edges curled and flaked away. Within a minute the last ember had blinked and died, leaving nothing but a thin breath of smoke, and that too soon withered in the ashes.

Staring there Diana felt a pang of remorse at the burning, like a window closed forever on another life and time. Then she raked it over and left it, anxious to fill the house with her life and time. Jessie simply wished the fire had lasted longer as he grasped his mommy's hand and returned to the house.

Like the fire the day ended too soon, without its customary slant of shadow and soft evening light. The sun having not once shown its face, it was like they inhabited a lone, isolate world, she and Jessie, closed in by a deep mist and fog while beyond the big house and lawn laid nothing but trackless wastes and indefinite forms. Every tree and limb etched black against the enveloping night; what leaves remained hung shriveled, their colors muted, browned in decay, awaiting the earth, lifeless, unburied. She felt utterly abandoned, forlorn. More than loneliness it was a haunting she sensed, like she and Jessie were the last of the living and all else lay dead in wait.

She turned from the window, the darkening scene, and shuddered at the thought of night. Jessie had grown fussy after his supper and she'd put him to bed with a story that seemed to quiet him. But nothing could quiet her own unease; she wished Lee were there. The darkness grew so dense that light bulbs barely lit the immediate space. The same when she stepped into the living room and gazed through to the grand staircase ascending to the shadows — witnessed a heavy encroaching darkness, indistinct, without shape or form, yet incipient and strangely hostile, like she'd felt while cleaning out the third floor earlier in the day. A broad empty space where she'd dreamed of dancing, but working there she felt watched at every turn, a looming resentment of her very presence that seemed to intimate, *No dancing, no cleaning...*wishing to be left undisturbed. Floors bare and unfinished, like the walls simply plastered over and left unpainted through the years, etched by ugly brown stains from the leaking roof. Diana had touched her broom handle to a damp spot on the ceiling and the plaster gave way, exposing the lath like an open wound. She quickly swept up the debris and soon finished cleaning, glad to return down the short flight of stairs and latch the door. She glanced to the diamond-shaped window and wondered for the hundredth time at its odd placement there at the end of the hall above the grand stair and before the entrance to the attic - like a stern red eye set glazed in warning. But she would not be intimidated. That's when she went to Jessie's room and cleaned out his closet. Though now, gazing through to the grand staircase and the shadowy glum, she again sensed the threat. She switched off the light and returned to the kitchen, clutching her shoulders against the rising chill and the darkness seeping in through every window and door.

Then she heard something. *A voice? No...*several voices. Upstairs. Seemingly from her bedroom. Her first thought was that the clock radio had abruptly turned on. But the voices quickly spread through every upper room and down the grand stair. And no horrendous howls or screams or grave whisperings as one might imagine, just peculiarly common voices of people engaged in conversation, exchanging pleasantries and mild laughter like at a party - she even discerned the clink of a glass, the swish of a dress, the light rhythmic footsteps of couples dancing, as if all her cleaning had somehow awakened the house and every memory was being replayed. She stood vaguely amused, curious at what was happening, then transfixed in terror as the voices drew closer, louder, nearly deafening, passing all around and through her like shadows, only willful shadows, voices too numerous to decipher or name. And suddenly one did name her.

Jessie cried from his room, calling for his mommy.

Diana broke and ran up the back stair, following the rise of her shadow, frantic to reach him. She turned at the mid-landing and saw a further shadow leaning into Jessie's room. Diana, angered at the violation of her child, continued up the stairs, determined to walk through ghost or wall of fire if need be. At her approach the shadow whipped like a dark wind and vanished, leaving nothing but a chill space before the door.

From the room Jessie stood crying: "Old woman! Old woman!"

Diana rushed in and held him in her arms, clasping his warm life to her.

"It's okay, honey. We're leaving now," she said and gathered him up.

She carried him down the stairs through the spawn of voices clinging like broken webs, no longer the least familiar but emphatically dark and menacing. She snatched her purse hanging from a chair and ran out the door. She didn't stop till they reached the pickup, nor once look back. She could still hear the voices spilling onto the porch. She strapped Jessie in his car-seat and started the truck, both of them in tears as she revved the engine and sped down the drive then swerved onto the road, all the while blinking her eyes to see, trying to calm herself and Jessie. And she didn't slow down till she'd passed the Shafer place and turned east on the pavement – at last breaking free of the haunting, ready to follow the road anywhere but back to the house.

THE BELL RINGER

Watching me pin up a music poster at the grocery store entrance, he wore a cagey grin and raggedy clothes, standing there in the cold with a red tin bucket, ringing a Salvation Army bell, close to Christmas.

He nods and says, "I rang this bell 3013 times the past hour. Yep, and I'll come 'n count while you play. I do that, I can count each strum. And when you finish I'll step up 'n say before all them ladies and gents, 'Congratulations, you have just strummed your guitar a total of, oh let's say... 8069 times in the course of this evening.' Yessir, I'll be there. Last Sunday at church I counted every word the preacher said. People were amazed, they said, 'What else can you count?' I said, 'I can count my footsteps for a week and let you know how many steps I've taken next Sunday.'"

I stuff a couple wrinkled dollars in his bucket and turn to exit across the parking lot. He leaves his post and joins me, still ringing the bell, and says, "Yep, and right now I'm counting each step you take 'n my own as well. I can count sixteen separate things at once. For example, listening to a sermon, how many times the preacher says 'God' or how often he scratches his ears or adjusts his tie...that and a dozen more different things and never miss a beat."

He pauses then in deep scrutiny and says, "I can even look into your face and count the tics of your heart. Even name the days of your life."

"Think I'll pass on that," I answer.

"No worry," he allows, rolling his tongue, "you got a while yet..."

FIFTY CENT TIP

(*A roadside cafe, early 1970s, a play of thought between a waitress and a drifter...*)

Feel like a mother robin. Glutton. Feeding on worms to feed my hatch. Only I have none. Glutton. Hunger like there's no tomorrow...hunger for tomorrow and yesterday too. There's the rub...mere worms of thought. I feed on nothing, just gulping air. Growing old here. I'll be twenty-two next week. Giving orders to the cook. Myself to no worthy man. Not one.
 "The roast beef special, Jerry..."

Fork it...searching through salad greens for tomato's deep red fruit. And searching for *'A Heart of Gold'* with Neal Young...reaching in my pocket for another shiny dime...

I'd cross the ocean if I had half a cause and money...leave these harvest hands and hitchhikers. Maybe the Paris sun wouldn't dry men so. Makes them old in their heart, not one of poetry have I heard. Oh, sometimes they call me *Honey*, all thick and sweet. Makes me so mad. The other day I told that rich-ass Jonson to go ram it up a beehive if he wanted honey. Well, that's the only way he'll get some anyhow. Hate it...*Honey*! Last summer at least I had a nice tan and cause to show it...

D-7 and *'Proud Mary'*...keep that music rolling, hopping like flames off logs in a wood-heat stove. Don't feel so lonely then. Friendly ol' jukebox...probably the only friendly machine I know. Christ, it's August and my coffee's getting cold. Ought to set it outside. Damn, try and catch her eye.
 "Uhmm...Miss? Mam? Yes, please, more coffee."
 Sullen waitress...

At least he's not loud, like most. Seems a little shy. Though he could stop chewing long enough to swallow...and spills his coffee.

"Everything fine now, Sir?"
"Sure, thanks. But...could you bring two rolls with the main course...please?"
"Certainly."
"Thanks...it's just I like lots of bread. A bit like the French..."

As you wish, two rolls, three or a dozen...butter too, anything you please, Sir, but me! Don't touch the bunny! Ah well, he's not bad looking and he's clean. A pity... hmm, *like the French?*

Damn, seems like she only speaks to me when I'm chewing...like being caught with your pants down. Swallow hard and try to answer with her looking on...sullen, judging my tone and manner. What the hell...can hardly look her in the eye or find my tongue to say *yes mam please.* Damned irritating...and damned I'll let any woman-wife-waitress corral me again...then let me out once a week just to show she can. The past...

I wonder if there really exist people who give. There have been times...down by the river...when it almost sang to me. Oh shush! I've washed a ton of plates and more tears...and never been to Memphis...

A good feeling can destroy bad ones. A good woman can erase the memory of a not so good one. I guess every heart carries a seed that if planted would grow into a bitter tree. Yet I can't help wondering. And can't help remembering. But digging up the past is a worthless stinking void of twice smoked cigarettes and old ashes. So...must pull myself out. A warm feeling, a warm urge. She's damned pretty, if a little sullen...though maybe just proud. There's music warm, air warm...sun warm. And woman warm...

No, never been to Memphis. And I'm tired of these college boys home for the summer. So starved and arrogant. They whine...I say, No! They whine "Oh please..."

Think I'll call the pretty waitress, Proud Mary. Think I'll let her sullen mystery draw me up like well water on a hot thirsty day...

God, if something would just happen...make me feel like I'm...*me!*

Yeah...Proud Mary's got me yearnin'...big wheel keeps on turnin'...pump that tane, Lordy me. Always thought it strange New Orleans would have gas stations, cars, traffic, businessmen. Always pictured Gypsy thieves, cobblestone, misty graves and wrought iron gates, moss, cypress, and jazz...lank black jazz...strolling down Bourbon Street past sultry women...fishin' in the French Quarter... fall in love with a Creole girl's languid cool accent. When the sun sets maybe even Proud Mary has a languid cool accent...

And not one word of poetry have I heard...

Never a good job, no-o-o...but I've been to the city, o-o-oh yeah. They say a winner never quits and a quitter never wins...so how are you to play if dealt no cards? Guess it's a game of chance. Lean in summer, might be flush come winter. Myth of the poor boy and the pot of gold...keeps people goin' though. Even poor boys. High August out there...*Jeez, it's a hot mother.* But a cool cafe...food warm, woman warm. Ah, here it is...odors to swell my tongue and take my breath. Good flavor, great taste...feed my hunger hunched to the plate...in fever, orgasmic, with runny nose and teary eyes...eating. God this is *great-full-ness...*

He has tears. Tears...? Perhaps a young heart...

Roast beef, taters, gravy, creamed corn, hot rolls, butter. God...she might even smile. I can almost smell her starting to smile. Like an instinct some have for weather, I have for smiles. Sometimes, when it's good...I sense it...like the moment the coffee percolates or the corn starts to pop...a shared expectation, a promise of pleasure. Her movements are too polite and subtle not to be a smile. Even her perfume is a smile...and this is a game of hearts and I'm the Jack to her Queen. Feel better than I did an hour ago...a minute ago. The past...good erases bad. Drop a dime and punch G-9...Jerry Lee Lewis and *'Chantilly Lace'*...now there's dinner music. This cafe coffee beats vintage wine...for sure with Proud Mary coming my way...

"Would you like more coffee?"

Sweetly spoken...smiling now...and didn't call me 'Sir.'

"No thanks, I'm good..."

Nice teeth. Perhaps my cowboy is no cowboy after all...anyhow, not like the rest. And I like the music, his choice of songs... never noticed his guitar before...propped by an old army bag...*I wonder how his voice?*...t-shirt, faded jeans...*has he any songs or dreams for me?*...boots, straw hat...all he seems to have. I like the simplicity...traveling light, living free. And he looks a little like Hud, this cowboy. Only Hud dispossessed, without a ranch or rich father...perhaps no one. Makes him more interesting somehow. Feeds my fantasy...while I feed him. But this is real...me, him. An event...one sad waitress and a lonesome cowboy met in an empty cafe one terribly hot day in Kansas and...*'ya giggle and ya talk...wiggle and ya walk...'* Stop making eyes and let him eat his food. Such nice teeth...

Proud Mary and no wonder...sure a pretty one. Got a slight 'S' curved figure. About 5'4", I'd say...standing there, leaned to the counter, trying to ignore my gaze...feigning concern for your nails. Throwing back your hair, exposing your creamy profile and your defiance. Yes, defiant, like a flamingo dancer. Proud Mary. At any moment jump onto the counter and dance the passion and deep rhythms of your soul. Call it seduction, a cry untamed, a ritual, a crime...or religious act as well. Sullen, furtive, only for its silence, yet willful as thunder. I'll take my guitar and play a fiery *Algerias* while you lift your petticoats and colored skirts and snap your moist thighs. Toss your head in defiance as I follow the long fall of your lustrous hair down to the small of your back...where I'd let my hands caress and search the path to your longing and mine. A brunette, no...a reddish tint, auburn, like a bay...yes, and coltish face...ponytail and flowing mane. And delicate shoulders. At times a woman's shoulders are as sensual as her breasts. I wish this were Spain in the 16th Century, the world receding from us, then we would do this Gypsy dance of pleasure and pain...

There are some possibilities which should never go unnoticed, and promises that needn't be avowed, and movements not to be hidden...

She's walking past again...to the window to adjust the blinds. Perhaps she's an itch between her thighs and walks to caress her feathering need. There! I could almost scent the earth of her...almost grasp the moist dark soil of her...*Chantilly Lace?* Yeah, she knows it too, she knows...

He thinks he's got something for me. Well maybe you do, cowboy, maybe. Am I your nightly dream, your Lady Jane? Do you know where the woman in me lies? She's deep in my abdomen, behind my loins...the passage to her is through my thighs and no man has ever found her though several have tried. Would you try? I think you might want to. Yes, and I think I might...

My hunger fed, another hunger builds, more lavish, painful, and urgent than the last. Racing with the raucous rifts of Jerry Lee Lewis...need to slow it down. Play a Neal Diamond...*'Song Sung Blue'*...it's meant to savor. Temper my breathing, my heartbeat, as I sip my coffee and listen...*'weeping like a willow...'* And damn, blushing like a school boy...

Not a force to be ignored. Nor wishing to. I've had your poster on my bedroom wall for five years, Hud...you replaced James Dean. Since age fifteen I've been waiting. Tonight will you be sleeping on my pillow? Will you sing a liquid song of heat into my flesh? Will you dare? This, his eyes...intimacy fueling chemistry...now magnetism...is this possible? I'm smiling, so is he...

Fire, fire, fire...we were born of fire, not dust, and it's fire to which we return and seek again and again...in life and death. Dust comes with the wind to cloud and threaten the certainty of flame. Fruit is ripened by the flame then consumed. They say the cherry came from China and that other worlds are more exotic. But red was not the inspiration of the Orient...the color has a broad, prior appeal, mixed of fire, ash, and dust. Nor was the sun hatched in Kansas, though it sets there each night, bleeding red in the sky, as if spread by the wind, rendering passion and breath eternal. Buffeted, nourished...flesh born of the American steppe...barbaric, elemental, urgent to share...desert, water, fruit...and tonight upon her cool sands feed my masculine heat to her feminine flame. By flesh made holy, by passion crazed...it is not our fate to be sane. But to sin, succumb, and emerge as saints with dusty aura about our jagged bones. Holiness is fire, is heat, is darkness. Man... woman... life...?

I wish to tell you how I saw the moon, its colors...the blue, the yellow, orange, green, and lavender. The green surprised me most. I was looking for darkness...but found color. The clouds, the moon and I had discovered a rainbow in the night. The vision trailed off with a coyote voicing my name. Strange utterances echoed in my mind, alien cries in another voice. Hot spasms fingered through my flesh like wind upon the water. You were inside me and I hadn't seen your face...still a darkness, a void, yet a presence. I couldn't breathe...then I fainted. A possibility...?

'Ring of Fire...' One of Cash's better recordings, alchemy to serve the sinner. Down, down, down...to the bottom of the cup...coffee's an aphrodisiac, so is lettuce and butter and fresh milk. Life caused it all...desire, the living testament to the soul...that I have found my way but for a moment. A pressing song, encircling...*'Love is a burning thing, it makes a fiery ring...'* Down, down, down...in a riverboat dream...from the past to the moonlight...the good side, to the warm and the woman...standing by...

"Your ticket."

"Thanks."
"Was everything okay...?"
"No...I mean...sure..."

Christ, fool...cat got your tongue? If we were alone, I'd know what to say...but no, not here. Say it with a touch...you have a way of smiling...proud and sweet as your answer:

"I know what you mean..."

Do I...really...? What has happened? Hours, minutes, days... have passed...since?

Proud Mary smiles and turns...I follow. Follow her to the cash register.

"That'll be a dollar fifty...plus two cents tax."

I look from side to side...suddenly realize I'm five dimes short.

"Sorry...only got a dollar. Kept feedin' the jukebox and..."
"That's okay," she says. "I enjoyed the songs. Just call it a fifty cent tip and I'll cover." She winks and rings up the register.

"Thanks, I owe you..." then catch her eye and add, "You have a pretty smile, ya know?"
"Why, thank you."
"Say...? Would I be able to find you somewhere...out and about tonight?"
"Perhaps...you might try The Captain's Inn...the south side..."

At times the heat is nearly terminal in Kansas — the August apocalypse spawns a restless quest for cool relief from the grating wind-dust whose only generative life is the windmills' iron-rasped refreshment that grudgingly endures the siege to maintain a limbo existence upon the plains, this parched lady so many have perceived and grieved for. Little wonder the body seeks the night at such times when the stars, though not cool, at least bear the semblance of snowflakes and ice. It's the simple, slim attraction of these nights that keep the people stirring, touching, and sweating...

Gus Cole found The Captain's Inn on the south side after working in a hayfield past sundown – cleaned up, cash in his pocket, joins the evening rush of air fanning through the tavern at 9 p.m.

"Is the captain home?"

"Sure 'nuff," the bartender replies.

"I'd like a six-pack of Coors."

"To go or stay?"

"Maybe...hard to tell."

The bartender stares a moment then lets it pass and goes to the cooler for the beer. Meanwhile Gus turns from the bar and scans the scene.

"You want bottles or cans?" the other calls, lifting the lid to frosted air.

"Bottles!" Gus hollers back over the din of youths gathered around the jukebox. The bartender slides the six-pack to his elbow. Gus turns and hands him a five. The bartender goes to the register and returns with the change which Gus palms to his pocket.

"New here, aren't ya?"

Gus merely nods.

"Where ya in from?"

"On west."

"That a place or direction?" the bartender prods, a tad more belligerent than curious.

"Depends, somewhat both."

"Okay then...where ya headed?"

"On east."

"East, huh?" the bartender mocks, continuing his game: "Goin' far?"

"You bet!" Gus laughs him off. "Ride a pop-bottle rocket all the way to the stars!"

Wry and jocular, but his gaze is firm, unrelenting as headlights in the night. The bartender gives a dubious grunt then turns aside in answer to two fellows just bursting through the door.

"Hey Moose ol' boy...get us two draws! In them frosted mugs!"

"Sure 'nuff Stan! Hey-ya Darrel! How's the fieldwork goin'?"

"Bloody hot! Make mine a red beer, will ya?"

"Sure 'nuff..."

Gus moves to the far side of the tavern and rests his shoulders against the dark mahogany paneling which blushes and darkens beneath washes of blinking *Budweiser* and *Falstaff* signs. He leans his head slightly left to catch a jet of cool air streaming from the ceiling vent.

The tavern is laid out somewhat like a ball diamond. The bar at home-plate, Gus opposite at second, the bandstand at third, pool tables at first, the rest of the infield a scattered array of tables set with pitchers of beer flanked by young men and women of various shape and manner; the outfield is the parking lot. The pinball machine which usually offers a deal of excitement for trifling profit has been sent out for repairs to a Kansas City factory, guilty of losing too many games to dexterous farm hands. It's the grim nature of the tavern relationship that it soon ceases to be an attraction and joy and grows into a need, dark and despondent like the void between doors ajar in abandoned houses...or the empty moments between two hearts opposed. So the tavern to no one's particular shame or chagrin, save older alcoholics', is often zoned beyond the city limits where many former little league players, the pitchers, catchers, and fielders commonly come to initiate their drudging careers as citizens.

Gus broods in such thought, leaned against the paneling, metamorphosed by the angling colored lights like a patient spider on its web, waiting nothing in particular, seemingly without energy or course. He casually unfastens his belt and uses the buckle to snap the cap off a beer bottle. Pleased at the taste, he chases the beer with deep breath then finishes the bottle and pops another. He rolls forward on the sole of his boots then heels back against the paneling, his hair dancing gently beneath the vent, his head in slow nod to his chest, relaxed in limp doze...wheat straw odors and April soda rains join a flux of memories, thirst, and satisfaction all adrift through dusty haymow coughs and crisp beer hall laughter...

In the afternoon he'd found work and the alfalfa stems had bit into his forearms and chest where his skin carried their tiny scabs like a child's scratched mosquito bites. The August sun had burned its mark upon his brow, darkening his features from earlier in the day. The vent air sooths and cools his flesh, stirring slowly, sifting finer seeds of former scents which beckon through his tousled existence...beer and tobacco vapors meet auto-exhaust and hot pavement air sweeping in through the tavern over the dance-scarred floor coming to rest near a slick vinyl barstool below the spin and rattle of a quarter as a dry voice orders *"One cold draw..."* Is it the sweaty brow, the blistered hands, or the parched lips that thirst to lap the foamy brew? There are many paths from the sunburnt, windblown day which lead the gaunt angular stride to the salves of night where like a sponge the body absorbs refreshment to sustain its mad wayward course, seeking carnivals and fairs or other festive delays before sleep and dream...along with darker remnants of tobacco and whiskey and gasoline, or perhaps the taste of popcorn from a theater matinee or the glimpse of a young woman's tender thighs edging towards the lakeshore in a soft summer night...

Gus jerks awake to a lilting song, *"Those were the days...,"* a slow concertina waltz, sweet like want and loss, and he thinks an echo always has more distance than its source, and a wave goodbye has a longer grip on the memory than the strongest handshake.

To the snappy rift of "Jailhouse Rock" the barroom floor begins to bounce as fresh-shaved youths and eager lasses enter to fill the cash register with their signatures. Small-town bank checks of five and ten dollars cashed for beer, cigarettes, music, gas. Quarters and dimes to the jukebox, half dollars for cigarettes, that is for popular filter brands, only forty cents if you smoke straights such as *Lucky Strikes* or *Camels*. A dollar a pitcher for beer, and if you want a frozen pizza heated up that'll be a buck fifty. The Captain's Inn is fully alive and friendly, too early yet for the hard raucous laughter that comes later, the feints and blows and parking lot fights, low drunken spirits of melancholy birth, and the very real and dreadful stink of men's room vomit. For now the ship is buoyant, if a trifle tipsy, all jubilant and frisky at prospects.

Gus sees her seated at a table, watching him through the crowd. She smiles as he pauses to drop a dime in the jukebox and punch B-14, approaching her table to Hank Williams' *"Jambalaya."* He passes through drifts of smoke, sweat, and rank perfume, but reaching her table the air sweetens with scent of fresh shampoo and lilac powder. Her reddish hair curls to her shoulders, wreathing a sleeveless white blouse belted in a short denim skirt – her slender legs crossed, a sandaled foot dangling.

She notes his smile even whiter against his suntan and coyly nudges a chair out from the table. He slowly sinks to the chair as she asks, "How ya been, cowboy?"

"Well now…uh…butter-fine. Yep, got my bellyful an' a pocket full. Feelin' gay-o. Say…," he adds, reaching into his front pocket, "I can pay you that 50 cents."

She stops his hand with hers on his thigh, blushing slightly.

"There's no need. Really, please…you needn't. I enjoyed the music."

"Okey-doke. But then you must have a beer."

He swings the six-pack on the table and offers her one. She shakes her head and glances toward the bar.

"Umm, cowboy…doncha know you're not supposed to drink that in here?"

"In here?" playfully indignant, "Why it's a bar ain't it?"

"Yes, but the rule is only one bottle, a draw, or a pitcher in here. You see, the six-packs are only to-go, because they are actually cheaper."

"Yeah, I know. The barkeep's been eyeing me in that stern silent way like he might wanna pay me a visit. Keeps hinting, but he hasn't."

"I wouldn't mess with him, cowboy. He's pretty big."

"He's fat," declared succinctly as he uncaps a bottle under the table with his buckle and hands it to her, smiling, "Call me Gus…" The jukebox whirs like a shout of laughter at the ripe sweetness of first touching, *"Sunavagun, we'll have big fun…"* and the song spins on in wink and holler, seeming to portend this winsome discourse and offering as she accepts the beer and begins to drink.

At a pause she leans and asks, "So, Gus…you got a last name?"

"*Co-o-ol-e*" he sounds it out in a throaty drawl, like a low growl.

"What?"

"Cole...c-o-l-e...same as coal. Like you burn, ya know, black...fire. If you put a match to me, I burn." They laugh. "Not like some wet logs that only smolder."

"Well, Mr. Cole," she aims her eyes at his belt, "I don't doubt that you burn. But why are you sitting there with your belt unbuckled?"

"Oh, that...," peering down, "does seem a bit moronic, doesn't it?"

"Some might wonder what you're trying to advertise."

"Me, advertise? What might that be?"

She gives a playful kick and says, "I'm not going to call it by name. But that shiny buckle flipping back and forth against your Levis looks as much like a neon sign flashing on and off as any I've ever seen."

"I wouldn't think your pretty little coyote eyes would notice."

"My eyes notice lots of things."

"Then you surely know even motel signs blink 'no vacancy' when they're full up."

"I don't read a 'no vacancy'," she answers pertly, unflinching, matching him move for move. Her manner forthright, escalating, cutting off his options for maneuver. And he's quietly pleased and surprised, though briefly hesitant, amazed by her poise.

"Well, actually, I use the buckle to pop the bottles...like so," he offers, uncapping another beer for himself. "You see? Innocent. Merely a utility. An old carpenter taught me the trick out in Denver. Fairly handy, saves splintering a table edge or busting your teeth, but if you're offended..." He starts to buckle his belt and she moves her hand to his, their faces brushing as she smiles, "No, don't. I kinda like the 'vacancy' sign. Besides, you'll need it again...once I finish my beer."

"You mean...the buckle?"

"What else?"

With the first chord of intimacy struck they fall into a flood of anxious flirtation, rushing, driving them, touching...first their feet beneath the table, teasing, then finger-tips and laughter, thirst, the beer and music adding that vibrant sexual pulse inherent in certain perfumes.

"Now coyote eyes, lovely *wild* eyes...what's your name?"

"Joy. Though, actually, Joyce. I was named for my mother...and so to distinguish between us I've been called Joy since I was very young."

"That's it...that explains the fine arch of your brows...and the twinkly blue flame warming your eyes. Joy...a most joyful name. And god created the heavens and the earth. Created man and woman and they him. And from their union came love which brought sweet Joy to Gus. You really are quite pretty, more like beautiful, I'd say."

"Don't play with me."

"What? But I mean it."

"No one has ever told me that..." Her tone and expression sobers, almost sad.

He casts a doubtful eye. "You mean no one, ever...?"

"Oh sure, they shout, 'Hey beautiful!' from a passing car...and add something dirty. But no one ever said it...like they meant it."

"Then they're just...blind fools. You are beautiful. It's plain to see. I'm not being flip or maudlin...I've only had a few beers. Though I did sweat a lot today. Out in the heat and sun...but it was you...you never left my mind. Like I was transfixed. Like there was a weight on my chest and I couldn't breathe, not like normal. After seeing you in the restaurant I saw you in everything."

"Your eyes burn."

"What?" he laughs, perhaps to ease the pressure of their too rapid intimacy.

"Your eyes burn...I can see it, feel it. They're intense and different."

"Well they oughta burn. I was in the sun all day. That and the damn dust in the hayloft, worse than smoke. Just bloodshot is all."

"No, I see that. The bloodshot. But they are different...," she pauses in struggle to express her thought, "they burn like a man's I saw in a magazine once."

"Yeah, so...who was he?"

"Some man. It was an article about him. He was on death row."

"Really...?"

"Yes, for killing his wife. I think his lawyers were appealing for a retrial on grounds that it was a crime of passion."

"Had she been with another man?"

"No. The article said she'd simply left him."

"Great. Did it say why?"

"I don't think so..."

Gus leans back in thought as the music fades to vague chatter and dim surroundings. Feeling dry and sober, he stands and says, "We need more beer," then leaves the table. The bartender Moose reaches left and right to serve the bustling crowd and at Gus's approach shouts, "No six-packs inside!" To which Gus laughs, "No problem. Got a pitcher of Bud and two glasses?" Moose nods, "Sure 'nuff..." and Gus shortly returns with an overflowing pitcher. He carefully tops off each glass and he and Joy sit for a time, pre-occupied, immersed in thought of the nameless man and of one another.

"I think my eyes burn from the sun and dust," Gus finally assures her. "May even need glasses."

Joy nods in concurrence then abruptly, eagerly asks, "What do you do?"

"I hunger," he sits up in answer, "and wait, wanting to kiss you."

"No really. What do you want to do with your life?"

"Kiss you..."

He leans forth and lightly touches his lips to hers, then brushes her cheek and softly kisses her neck where the perfume lingers strongest. She draws to him for a brief warm kiss, lets him taste her sweet tongue and hot spicy breath and feel the press of her lace-covered breasts. Slowly, reluctantly, they part, resuming prior postures, quietly drinking their beer, looking about the bar and occasionally at one another, smiling.

"Okay Joy...you asked what I'd like to do."

"Yes?"

"I'd like to play guitar for people and sing...really well."

"Like Hank Williams?"

"Sure, like him and others. Just make people feel...ya know, warm and sad, then sometimes glad, make 'em jump 'n shout. Make 'em dance and act a little like kids..."

"And drunken fools?" she suggests as they laugh and touch glasses.

"You bet, that too. Somehow ease the stress and pain of all the get-go 'n gain that we're taught to strive, cry 'n die for. The vast number always falling short in wonder of what-the-hell 'n why? And that…I cannot answer."

"Whatever set you to thinking such thoughts?"

"Ah well, I's born very young and had little experience in life," he grins. "Pardon, that's an old joke…probably old as Adam. But here's the truth, the real base fact of the matter, the hard nut dug up like an elf's treasure and offered to you. Yep, pure gold, or nearly so…all started with a little flower, much maligned, the dandelion."

She leans to one elbow with the eye of a skeptic. "Now you are pulling my leg."

"No, much as I'd like to," he grins in glance to her bare thigh tempting the hem of her skirt. "But it was the dandelion that set me…on my wayward path. You see, one day when I's a boy my mom made me dig dandelions in our front yard. Said, 'Dig 'em all up before you can play…' Well, ya know, I wanted to please my mom, I's a good kid, sort of, partially, some of the time…so I set right to the task, poppin' the little fellas out of the ground. But it wasn't long before I realized I'd dug nearly two hundred and hadn't made a dint. Furthermore, I'd taken to their color…pretty a yellow as ever was…a dandelion. And fragrant…a fresh virgin grassy flavor, wonderful, like clover and alfalfa breezes in a summer pasture. And the leaves made a tasty salad, I knew that. And dandelion wine, though I had little notion of that as yet. Still, I suspected something out of kilter, people killing off this dandy little flower. Christ, what did they have against a dandelion?"

"So? Did you finish your task?"

"Nope. I think mom looked out after about an hour and saw me dawdling 'n gazing off, took mercy and set me free. Knew I was a lost cause. Besides, only snooty church folks had dandelion-free yards and she never cared much for their kind, so our yard grew a glorious puff of dandelions from then on."

"That's a wonderful story, Gus. And me too…I've always

loved dandelions. When I was a little girl I'd gather them, and you know what they made me think of?"

"No, but I bet your gonna tell me."

"Tiny little male lions who instead of mangy manes had beautiful yellow petals all around their faces."

"Why, that's crazy" – they both laugh. "But I had a similar notion. Dandy little lions, the very same. Yet here I am all of age and still haven't sipped dandelion wine. There's something wrong with that, Joy. Almost a sacrilege, like missing communion. And look at me, spent all day throwing alfalfa bales, stems of another flower crushed together by the thousands, cut down, wired up, bundled and stowed…to feed cattle cuds, horse droppings, sheep manure. But what the hay, critters gotta eat, right? Same as us, so we spend most our lives slaying things we love, craving things we don't need while praying to something we can't see. There you have it, pretty much the twisted trail of thought I travel, the nugget of gold I seek, all a dream, and it may not pan out."

"You do have a way with words."

"Words are easy. The guitar is hard…and convincing folks to listen."

"So…where's your guitar?"

"In my room. I took a room at the motel…out by the highway."

"Oh, I see."

"Would you like to dance?"

"I'd love to…"

Again Gus plays *"Jambalaya"* and leads Joy to the floor, their smooth happy movements more celebrant than seductive. They dance relaxed, without tension, allowing their bodies to sway and touch in mutual, casual massage. They laugh and sing along *"Me-oh-my-oh…"* with a looser south-of-the-border version of the jitterbug.

The song ends in a sharp crack of thunder that silences the bar and cuts the lights, then a murmur of surprise and laughter as the lights flicker back on. A man enters the front door dripping wet and Moose the bartender yells, "Christ O'Molly, it's raining!"

"Hell yes!" the man shouts back. "Blows hot all day then slaps down a gully washer!"

"Sure sounds like it."

"Dern straight!" the wet one affirms...

As the jukebox and crowd whirl back to life Gus and Joy take their exit, thrilled in their rush through the downpour and soaked when they reach her car. But in their leaving the storm already begins to break, intermittently mirroring headlights and far lightning in puddles along the highway. Joy drives as Gus hangs his head out the window to catch the gusts of cool air and rain, thinking of all such nights he's known...massive onslaughts of opposing dark fronts muscling forth, casting turbulence through the arena sky in dance and spar, charge and slash, stunning the senses with wicked bolts and jabs and thunderous tumult, cleaving the heart and scattering shadows to lurk about the night. Horses neigh, children jump and scream, then a few miserly drops fall like blood from a superficial wound to curl the dust. The storm soon passes...hopes wane. Those with fates and crops in the balance turn again to whiskey and despair.

"I love the wind," Gus muses, "constant, wild, untamed."

Joy replies that the wind frightens her, "Makes me feel alone."

They drive on to the motel in silence.

Entering his room they quickly embrace, then stumble and giggle, faint with passion. Joy looks around, puzzled, and asks, "Something smells like a greenhouse?"

Gus laughs and pulls her to him.

"It's your hat," she says, "your straw hat. The rain makes it smell like a greenhouse."

"You're so fresh and lovely...a budding flower. All petals and pulse..."

Gus kicks the door shut. Joy moves to the bed and sits, hands folded on her lap, looking up, anxious, as he pulls his t-shirt over his shoulders.

"Wait...please," she bites her lip, hesitant. "I don't want this to be just one night."

He steps toward her, belt unfastened, almost belligerent in tone.

"Look, I could promise you two nights. Twelve, eighteen...all the tomorrows. An entire lifetime, sure, why not? But it wouldn't affect tonight. Now. We love, we desire, it's real. Like our flesh, our need...so don't qualify it, Joy. If not now...when?"

"Gus, you...your eyes...you do look like you could kill."

"Then go to your car, leave if you want. I won't touch you," he says, standing back.

"No," she smiles weakly, "I'll stay," reaching to unsnap his jeans...touching, wanting, awaiting the pain, the pleasure, his hay-loft breath to her budded lips and sting-froth filled entering the moment's embrace while neon strobes through blinds with heat cast from gone storms and headlights passing...hot flesh on cool sheets, his skin to hers taken-given utterly in hunger and need, their blood in rush to the sea...hands, feathers, fins, grasping, reaching one to the other lost in depths and memory primal to knowing, unsought yet surfacing in salt sweat, breath, and gasp...heave, pull, arch, and thrust, limbs like oars dipping to waves of passion and lust too intimate to forgive or forget, tender, vibrant, uncoiled, consumed...at last lying still, becalmed, silent...

(*Several hours later: the same motel room. Occasionally a truck or semi passes, engines grinding on for Denver or Saint Joe. The room is spare and commercial, neat but gray, colorless. One large bed, a bureau, chair, and floor lamp. A bathroom off to the right. The room is dark except for the flashing motel sign outside the window. Finished with their love-making,* Gus *and* Joy *lay half entwined, drifting through the early morning nuance of hunger, fatigue, jaded nerves and aching eyes, and long beer-breath sighs of insomnia blues strained through a night of wayward circumstance.* Gus *sits up on the edge of the bed and gazes through the darkness toward the bathroom door and the stool that won't stop running...*)

Gus: Seems kind of sad now it's over...you 'n me, here, but separate. Odd how loving someone only reaffirms you being alone (*speaking with no particular motive or reason, rather quiet and rambling over his thoughts*). It's always so fast, abrupt. A quick for certain union then Wham! (*slaps the bed*) all the magic glitter falls to the floor and fades away. The sandman throws dust in your eyes. You sleep. The night's hot embers cold by the time morning comes and the damn birds start to sing. Remember how fast a stick of gum would lose its sweetness...or a carnival its excitement? Everyone and everything wearies of the day, all its odd and familiar proposals. Remember those late nights as a kid riding home from a fair or a movie? Summer crickets singing over the country night, the pageantry dead before the dream...and we were dead to the world. Remember?

Joy (*turns on her side as the neon illumines all the fear, misunderstanding, and worry in her eyes*): But I thought it was perfect. And the sweetness isn't gone, Gus. I love you. I didn't realize it had gone wrong.

Gus: No, no, that's not it. Truly (*he leans back and kisses her*), I'm speaking of loss, of endings. Of our inability to sustain rich moments. No, it was good. Beautiful...like you...and I'm all the more diminished for its goodness.

Joy: But it hasn't stopped...not for me (*she takes his hand and moves it over her pelvis and loin region*). Feel...here...see? Tiny heat spasms moving like waves from a pebble dropped on water. From my thighs to my throat, and I feel as if they could last forever. See, you can retain the feeling... (*both glance up at a truck screaming past*). Already my love grows beyond where that truck will travel tonight.

Gus: Okay, sure, I feel the warmth...like an afterglow of love. And that's a potential that can't be measured...somewhat along the lines of hope and faith, nearly infinite, at least in theory. But each day we have to deal with endings...if only in thought.

Joy: But what about beginnings? Aren't there beginnings?

Gus: Yes, but more deceptive. The embryo is born into a void. Not from, but hatched into a void. Love, a puzzle of all white pieces. A sort of hiatus, a twilight of being. An anticipation, a profound belief, a certainty in something... illusive...ever near, wanting to touch, embrace, but falling short. As if our lives were passing on close parallel paths that never really merge. A separateness that tempts like neon splashes colored with anxious heartbeats, hinting of 'beyond-beyond', echoing through the night in urgency to become the day. A futility without end...like the distance beyond those headlights...always some arbitrary moment, place, or person along the highway...

(*A confession of his restless nature, his wanderlust, while* Joy *is in fact still anchored to the act, their passionate exchange,* Gus *already moves beyond, however unwittingly. He quietly pulls on his jeans and begins pacing the floor, barefoot, silent, in fumble for words, sensing the vague fraught meaning of their experience and what waits. She's rooted to him while he's rooted to the world and all its uncertainty. From pleasure to despair, feelings discordant, each drawing back into themselves.*)

Joy: I don't know what you mean (*she half rises, clutching the sheet, doggedly asserting herself and her experience*). I...I love you. What are you saying, meaning?

Gus: Sometimes we must live with the burden that there may be no meaning.

Joy: And no love?

Gus: Yes, even that. At least not as we wish. Not an absolute, to have and to hold... (Joy *begins to weep – wounded, unable to deflect or refute* Gus's *stern assertions.*) Hey, don't do that. Don't cry. Look...it's not like you think (*he sits back down and draws her to him, her head to his shoulder, in attempt to break through the angst and abstraction, his grim mood...*) It's the beer, the highway...the trucks. This room, the cinderblock and tiled floor, and that flushing stool...all point to the sterility and stink of modern doings. Thoughts driven ajar, everything counter of what it should be. It's not you, Joy. Listen, it's...the past...tensed up like walls closing in. And life...women...yeah, count yourself lucky if you can take and hold the moment... linger in the mist of the love act for a time...enveloped, radiant, renewed. Seems men can only jump in 'n out. Blam! Like a shotgun blast...shoot our pattern once, twice then collapse. Left wrung-out, empty. Women are absorbed, men merely plucked, consumed...like a grape from a vine. All that potent heat 'n juice vanished, gone in an instant...leaving a sort of gnawing void, a perplexing mix of want, loss. A sudden restless urge that pulls you back and away...not in dislike or disfavor, but a lax weakness...like the magnet's lost its charge and all the filings fall to dust...(Joy *has stopped crying and is listening, dazed and dreamy.*) Is any of this making sense?

Joy: I love listening to you speak. Your voice...

(*He half-smiles and leans back, squinting to the vague darkness in search of meaning.*)

Gus: You see...men have this big ego. More so than women. And we're prone to get humbled...awestruck, if we're lucky, but more often beat down. Sometimes by an astral event...an eclipse, or a passing comet. Sometimes a drought or flood will drive the bitter blade of doubt between our ribs and end our arrogance. And sometimes a lovely woman like you will cause us to totter and gaze to the ugly depth, or truth, no longer cocksure of our path, ourselves. Faced with our meager reflection, suddenly cornered, swallowed up, we try to jump free and escape the event...its power and hold.

Joy: So you want to run away from me...is that it?

Gus: Not my want, it's my instinct...because I've never been so at ease with a woman. Never spoken this freely or felt such warmth. And this is where it gets ugly, because it's untimely, unexpected. Men want to aim straight but miss, always at cross purposes. We try to draw more from life than we've any right to, waste the greater part on profanity and poker and so squander what chance we may have in reach for what we can't have. Then, finding ourselves dressed up fools, left desolate, empty, mocked by the vanity of our lives we grow reckless.

Some turn to drink, others…suicide.

Joy: It doesn't have to be that way.

Gus: No, but it sure tends to. Women, not so foolish, are less prone. Still, it happens, victims of unmet desires, or another's need. Used by men in our wildling quest, you are the oasis, the fruit, the well to drink from when we thirst. Call it survival, right or wrong, I don't know. But seems love and passion are two distinct forces, like man and woman, that converge and conflict and leave you wondering which. And what it comes down to is this…when a man feels strong, drunk on life, he wants to challenge the gods and seek his destiny. At times he sobers and draws back, perhaps weakens, and cares only for the human path, and a woman's heart…

(*Two trucks roar past, battling for the next stretch of unclaimed highway.*)

Joy: Do you want a woman's heart?

Gus: Sure. But I also want to battle the gods.

Joy: What about a home and children?

Gus: Nothing against a home and family, someday…so long as it doesn't undercut or hinder the other…the battle. Why I live and what I am.

Joy: Isn't love enough?

Gus: No, it's not. The other, call it the quest, is not a wish, it's a curse, a demand that also pumps the blood…without which life becomes a mask of decay. Even love, our finest emotion, soon wears the mask. It changes feature…checks the heart with new terms and definition, mostly negative. Wears the mask of finance and responsibility, the mask of the father, husband, bearer of the seed and original sin, sire of the children and their malleable souls. Eventually love dissolves and decays. What remains is a jealous, guarded, fenced-in partnership, cool, utilitarian, life-insured. The couple no longer share their hearts...they share a policy...call it marriage. Ultimately they take responsibility by the handle and dig their graves with it.

Joy: This morning...I mean yesterday...in the restaurant, while you were eating, everything seemed so simple. You were like a movie poster come to life. Interesting, carefree, vital. From listening now I know more about you than if I had known your mother and father and the events of your life. Yet it's all so confusing that I actually know less than if I knew nothing at all. Less than yesterday...in my fantasy.

Gus: And yesterday, I never guessed that I'd love. That I...I wasn't expecting to love anyone. Not like this...

Joy: You can say that? And still leave...like you're going to?

Gus: Look! Love doesn't give you the right to ask for more than what just happened between us. We shared tonight...and there were no promises. So you have no right!

Joy: I know. I'm sorry. I know... it's just that one night is so little.

Gus: Now you're beginning to feel the emptiness, the loss. The gum is losing its sweetness. The moment is gone. You're realizing it now.

Joy: Yes. Perhaps I'm selfish. I've waited so long...only one night.

Gus: I never said I was leaving.

Joy: No. But I bet you do.

Gus: Don't bet. I might stay...awhile. I don't know. I don't know...

(*A bird sings and the neon colors fade before the graying dawn. The 5 o'clock train whistles several miles south out over the valley. Joy throws back the sheet and begins gathering her clothes and dressing.*)

Gus: I hadn't noticed the birthmark on your spine before. (*She continues dressing, turned from him, not speaking.*) You're sad, aren't you? Probably even sorry.

Joy: No (*in a soft whisper, still turned away*). I'm not sorry. Not for anything.

Gus: But you are sad, aren't you?

Joy: Yes (*turning to him, now fully dressed and prepared to leave*). But only because I love you and don't know if I'll ever see you again. (*She pauses.*) Will I?

Gus: I don't know. They said they had a week of two of fencing. So yeah, maybe…

Joy: Well, goodbye…

(*She exits into the pending dawn, the night dead to the day. Gus swings to his feet and switches on the radio. The early livestock report hums rudely in from Saint Joe: "Lambs down a quarter. Beef 'n pork up a half…"*)

THE FAIR

The wind blew like a curse while the sun, the great robber baron, seized the lion's share from all that lived. Dust and heat coalesced with a skiff of clouds as a blue-gray haze dimmed the sky. Through the pastures and along the fences native grasses baked to dry blonde and brittle russet, dormant, the juice of life drawn to the deepest roots. Even the green in the leaves hung on, flaking like a fool's illusion.

The farmer knelt in the wheat stubble for a time, elbow to knee, his right hand stirring a small pile of grain spilled earlier from the auger. Standing, he cast a handful aside, not in disgust but weary resignation, like a sower who knows he will never reap a bountiful crop. For harvest, nature's promise of surplus and feast, her banquet of hope, had fared poorly, a miser's gift to the needy. He was not inept, to the contrary, he was diligent and hardworking and it was a minor miracle the land produced at all. Simply, his acreage was insufficient and he lacked the means to gain more. Bound to a tenant farm on the marginal prairie, snared by time, inertia, and a landlord's deceitful promise to one day will him the farm, so caught in a grinding cycle of labor, worry, and bitter reward.

A dust-devil grazed his face like chiding laughter. He pulled the bill of his sweaty cap lower to shade his eyes then slowly wiped his hands on his soiled overalls. Turning, he glanced to his wife and four children waiting anxiously at the edge of the field by a faded-green Ford sedan, fender-bent and rusty, their hopes tied to the trail of dust left by their neighbor's truck heading for town with the last load of grain to be tested, weighed, and sold, all hopeful in watch and wait for it had been weeks since they'd seen a movie, visited for pleasure, or spent a dime other than for bare essentials or machinery repair.

There was a fair, with carnival, that very evening at a town twenty miles east, and they were wondering if with the cash from the harvest in hand whether he'd hold it all in reserve for planting costs and winter needs or relax his grip and take them for a little fun. Just to see it all would be grand. His wife, still in the bloom of youth, stood outwardly stoic, veiling a gnawing weariness from years of doing without.

He smiled inwardly...for her there was a blue satin dress, boxed, hidden in the closet, waiting at the house. And the children, ranging in age from four to fourteen, the oldest, a budding brunette, then another daughter and two sons, towheads like children of the grain goddess, all beautiful to his eyes, proof that fate had not forsaken him entirely of blessings, so he took great care to cultivate their dreams...for them, if not a full glass, tonight at least they'd have their sip of joy.

Through the heat-waves they watched his gaunt frame approach, emerging much like a shadow from a mirage. Lean, hollow-cheeked, as the truly impoverished often are, his dark weathered face seemed cast by the ancient mark of Cain, as if he carried that old scar of feudal endurance against some Lord's cruel indifference. But not a mean face, his eyes when not glinting black in anger or frustration sang, moist and playful, and he could smile, though the smile and laughter always tore against a grim knowing. For etched in his face lay a hardened sorrow desperate to strike out as he had many times in his youth, leaving the fingers of both hands scarred and bent. Though he told his sons that he'd broken his hands taming wild horses, truth was his family, hill folk transplanted from eastern Tennessee, had provided ripe gossip for the local rumor-mills, and his fists had dutifully erased the smirk from many a startled face. Even at that his fighting hadn't changed a thing, and now...it was clearly futile to pound a fist against the hard-packed earth or against a banker's vaulted door, and the fight in him was being swallowed up like a fleeting rain in drought, swallowed up and turned inward.

They waited, his wife and children, watching his fierce silence stop before them, watching the fight-scarred hand tip the bill of his cap back from his eyes as he gazed on the dust-trail slowly disappearing from the hill east. Waiting, watching, listening as he finally said it was time they head back to the house. Another breathless moment passed before he added, "There's lots to do if we're going to the fair tonight."

Shrieks of joy erupted with his smile.

Their jubilation accompanied all the remaining hours of the day. Buckets of bath water drawn from the cistern, commonly a considerable labor for his wife, rose buoyant as circus balloons on a string. And the daughters, using irons heated on the oil-burning range in the already stifling kitchen to press their pleated skirts sewn for blue ribbons in 4-H, fairly danced through their task as though inhabiting a cool breeze of delight. While the two boys, after gathering eggs, eagerly helped their father finish feeding and watering the livestock. All through the chores their father, presently free of worry, overflowed with wit and good-humor. Even the horses nibbling at the grain pulled back their lips and seemed to laugh as they chomped and snorted.

That evening after his wife had cleared the dishes from the supper table and he laid the surprise box before her, all watched expectantly in hushed silence...then overjoyed as she unfurled the dress before her. It was like Christmas in July and her love for him was tangible as the touch of her hand tracing his smile as she whispered something he alone could hear. The moist tearing of her eyes was his wish fulfilled.

Soon all were dressed as only people who have so little can – resplendent in their pride and cleanliness. The farmer's pressed work jeans fit him neatly from the waist to the heels of his polished boots, while the white shirt and light-gray Stetson highlighted his darkly handsome features. His lovely wife blushed like a bride in her new dress; the daughters blossomed pretty as daisies in their pleated skirts and blouses; and both boys, bronzed, grinning ear-to-ear, wore blue jeans, t-shirts, and tennis shoes. All dressed and ready for the fair. Resplendent and happy. For country people love a fair like kings love grand parades, as if the purpose of their long labor was this brief joyous occasion.

With the evening sweetened by cicada song and the sun's white heat softened to a warm red glow in the cool blue west, the old Ford turned out of the drive onto the road heading east. At the crest of the first hill they glimpsed the long beam of the revolving spotlight calling all to the fair like a great magnetic pulse funneling their souls toward the vortex of a dream. Immediately their voice-heart-minds filled with sights and sounds of the fair – a vivid swirl of acrobats, clowns, Gypsy fortune-tellers, spellbinding rides, and the crowded midway lined with intriguing games rigged to pick their pockets through sleight-of-hand and eye-alluring prizes. The attraction was visceral, an elation felt in their stomachs as they journeyed over the hills with the rush of a roller-coaster, literally floating an instant, weightless on the descent, the effect heightened by the acceleration at each crest, propelling them airborne briefly before bounding down then up again, soaring on the magical anticipation and excitement of the fair.

And perhaps it was this added mechanical stress that broke the axle. Most likely it would have happened anyway. In any case their levity ended in the utter silence of their car broken down at the side of the road, stopped five or six miles shy of their destination, so tantalizingly near it was heartbreaking, for they could clearly discern the lighted whirl of the Ferris wheel on the horizon. Mute, sullen, anchored by the firm gravity of the fallen, they slowly dislodged from the unfaithful metal beast. A flat tire could have been replaced by the spare, but a broken axle ended their dream – its pitiless phantom circled with the taunting beacon cast through the shrouded sky.

The farmer gave the left front tire a perfunctory kick, mumbled his intentions to his wife, then quickly left seeking help that would be a long time coming for he would not approach the farms close by. And the reason was not that he had at one time or another blackened an occupant's eye, though true, but because he retained his hill-people's deep-rooted distrust of strangers. He would walk three miles north to his sister's place, to one who had spawned much of the scandal that had embittered his life, and it would be late, nearly midnight, before he returned with a borrowed car to take them home.

And he left quickly to avoid the combined stare of their crushing disappointment. Bitter rage tore at him. Happiness had been so close, like the vision of the Ferris wheel come into view till you could reach out and touch its arcing light and life, yet all now flung to pieces. And he felt a groundswell of hatred growing behind him, felt his own culpability for maintaining their poverty through a vain stubborn attachment to the land, felt as well a deep groaning in his bones, like blood-mixed urgings from a Druid's ghost whispering dark intimations of sacrificial death. Was it then that he first thought of the brass-encased bullet, in those few grains of lead, a dream of peace aborning? Perhaps his death could one day bridge their disappointment and bring celebration to hand...

But it was not hatred they felt. His wife, her eyes burned dry in the disconsolate wind watching him walk away, knew the realities, the fruitless cycle of all his labor, knew his goodness and feared for him and herself. True, the daughters were quietly scornful, harboring the resentment common to all adolescents for a parent who cannot fulfill with a wave of a wand their urgent, confused desire. And the boys were merely stunned, mystified at such a God who would strike them down in the midst of their glory and leave them abandoned on this bleak, desolate hillside, and their father swallowed up in darkness as he soon would be forever in death.

Silent, their festive raiment aflutter, festooned on the hulk of the car, they all watched with faint pleasure the brief fireworks display, too distant to inspire the usual gasps of awe-struck wonder, though the moment did attain a flicker of delight, only to quicken their thirst and leave them hungrier than before. Fading to a deeper silence till even the stars that had shone through the hazy veil now vanished, leaving nothing but the spotlight, the teasing echo of their longing, throbbing through the night, and the empty ache of never knowing that plateau of happiness they might have shared had they arrived that evening at the fair.

OF BIRDS AND TIME (from *Skin for Skin*)

A half mile west of Elim, Kansas, a tall sandy-haired boy runs along a dirt road south of the railroad tracks. Odie Nietenthall lives on a farm a mile on west and two miles south and runs everywhere he goes. The previous spring he took first place in the quarter mile at the 1933 Hill County track meet, only a junior. And a year ago this very day he scored the winning touchdown over LaBelle, their arch rival. Tied 6 to 6 at half their coach said, "You boys win this game...I don't care if you gotta kill 'em!" They sent three LaBelle players off on a stretcher and Odie busted his nose in the effort, sniffs now and then as it wasn't set right. But no football this year, the coach hired away to Ft. Hays College and no money to replace him. Every Saturday gone silent, no band playing, no drumbeats, no crowd cheering – a bum deal for the fastest boy around. Still, there's basketball this winter and track next spring, so he runs his three miles to school and back each day. Now running into town for the Saturday night movie, he carries a fresh-dressed chicken wrapped in newspaper tucked under his arm like a football. Joe's Cafe pays 75¢, which buys him dinner, a movie, and leaves change to jingle in his pocket.

The sun setting fast at his back stretches his shadow a good 50 feet which makes him feel like a giant, like he could reach there in a single step. Along the track from the east he spies his friend Faris Clayton walking his way. He gives a holler and strides out, aiming to sprint the distance. Out front his shadow sets the pace, edging to a large flock of blackbirds, hundreds of them spilling over the road and ditches and adjacent field. At any moment he expects them to rise up and funnel off like smoke in the wind. But they remain set, feeding on weed pods and grain leavings, and not until his flesh threatens do they flutter up and fly and then only ten or twelve feet in hover and swirl like a moving canopy under which he runs. Hundreds if not thousands of sun-tipped wings beat the air close above and all about, creating a symphonic rush beyond any band or cheering crowd that lifts him as if he were all but weightless, himself flying. And so cocooned he runs through the greater distance until he exits, gasping for breath, not from fatigue but the sheer thrill and exhilaration. He staggers down the embankment and crosses the tracks, wearing a big grin like he's won the greatest race of all.

"That was…that was wild!" he says, greeting his friend.

"I watched all the way, Odie. You near disappeared in there. Thought they's gonna carry you off like that twister did Dorothy and take you to Oz."

"They dern did for a spell. That was magic, real magic!" he swears.

"You headin' to a movie?"

"You bet I am. *The Black Cat*…they say it's scary. You oughta come."

"Naw, need to save my money, I want that cycle. Besides, I had the best day ever."

"Really?"

"Better than any ten movies. I drove Mira Rose to Red Cloud and back in the Blue Roadster."

"Gol-ly…clear to Red Cloud?"

"Yep, my best day ever. Like I was thinking on the way out just now, if this track was my life, that spike right there" – he taps it with his shoe – "that would be today. The golden spike of my life."

"That ain't gold. Just a old rusty spike."

"No Odie, you gotta imagine it's gold. And that spike is today. See, right here along these tracks where we stand, this span of tracks is our life, our time. On west, toward the sunset, that's way beyond where we live. We can only live to where we see the tracks end, up by that far tree about a mile 'n a half west, beyond the Hinsen place. And back yonder where the tracks curve around Krouchek's pond and head east, that's where we started out, where we were born."

"I wasn't born down there. I's born over to Mankato."

"No, listen Odie, not the place, but the span of time we live. You got to imagine. Look, up there where the sun's near gone, that's the future where we'll never live, only our children and theirs after them. The tracks will lead to a new terrain 'n time. To mountains, deserts, the great ocean beyond. Events and lives we can't even name, for they are yet to come. And back yonder beyond that curve is the past, where our folks were born and their folks before them. And the tracks lead back in time through timber 'n hills and deep forests to another ocean all dark 'n hidden. That's the past. And up ahead, that's the future. But right here, where we stand along this span of tracks is our time, where we live."

"This…right here?" Odie motions with his dead chicken. "You mean that's all?"

"No, there's trains passing each day, carrying people 'n freight. All the things happening beyond ourselves. Like war in China or the elections coming up. Or the World Series last week between the Cardinals 'n Tigers. Like a newsreel, Odie, or a movie, and we watch it all go by. Then it ends."

"Ends?" Odie sniffs as much to clear his mind as to clear his nose.

"Yep, somewhere up by that tree."

"Heck, I can't even see that far it's so dark. You're makin' me sick to my stomach with all your dizzy talk, Faris. Sometimes you think too much."

"No, I wonder is all. Thinking is more like figurin' interest on a bank loan. Or how I'm gonna get the money to buy that cycle off Lyle. I'm only wondering, Odie."

"Then I'm wonderin' why we can't just hop that train 'n ride past that tree on out to the mountains 'n ocean and see all that time up ahead?"

"You can't ride that train, Odie."

"How come?"

"Because it's not a regular train, it carries things that happen outside us. Things we hear on the radio or read about. It's not a train we can ride, but we can listen…" In the gathering shadows Faris kneels by the rails. "Put your ear to a rail like this, sometimes you hear your death comin'. Try it."

"No, I don't want to."

"Well I hear mine. The death train will come when I'm about 40. A man shouldn't live past 40."

"Beans to that. I'm gonna live past 90."

"You just might."

"And I don't like your danged ol' trains. Time trains, death trains, none of 'em."

"Don't sweat it, Odie. There's trains we can ride. The Rock Island Rocket, the Jersey, they hit Elim every day. They take us on to Mankato, Kansas City, or way out west to Denver, clear to California."

"Well that's better."

"And look, the sun's gone down. See the stars coming out? Soon be hundreds, thousands. The Bible says, *'Tell the stars if thou be able to number them...'* Just think, millions of stars aglitter in the endless night. A night without time or end."

"I ain't lookin' up there, makes me dizzy, Faris. And I ain't thinkin' no more. Need to get some food in me 'n see a movie…" He dashes off before he hears another word.

"Watch out for near-things!" Faris yells as Odie one-hops to pull a devil's claw from his heel. "They'll snatch you up 'n carry you off like the birds nearly did!" He laughs watching his friend high-balling for the lights, fading towards town.

THE CACTUS FLOWER

The sulfur moon had not quite stilled behind the earth when morning came. Cock pheasants barked in dance beneath the dawn which briefly held then spilled into the day. The meadows and reeds soon shed their dew as prevailing winds swept forth and heat phantoms roused over the broad grain fields and rolling pasture lands. Beneath the aegis of the October sun, Indian summer bloomed with a brilliance equaling the warmth of June. Not at all a shy sun which unresolved as a child in fear of strangers will attempt to hide its face, but a proud, regal sun which bids all others abate their gaze and boldly shows forth his massive yellow plumes.

Far below, the colors echoed and mushroomed in flumes of rival river currents splashing over a logjam. Their pulse carried the painted memory of the land and its elusive song to where the colors pooled in softer, deeper hues, the golden browns and russets of autumn mixing in the quiet eddies. Overhead, the breeze purled among the cottonwood limbs, its psalmody immanent in the orphaned leaves. About the hills and distance all loomed larger, the present made grander by the close-whispering past.

Even the two men who now walked past a cistern at a nearby farmstead seemed twice their normal size, made archetypal by the strong distortion, a magnification with which the past oft imbues its subject. The older was the younger's uncle and each bore distinct resemblance as uncle and nephew sometimes do. Both faces were sculpted in similar lines of sun and shadow, though the uncle's brow was broader, low and Spartan, while the nephew's narrowed in a more fitful countenance, especially since his hair was longer and blew awry – his eyes brown, the uncle's deep blue, reflecting the sky where he'd flown in two wars. In their carriage and stride both men were lean and supple; the uncle taller and more tautly hewed. As they strode their thighs forged against their faded denims; their bare forearms swung rhythmically with the steel-blue veins of labor and the swarthy print of the sun.

They disappeared behind a small shed briefly then reappeared on the other side. The uncle proceeded slowly some ten paces into the fireweed and clover then stopped and turned to his nephew, showing the gray of his temples against the sun.

"Now I've stepped them off," he said, his rich brassy voice resonant and bemused, "right from that north corner post as before. And it should be here. Could have sworn I left it here the other day. By the gosh," he drawled, his mustache bristling sharply above his grin, "is this any way to run a farm?"

"I don't guess," the other laughed.

"Hell's bells," the uncle grimaced, rubbing his jaw as the nephew kicked in search among the weeds; "the old man can't seem to keep anything straight these days. Gettin' as bad as those two boys of mine…"

He meant to use the singular of course. During the preceding winter his eldest son had been killed in a car wreck and the uncle still had lapses when he spoke of him in the present tense. The nephew was accustomed to this happening, but lately he'd begun to wonder if his uncle would ever accept his son being gone. And while he realized that the sense of him, like a shadow, may have lingered for a time, it was painful to see his uncle carry its presence so long. For the other son, too young for a man's labor, waited eager for his father's eyes to turn to him, yet his father continued to gaze off in want of the first, a constant, gnawing grief. So the nephew came often to help his uncle, and they'd grown close during that time.

"Couldn't we use the truck?" the nephew offered. "I can load while you drive. It wouldn't take us too long."

"Oh, reckon we could," the uncle offered vaguely in wry glance, "but wouldn't want to take advantage of a young man…give him a hernia. You'd have to drive."

"No, no," the other countered, "you don't need to be throwing bales. I'll do that."

"Well then," the uncle chuckled, "since neither of us wants to drive, guess we'll have to find that gear-box, wherever the devil it is, and do it the lazy man's way, with the Farm-all."

"You sure ol' Milner didn't grab it when he borrowed the Oliver?"

"No, not sure of many things these days," the uncle frowned.

"Gettin' forgetful. Oh, it ought to be layin' right here. Like those pliers ought to be in my pocket. But bet they're layin' over in the field somewhere," he continued in self-parody. "I could do a better job of managing, I reckon, put the place in shape, but you know how it is...the old man likes to talk. I stop in to check on my neighbor more'n I should. And I imagine my absentmindedness and visits have cost me some over the years. But tradin' such for all the work I might've done doesn't strike me as a bargain. Besides, and this I admit," his tone more sober, "I don't have much get-up 'n go anymore. When I started farmin' with Dad there after the war, I worked hard. Put in a new barn, corrals, built up a good herd. Played town ball..." He'd pitched, cool and lank as a whip, favored the knuckle-ball and threw a no-hitter in '49 that folks still talked about. "And I got to fly my Corsair each month in the reserves. It was a good life. Then Korea came along, I was called back up..." He'd lost three planes, too shot-up to fly again, and seen good buddies go down, and after his son's death often wished he had too. Left embittered at the sorry stalemate, the war seldom mentioned. The one story he liked to tell was of his and a buddy's liquor run to Japan – they'd smuggled a crate of whiskey, weighing nearly a ton, and brought it through by bribe and bluff, cheered by their thirsty fellows at the front, reward enough for two bold Marines. "So...that done with, I returned and we went back at it, Dad 'n I. The place really took shape, felt like a home. Then the government put in the dam up there and we had to sellout 'n move from the White Rock. You can only start over so many times and, well...that took it out of me. And it's taken a long time down here. Then Dad died and I sort of took a rest...almost gave it up. Then, gradually, these past few years the place started feeling like a home again, like White Rock. And the boys 'n me, we've worked it hard. It's slow, but improved. And then...well," his voice began to break and fade, "I was hoping to leave it to him..."

The uncle's face winced with stoic shame as he turned from his nephew to gain control then failed and sobbed with long abandon. Embarrassed, respectful, the other also turned aside, had a few tears of his own to blink away.

A red-tailed hawk circled in vantage above the land as the nephew cast his eyes west nearly a quarter of a mile to where a black locust stood like a lonely gallows on the pasture hillside. And memory seemed to hang upon the land, seeking the least scent or sign of movement. From the raptor's wing to the far tree the colors whirled slowly back, matching a midsummer scene when the nephew and his cousin were no more than nine or ten – when the windrows came like spaced hedges before their galloping leaps as they ran across the alfalfa field up to the old tree, well distanced from road and creek, isolate and secure, as children often seek out a wild microcosm all their own. They fancied it 'the hanging tree' for it was black and hoary and sprouted many thorns along its limbs. The evidence seemed to them solid and compelling for a pioneer dwelling lay fallen in the grass among remnant stones and rotted timbers. Clearly to their minds this had once been a hideout for horse-thieves or rustlers, the culprits surrounded and hanged from the tree. So they imagined, playing there often as children do, blending easily with all things past and apparent.

On this particular day the two cousins happened upon a cactus approximately fifty yards from the hanging tree, and on the cactus was a single flower as brilliant red as ever distilled to the eye. The boys quickly crossed the creek and raced the final stretch to the house, eager to tell the mother and aunt, for she was a woman of natural spirit who loved her garden, orchard and flowers, who breathed life into frozen lambs and once braved a flooded creek to save a drowning calf, so the children knew she'd be pleased with their find. Also, being a passionate woman, she had a quick temper and the boys often earned a sharp rap on the noggin for their rowdy ways. So they doubtless hoped to appease her. And she sparkled with joy when they told her of the flower and followed them back with a spade and box to fetch the prize. But the flower could not be found, only the cactus. They searched until the sun's descent and returned sadly disappointed. She noted their bewilderment and quietly allowed, "Some beauty lasts only a moment...like birdsong." Yet they could not fathom this, what was absolutely there hours before, and still vivid to their mind's eye, now vanished.

Years passed, a decade in number, and his cousin was killed. And the nephew remembered a day that recent summer when he walked into the same pasture, walked unknowing, without reason, relaxing after finishing the alfalfa harvest. Simply gazing about, not searching a thing, he glanced down on what appeared to be the same cactus with a singular red flower equal to the one long ago. As he knelt to touch it a distinct chill swept forth, as if cast from the locust tree, freezing him in the act. And it was not fear, but a nameless brother emotion that drove him from the pasture that day.

"Ah the heck...," the uncle wiped his eyes, calming now, having vent his sorrow. "It's just...sometimes I forget. He seems so near."
"Yeah, he loved this land."
"And it hasn't been long, has it? Not yet a year..."
They began walking back towards the house, deliberate, slow, and rather peaceful. The sun had climbed to an angle higher than mountains ever rise. The uncle stopped and squinted there, again smiling.
"Why don't we give the day up to the sun? He's got the better share of it anyway."
"Why not," the nephew grinned, glad of a day off.
"Besides...," the uncle mused, "I may leave the rest of them bales out there. The barn's full, doubt I'll need 'em. Let 'em keep the land warm this winter. If need be, I can always feed from the field..."

And the sun's violent splendor funneled down from its great summit and faded to the west. Not only the masculine season stalked the cooling air that evening but memory and memory's presence which hung upon the land like the fresh cicada shell latched to the bark of the old locust tree. The pheasants huddled quiet and the yard light glowed and the sunset was as brittle and short-lived as a dead twig snapping. The nearly full moon did not rise till on past midnight when a raw anima awoke to squall about the land. The coyotes cried awake in the swirling wind. And the spirit moved out from the tree, abandoning it in all directions as the breath abandons the body, spreading like a solemn vow over the niches and recesses of the land to assume the character it would hold for all the years to come.

BENEATH THE CEDARS

A hallowed acre on the hot dry plains, the sun so bright like film overexposed as they walk through a small hillside cemetery, an elderly woman and her middle-age son, their bodies nearly transparent, ethereal in the heat waves, grainy and faintly edged till closer up they focus. A pasture borders on the south, a broad plowed field to the north, and a gravel road runs east, the cemetery no larger than a football field with assorted stones of various size and color and a few scattered cedars that stand in testament to birth and death and the steady churn of wind and season. The swath west remains vacant with no mound of earth to mark a passing, while most graves lie in neglect, the ground sunken, and here and there a stone tilts askew in the glacial shift of feature and terrain.

Likewise the woman seems slightly out of kilter, shuffling for balance from stone to stone, her hands knit at her waist in earnest search and query. She halts, wavering a bit as the wind catches tufts of her white hair cut in Dutch boy bangs, white as ermine and brilliant as a flower against the droughty grasses and dull-green foliage. A fold of her blue dress flutters lightly in the wind. Her son stands at her side, quietly observant, his straw fedora tilted back, waiting to steady her if need be. She raises a hand to her lips, sifting layers of memory and the immediate substrate of earth, flesh, and bone, having passed her father's and mother's graves, now those of her grandparents, uncles, aunts, and cousins, pausing occasionally to recall a trait or incident, speaking as much to them as of them, as if those below ground were more alive to her than those above.

She chuckles fondly reading the name etched on the stone, "*Van Lee Churchill…*"

"That's Uncle Van," she notes. "He'd first courted Aunt Claire then dumped her. Claire was my Grandmother's sister, both Jones girls before they married. And while Grandmother was quite a pretty woman, Claire was fairly plain. So another girl caught his eye and got him hitched. Then he got what he gave. On their honeymoon trip to the Chicago World's Fair of 1893, she ditched him right there in the train station. Took the money and luggage and vanished in the crowd while he was in the men's room. She got what she wanted sure enough, a ticket out of LaBelle, Kansas. Years later he often laughed about it and didn't mind telling the story, but he came back feeling like a fool. Once burned...they say...

"Aunt Claire was living out with my grandparents at the time, working as their cook and housekeeper. And by and by, one evening, Uncle Van Lee showed up on the porch, looking all shamefaced. He tossed his hat in through the screen door then stepped back and waited. That was an old custom, a man tossing his hat in to see if a girl would have him. Well, in a short while Grandma appeared and said for him to come on in, that Claire would see him. So they patched things up and were soon married. And theirs was a long happy marriage. Though they never had any children, they were always good to us kids, my brother, sis, and me..."

She moves beyond the family plots, angling several rows north and west, carried along in idle drift, flesh and footing tenuous, like filament woven of sun and wind.

"Oh my...," she pauses before a low pink stone placed nearly level to the grass, slowly kneels down and touches the lettering. "Kathleen Thornsen. She was a senior when I was a freshman. Just the nicest girl, kind and pretty. And look, she died in April 1935...only 17, so sad. They claimed it was a burst appendix, like with Dad's youngest brother, David. But it was a botched abortion, one of those back-alley deals, and she hemorrhaged. It was the music teacher that got her pregnant...with his slick black hair, handsome devil. He ran off to Kansas City and left her hanging. Poor desperate kid. I hadn't thought of her in years."

The son helps her stand and they amble further north, then back east in a seemingly aimless pattern. She blinks in one direction then another, apparently confused as to time and place. It happens often of late, and the son is about to ask if she'd like to leave, when she stops before a chest-high obelisk of dark gray granite.

"Why, that's odd...," she says, leaning closer. *"Marlin Dahl...November, 1938.* Well, that's surely him alright. I had no idea he was buried here..."

"Mom? Is there a problem," he asks, fearing any moment she may falter.

"No, it's just that the Dahls come from over around Elim. I thought he was buried over there. Of course they were quite religious, holier-than-thou...holier than some of their own it appears. And there was some awfully hard feelings surrounding the murder. Some bitter dust never did settle."

"Murder? Who? Marlin Dahl?"

"No, another fellow named Rose was murdered. Dahl died in a car wreck a few years later. Though some thought he'd been run off the road."

"But why...I mean...was he involved?"

"Well, that's what some people thought. They were all gamblers, Rose, Dahl, and others. Rose ended up dead one night. They tried to fob it off as a train wreck. But his body wasn't even in the car. They found it a few days later in a well a mile north."

"So then...who did it?"

"Just who and how...was never determined, not officially. *Death due to unknown causes*...so they said. But all knew it was murder and there was lots of talk. Your father had a good idea who and why, he grew up over that way...and...but nothing...was ever proved. Not until...and even then..."

She wobbles a bit and steps back. He catches her arm and she steadies. She raises her hand to her lips in puzzlement and remains silent, having lost the thread, each strand frayed and broken till there are scores, each leading to an aimless distance as if her mind tumbles like a rootless thistle shorn of leaf and flower, brittle at the very stem. And as she turns to him and asks, "Who are you?" – he knows it's happened again. She's had two prior episodes. The first was a real shock; but both had passed in an hour or two.

"I'm your son," he answers calmly.

"I have a son?"

"Yes, two sons and three daughters."

"But I...? How can that be...?" Again she falls silent, utterly bewildered.

The doctor said it's to be expected at her age, nearing ninety, likely minor blood clots causing temporary mental lapses. They keep her blood thinned to forestall a major stroke, hopefully. But today it may be simply too much sun and too much memory, one layer too many, like peeling an onion till the mind tears up and loses focus.

"Let's go over here, Mom," he says, gently taking her arm. "Let you rest awhile..."

He leads her to a stone bench in the shade of a cedar and stands by while she sits and gazes about, twisting her mouth in quiet question of who and where she is – like a needle has skipped on an old record, landing her on another song in another time and place. Perhaps she's age 9 or 10, still a girl, in the time before the murder and before meeting his father. Who knows? He asks no further questions in hope a little rest will knit the moment and draw her back.

But what draws her now lays underground and all the facts of how and why and who lay boxed and silent. All died in a moment of knowing, like the shutter closed in one instant and left no image, each mind blank as a box camera buried beneath the sunbaked sod and dormant grasses where roots descend to the ever-moist region where life and death mix with the worms and flesh, where bones harbor old scars and answers not guessed, and no mote of light will reach the dark vacuity and rouse the silence. Yet there is a knowing that lingers in the bones laid side by side within arm's reach but never touching, a shared communion of decay, a breathless longing that slowly rises through deep tendrils to the surface where trees sprout and branch forth...

And the trees are now younger, more pliant and green, and the stones are fewer in number and the knowing is yet alive and the longing is fully fleshed and agile, daring, and the mind quickens with blood replete with memory, doubt, and dreams.

Her eyes blink moist and cast an eager glance to a wagon pulled by two mules coming up the road. Joy catches in her throat. She knows the driver, now seated beside him on the buckboard, gazing up at her father, still young, his hair black, hat shielding his blue eyes from the sun, chin whiskers bristling red. He winks to her and "Hie-ups!" the mules, flicking the reins in ripple over their rumps to their stout ears, speeding them on past the cemetery as not to spoil prospects of a happy day. She a young girl on verge of summer, her sis and little brother in back, their pouty mother home in bed – but the road beckons like the Promised Land, a special place another mile beyond the rise, off to visit her grandparents. But the gravestones jar her mind in sudden question.

"Do you know anyone buried there?" she asks.

"Oh, a few…," he says, mildly bemused by her question.

She keenly recalls the death of her Uncle David, but isn't certain of his grave, just where, whether here or at the site further south. Her dad is still bitter at the loss of his youngest brother – impetuous, wild, so full of life one day and the next day dead, a bit shy of 22. Some said he was full of sin and made God angry; others said he was most loved, so God took him home. And there had been an argument with the doctor over whether to operate. Her grandmother said no, fearing the results. Then he died anyway. Now two years on and she could not guess just why, all the reasons, but her grandmother still set a place for David at each meal and let no one use his chair.

"Do you believe in ghosts, Daddy?"

"That depends…," he slows the mules in glance to her, "on how close they are."

She's not sure why but him saying that makes her feel better. She smiles in wonder of all he knows, and his wry calm manner, hardly ever frets or scowls, unlike her mother.

Just then a black cat crosses the road, either wild or stray, and not a spot of white, coal black against the chalky dirt road. He halts the mules and they watch it disappear in the weedy ditch.

"That's a black cat, Daddy."

"Yep, sure enough is."

"He crossed our path. They say that brings bad luck, does it?"

"Well…some folks think so."

"What do you think?" By now her brother and sis both huddle forth in question.

"For good or bad…I think most things turn out not like you'd expect." He studies the haze of clouds to the west then looks to them and asks, "What do you say, kids? May be a storm brewing? Do we turn back or go on to your Grandma's and Grandpa's?"

"*On...go on!*" they shout.

He slaps the reins and the mules pull on up the grade, broad haunches in sync and thrust as they twitch their great ears seemingly in thought of recent questions – of ghosts, black cats, and luck – quite thoughtful creatures at times as her father often notes. While the day changes much sooner than anyone would expect, noticed first in a sudden rush of air, not cool and fresh like before a rain, but dense and gritty, foul with dust. Strange, the sun shining, the sky cloudless but for the brownish haze in the upper west.

Then they top the hill and spy the dark roll of reddish dust growling from earth to the sky all along the horizon, soon engulfing their grandparents place and churning their way like a vast locomotive, only broadside with a beastly gust and roar. The mules halt, and need no urging; they stomp their hooves as her father scans the terrain. Not a barn or homestead in sight. Only chance of cover at hand is the stand of cedar in the cemetery a quarter mile back.

"Well, kids," he says as he haws the mules around and heads them down the hill, "looks like we'll pay your Uncle David a visit..."

No humor in this, she sees him grimace and shares the tension as he grips the reins, checking their stride as not to panic them, covering the distance at a slow trot. And all slows in their desperate descent – thought, breath, hearts – all except the wind hurling at their backs. As they reach the cedars the storm rolls over the hill, masking the sun.

Her father jumps down and quickly secures the reins to a stout lower limb then shakes out two empty grain sacks and tears the seams. He covers each mule's head and tucks the excess under the harness, letting it drape over their nose and mouth. Wind and dust already closing around, he shakes out another sack and rips it into quarters, handing one each to the kids, clinching one in hand, shouting now to be heard: "Hold it over your mouths! It'll help filter out the dust! Close your eyes and breathe through it!" He hops in the wagon bed and pulls a tarp over all as they hunker down on the hard plank floor, their bodies snug to his, his strong arm hugging each, his deep voice calming, "Just lie still and wait it out...wait it out..."

Hearts pounding next their flesh like the wind flapping the tarp, but quieter inside, cocooned and muffled. She feels his body tense and flex even more than theirs, dreads closed spaces, having dug dead men out of bomb proofs – she knows he has nightmares from the Great War, seldom sleeps through the night, often sitting up, smoking in the kitchen. But he simply smiles when asked why he's awake and says a man doesn't need much sleep after soldiering then urges her back to bed. And she tries to imagine all the battles and bombardments of that war, the gas attacks, and senses it now amid the grim storm and darkness, the rusty dust, sulfurous and suffocating like they speak of Hell in church. And she thinks to pray and does so briefly but the Lord's Prayer seems too grand and out of reach and she tries the children's rhyme, *"Now I lay me down to sleep...,"* till it too fades as she senses another breath or presence, neither divine nor themselves, it's her Uncle David coming from beyond the wagon, the storm, from underground, nearby, beneath the cedars, his smile suspended in the amber of her memory, caught in a moment of song played on his accordion. And what song? – *"Cotton-eyed Joe", "Oh Susanna", "Home on the Range"* – she does not know, only that one long note held in comfort like his smile as she hums along in the variance of the wind. Now and then her father repeats, "Hold on, kids, hold on...it'll soon pass..."

And it does after 20 or 30 minutes, eases up and passes, though it seems like hours. A sudden quiet settling down like the weight of dust on the tarp and the song, wind, and her Uncle's smile all vanish as her father lifts the tarp and folds it aside, letting in the air and sunshine, the sky already clearing. They rise to their feet and stand now, coughing up mucky dust swallowed in breathing, their lips and eyes lined in dirt, but grinning, all smiles as her father dusts them off, tears streaming from his eyes, and she's never seen them so blue, sky blue with joy. He takes a deep breath and laughs, "Dern near buried, kids! Buried and resurrected all in one day! How about that?" And she knows he's not religious, not since the war, but he is grateful...

"Yes, he was always grateful…," she repeats softly.

"What's that, Mom?" her son leans close, trying to catch the first words spoken in the past ten minutes.

"Oh, there you are," her eyes clear in recognition, "wondered where you got off to."

"I'm right here, Mom. You had a dizzy spell. So we sat down."

"Well I feel fine, just fine. But…where are we?"

"At the cemetery…visiting old family graves."

"Oh, I knew that. But…those aren't our stones."

"No, they're back there a ways," he says, helping her stand. "We were just over here, Mom. You said the young fellow buried there had been involved in a murder."

"Sure, I remember now. That was Marlin Dahl. The Rose murder, yes…"

"I asked if it was ever solved and you said, *No, not until*…then you went silent and left quite a puzzle hanging. So…was it ever solved?"

"Well, no, not really. But there's no road so long it doesn't take a turn. There were six fellas involved and all died in a bad way. Many thought Rose's older brother helped them along. He swore they'd pay right there at the grave…but no, nothing ever proved. Just mostly guessed at…until the last one, the old barber, Pup Sorell, lost his mind and spilled the beans. That was twenty years on. Then he died in the nut house. Nothing was ever solved. They're all dead now and hardly even matters…" She pauses in faint grin to him and adds, "Funny how things often turn out. Not like you'd expect…"

They meander on down towards the car, voices soon fading in the wind like their bodies and the car, soon gone, vanished into the day, the dust and heat, leaving awkward rows of stone-marked graves beneath a stand of cedar on the empty plains.

WINTER MEMORY

(*For my mother, Neva Rebecca Bell-Litton*)

You sure didn't leave any gristle on the bone in those hard times, but we had good times too. Uncle Otis and Aunt Gladis drove over most Sunday evenings to play cards with the folks. All of us kids would bundle up out in their car and tell ghost stories till we were scared half to death. One time in particular in the midst of a story our old gray mule, turned nearly white in its winter coat, came around the barn...that was enough, we all screamed "Ghost!" and hit for the house.

I also recall seeing the Northern Lights for the first time. It's a rare event this far south. Very unusual...those great bluish lights streaming up from the horizon like fireworks in the sky. We all stood watching when one of the adults suggested that maybe it was Chicago burning. Seems funny now, but in the Thirties events and news traveled so slow...oh, we had radios, but batteries were pricey and often dead. So we did wonder.

No, in those Depression years darn few had cash money, still people got out, even in blizzards. Which reminds me...don't know why it was but Mom always insisted on going to town on Saturday nights, even in the coldest weather. Maybe it was us kids too, for there were the picture shows to see as well as Mom's trading to do. Dad might protest that it was too blame cold, but no matter, pretty soon he'd be hitching up those two gray mules to the buckboard. He'd lay down a bed of straw on the floor and we'd jump in and wrap up under the lap robes. Ours was made from Grandpa Kohr's old bay mare. When a horse died they'd send the hide in to be tanned then backed with a wool blanket trimmed in felt rickrack pattern. Grandad Bell had one made from his red 'n white pinto. Our bay robe still had some mane running part way down the middle. Anyway, those lap robes along with comforters kept us quite warm on the tree-mile trip to town.

Times were still hard, though by the late Thirties nearly everyone was driving cars again, but not Harry Bell. So at the edge of town George usually got out and walked the rest of the way alone. Us girls stayed and rode with Dad and Mom, but George must have felt a little ashamed. There were hitching posts in behind the grocery and the mules were left tied there while Mom did the trading, sold her eggs 'n cream to buy sugar, coffee, and such. Us kids usually took in a movie while Dad spent his time talking with a group of men around a big oil stove down at the hardware store. Of course Mom was always ready to go home before anyone else. As soon as we were out of the show she'd send us down to find Dad and tell him it was time to go. Well, Dad was never one to jump up from a good story, so he'd just say he'd be along shortly. Sometimes "shortly" turned out to be a good deal later...Dad as you know loved to talk.

I remember one night riding home, it was quite cold with a good foot of snow on the ground, and we were all of a mile from home when we broke down. I can't recall exactly what it was, whether a broken wheel or the tug...in any case it wasn't something you could fix in the middle of the night out in the middle of nowhere. So there we were. Dad unhitched the mules and we walked carrying the groceries that mile on home. We got plenty cold but we made it.

That next morning while walking over to Grandad's, us kids found some oranges that had fallen from the sacks, they were frozen hard as rocks, but we picked them up, carried them along. You can bet one way or another they were thawed out and eaten. Nothing went to waste. And I don't know, maybe it's all the conveniences, but winters don't seem nearly as long as they used to be...

THE SHARK'S TOOTH (from *Banks of the River*)

Third game of the evening – "Pee-wee" and "Midget" champs already decided. Sun had set, field-lights on, stars appearing. Boys paired off, throwing balls, warming up. Teams stationed at opposite ends of the field, Wolves in red, Badgers in black. Parking lot and surrounding ditches full of cars and pickups like at a farm auction. Stands packed. People standing three deep down either baseline fence. Moms, dads, brothers and sisters, grandparents and cousins – all kinds of grown-ups and kids. Big shots from uptown, renters from the outskirts. Men milling about talking grain prices, politics, and weather; women leaning close sharing beauty tips and shreds of gossip. But either team's prospects soon dominated. And there would be money changing hands – 5's, 10's, a few 20's – depending on the outcome.

The Badgers took infield practice first as they would bat first.

A warm breeze stirred the treetops, all still down below. Dust from grounders puffed and settled. The night clear and calm. The Wolves continued throwing back and forth, loosening their arms, gaining speed, some playing "burn-out" as gloves popped catching the ball. Most were chewing gum, blowing bubbles, rested and ready, as yet indifferent to the buzz of the crowd and their opponent's chatter. Each boy's thoughts governed by the pep-talk heard earlier at the jail...

Jack wanted to see the boys, and Guy okayed it. All met there at 6 o'clock sharp, entering single file, quiet and curious. Except for Ross, Johnny, and Arran none had ever seen inside the jail. They gazed at the bare bulb on the high ceiling, the bared windows and empty cells, perceived grim rumor and tragedy in every shadow. Paint peeled from the walls, leaving wounds of fallen plaster. Grimy, sticky floors. And the smell, like an attic, cellar, or hog shed, or a greasy filling station urinal that's seldom flushed. A dark sobering place, a little spooky, and hot enough to make a boy sweat clean through his jersey. Entering further, they grew tentative, as if expecting to view the dead or meet the "Mummy." Much relieved to see Jack standing there, big, strong, and lively. His very presence dispelled the gloom and sparked their courage. Even knowing about the murder not one of them feared Jack, to the contrary, they looked up to him, literally – all eyes fixed as if drawn to a flame, so rapt and attentive they hardly breathed. Because Jack never minced words or coddled, made them feel worthy and able. He gathered them in his eyes, waiting, glancing to each, making certain all were there.

At last he looked to Johnny, words for him shared with all.

"This is it fellas, the big game. Guy says you're ready." Some eager nods, a few *Yessirs*. "Now remember..." – his voice flowed to them like a river, deep, smooth, and heavy – "tonight is your whole life, what you're made and meant for. Don't be thinking of the fair, of tomorrow or next year. There's no pie in the sky. Life ain't somewhere, sometime, waiting. It's right here, right now. You gotta seize it, like this game and make it yours. Now I know what happened last time with the Badgers..." he paused, peering around, wrinkling his nose for effect. "It do stink some, don't it?" The boys grinned, careful not to laugh. "Yeah...they'll try to shake ya, they'll try to rattle ya. And if you shake and rattle, they'll roll all over ya. They'll stomp ya in the ground. Don't you let no one or nothing ever stomp you or take you down! Got it! Never! Now let me see you claw the air and hear ya growl!"

The old jail came alive, vibrant, as they showed the Lion their stuff. He stood smiling, proud of his cubs. Then he took a shark's tooth from his pocket and held it before them. They quieted, amazed at its dagger shape, like a deadly gem or a bullet from some old war.

"The shark is the oldest predator, boys. One of the few things I remember from school." Their interest heightened by his a sardonic grin. "It roamed the seas that swept this land ages ago. Right here underfoot, boys...right now in the air you breathe was once a sea, the shark's home. Now it's ours. This tooth's been buried in stone a million years till I dug it out yesterday. Here, son..." he handed it to Johnny, "you be the keeper of the tooth. Pass it around, share it with the fellas. I want you all to hold it. And tonight, waiting your turn at bat, grip it in your hand, each of you. It'll sharpen your eye 'n even your swing. It's waited a million years to bring you luck. Now you may get a hit and you may not. But you strike out, dammit all, go down swinging. Hear?" They nodded, reverently passing the tooth hand to hand.

"Tonight I want you Wolves to swarm in a blood frenzy, don't let one ball pass without diving for it...nose in the dirt if you have to. And Tommy!" - pointing to a chubby freckle-faced boy standing off alone, considered by his peers their weak link, but Jack wouldn't have it, swore any boy could play baseball if he only believed. "Each time we take the field you fetch that tooth from Johnny. Put it in your pocket. It'll bring ya luck. Tonight you show 'em. Catch a fly ball for me. Catch any that come your way." The boy, wide-eyed, held the tooth like it was pure magic – at the moment the envy of all his fellows. Then Jack winked, "If you drop one, Tommy, that tooth'll bite your balls."

The boys laughed, Tommy too.

"Now lissen, one last thing. You're all growing fast. Soon be young men. From here on you call me Jack. Got it?" They answered in a swift chorus – sang out his name. All fired up, ready to hunt, ready to swarm. "Now dammit all! Go out there 'n play hard ball and win! Whip their butts! Go on now, scram...jail's no place for boys..." he mumbled, watching them rush out...

Fresh strips of lime marked the batter's box and extended in a widening "V" on past first and third. Home plate swept clean, the umpire tossed a brand-new game ball to the pitcher. Johnny slapped it in his glove a couple times, gripped the taut stitched seam and fired it to Arran at short, who in turn threw it to first, then on around-the-horn in a successive blur to second, third, into Ross at home, then back out to Johnny.

The umpire hollered "Play ball!" The crowd stilled, anticipating the first pitch. The lead-off batter dusted his hands, tapped the dirt from his cleats, and stepped to the plate, the dentist's son, Darrin Fain Jr., one of the few boys who wore actual baseball shoes. He took a practice swing and dug in. Ready.

The pitch. A swing and a miss. "Strike one!" The Wolves erupted in a brisk chatter led by Arran and Ross. "Atta boy Slinger!" "Way to blister it!" Even Tommy from right field added his distinctly high raspy howl – "Hey! Hey! Hey!" – overweight and asthmatic, but heads-up and knees flexed, braced and alert, determined to make a stab for any that came his way but hoping like heck Johnny blew it past 'em all night.

Second pitch looked good, but "Low and outside!" according to the ump. And Howard Fritz, the ex-Marine, called 'em like he saw 'em – as good an ump as any, Jack and Guy often claimed. So Johnny shook it off, hoping to split 50/50 on the close ones. Next one he zipped about chin high, brushing the batter back a step. "Ball two!" A hair wild without a doubt. "Bring it down Slinger!" Ross shot back, a trifle irritated. Johnny nodded, took a deep breath and honed his eye, tried to imagine the knothole center of the glove. Then pop! put it right smack in the pocket. Ross never flinched. Nor did the batter. If you blinked you missed the pitch. That fast. Though he tagged the next one and sliced it high over the Badger's dugout for a foul. Still 2 and 2.

The crowd stirred, waiting for sign of how the game would go. Then Johnny drew back and let fly and the batter missed it cold – so far behind the pitch in fact he heard "Strike three!" in mid-swing. Johnny settled in and took control, struck out the next two on eight pitches. Same happened next inning – 3 up, 3 down – no Badger bat so much as ticked the ball. Meanwhile the Wolves scored two in the bottom of the first: Arran led off with a single, next boy struck out, Johnny walked, and Ross cleaned-up, driving both in on a sacrifice-fly to deep center. From then on it was a pitcher's duel through the second and third innings. Some scattered hits, several walks, all runners left stranded.

Top of the fourth, one out, one on, Johnny's first walk. Badgers still scoreless. Their dugout remained fairly tame, thus far hurling only standard taunts at the pitcher. Reluctant to draw Johnny's ire else he'd draw blood. Bad enough facing his fastball without it coming right at you. Gary Tottleson, the opposing pitcher and coach's son, approached the plate. Johnny relaxed a moment, kicked dust from the mound, adjusted his cap, then looked to his mom and Bonny, even saw his Aunt Ruthie in the stands tonight. A rare appearance, and looking flashy all in red, she really stood out, wouldn't miss the big game. She sent a wave and hollered with the best of them, nothing shy about Ruthie. Almost as loud and boisterous as May. But May could out-blast a trumpet when she got wound up, and had been so since the opening pitch.

Good to see them all there watching.

On the first pitch the bat connected blasting a low line drive between short and second. It looked to be a sure double, but Arran shot left and dove, making the catch for an instant only to bobble it upon hitting the ground. He scrambled to his feet and retrieved the ball, but checked his throw. Runners already safe on first and second.

"Good stop Moose!" Johnny offered. Arran shook his head, disheartened as he tossed the ball back, should have made a double play...sensing trouble. Sure enough Johnny walked the next man. Bases loaded. Badgers scenting blood, their best hitter, Troy Sewter, who was Lyle Sewter's nephew, stepped to the plate.

The chant started up: *"Johnny Marshal smay-ells! His daddy's in the jay-ell!"* At first a single voice, then another, and soon the whole bench in full chorus. Their coach and grade school principal, ol' man Tottleson, standing prim and smug, nose in the air, as if they recited the Pledge of Allegiance. Johnny wiped the sweat from his palm, glanced to his teammates; each wore that worried look like he'd gazed in a crazy mirror and saw himself reflected from a dozen different angles.

"Don't lissen to 'em!" Ross warned. Easy said, and he tried not to. But there it was, what he'd braced for and practiced against, imagining it over and over. And facing it, he felt a void like his stomach opened up and drained away, leaving him faint and empty, without will or strength, like reaching without a grasp, utterly alone, sinking, his senses numb. He heard nothing more, like being underwater, weighted and weak as he raised his arm to pitch in a world of greater density and altered optics. The ball floated towards the plate, seemingly big and slow as a child's balloon.

Troy hit a beaut – lifted it to left center, hitting the fence for an automatic double, driving in three runs. Badger fans erupted with whistles and cheers, horns honking, feet pounding in the stands. The shock brought Johnny to his senses – the chant scorching his ears, each word a branding coal that strangely now stanched the wound and firmed his gut, leaving only pain and anger burning within.

Don't let 'em rattle ya... the low voice growled. He gripped the ball, fighting for control, determined to reclaim his stuff, and held the runner at second while battling the batter to 3 and 2, a full house. Two more pitches fouled away before he walked him. The chant flared anew – *"Johnny Marshal smay-ells..."* – sweeping from the Badgers' dugout into the stands like a spark carried on the wind, threatening to engulf his mom and Bonny as a number of parents joined in.

Among the first was Birdie, standing with her friend Marge, bleating *"Johnny Marshal smay-ells..."* in that shrill partisan pitch that heeds no limit or shame, for it was her son Justin coming to bat. Without any warning from two rows back Ruthie reached forth and sank her nails into Birdie's fresh-permed hair and sat her down with a vicious yank and a few sharp words: "Shut up bitch! That's my Nephew!" And she meant to protect Anna and Bonny as well. The commotion and the victim's shriek promptly hushed the crowd. Doused the chant. Birdie fussed briefly, smoothing her hair then turned to face her attacker – flustered, indignant, trembling.

"If...if I weren't such a lady," she managed to gasp, "I'd...climb up there and slap your face!"

"Oooh dear, dear," Ruthie chided. "Pipe down before you blow a gasket."

Then a greater voice and presence intervened from several seats stage left.

"A lady?!" May scoffed, standing with her fists propped to her vast hips. "Why Birdie, what are you a lady of? A pig pen?" Then leaned back with a grand cackle like she'd laid the golden egg of wit, inspiring a wave of laughter all around. And while Anna merely smiled and gripped Bonny's hand, both were much relieved and grateful.

Birdie sat there utterly abashed, boiling. She a size 6! called a sow by *that* sow! Why...! She'd never been so humiliated. And to imagine Ruth doing that to a loyal customer. She always went to Ruth's Salon. Birdie felt betrayed, absolutely betrayed. Both business women, colleagues in a sense. Any number of times she'd special ordered for Ruth at no extra charge. Even complimented her figure, out and out conceded that she had the better body. Taller, more busty – and those legs! God...Birdie could have killed for those legs.

And what was she doing at the game anyway? She should be out playing with her new beau. "A lawman" as she hinted to the girls, adding with a wink that they should call her "Miss Kitty," then archly said no more. Well for certain it wasn't "Matt Dillon." Birdie's suspicion initially centered on the highway patrolman recently moved to town, Lt. Dwayne Allen, soft spoken, mannerly, and handsome as a Hollywood star. Wore a thin mustache. Always neat and trim, sharp and spiffy as a tack in his uniform. And despite a wife and child, every loose tail in town wagged his way. Birdie among others even chanced speeding in hopes of being pulled over. So far no luck.

No, she decided, scratching him from the probable list, more out of jealousy than doubt or proof to the contrary, for she quite preferred him in her own fantasy. And so stewing, hatching plots, her eyes fell to Guy leaned against the fence, trading words with a red-faced farmer. *Hmmm*...she wondered. No, surely not. Impossible. Definitely not her type. No class at all. Though Ruthie had varying tastes, a true Catholic. And then again he had that lean hard look like "Bogart" – hat tipped back, cigarette dangling from his lips, and stripped down he might prove entertaining. If a woman could forget *what* he slept with most nights.

But such musing vanished in a blink as she saw her son standing at the plate, bat ready, further drowned out as the Badger bench again roared to life, chanting *"Johnny Marshal smay-ells! His daddy's in the jay-ell!"* Though from then on the taunt remained strictly on the field, for no one in the stands dared join in with May and Ruthie present. All like notions effectively scotched.

Then a rival chant arose like a drumbeat countering the Badgers as Arran, anxious for self and team, suddenly voiced his defiance, shouting "Jack, Jack, Jack!" It spread like a contagion through the infield and up into the stands. Even Ruthie proudly chanted her brother's name: "Jack, Jack, Jack...!" The Wolves, so recently fragmented, once more melded into a team. Johnny looked to Arran and his teammates and calmed, no longer alone. "Jack, Jack, Jack..." rang in his ears, surged in his blood, steeled his flesh. He went into the stretch, cocked back his arm, and fired one right in the pocket. Then another. Confident, deadly.

Mr. Tottleson hollered for Justin to *stand in there and take a swing!* But to the boy that sharp incantation – "Jack! Jack! Jack!" – was more threatening than the fastball, leaving him all alone to face a focused enemy. He nodded to his coach, swallowed hard and made ready. Meanwhile Birdie held her breath, fingers crossed, praying like a good Methodist for Justin to get a hit and right the world. Restore her wounded pride.

"Please, please, for Mommy, please..."

The wind-up and the pitch. At the last instant Justin swung, cracking the ball in a high pop-fly to far right field. Looked like an easy catch from the stands, a smooth long trajectory. But that was Tommy out there and nothing looked easy and smooth to the one stumbling backwards, trying to keep his footing, eyes to the sky – ball zig-zagging like a deranged comet amidst the bright lights. Then he slowed, getting set. Okay....see it now, coming down in the ol' bread basket. Dang! Falling short! He lunged forth and felt it strike his glove but kept it in the air. He looked up. Gosh! Caught it! Also got stickers in his knees, right forearm and palm. But so thrilled he didn't feel a thing till he threw the ball into first. Then – Yikes! – started gingerly plucking stickers from his skin, gritting his teeth like a cowboy biting a bullet.

The runner tagged up and advanced to third, but was soon left stranded as Johnny retired the side on three blazing pitches. Running off the field, Tommy forgot the pain of the embedded thorns, accepting backslaps and praise from his joyous teammates. Down by one, ready to rally. Tommy, their man of the moment, first at bat.

He clutched the shark's tooth wistfully and passed it on. Whatever favor it had granted in the field was withdrawn when he went to bat. At 2 and 2 he ticked a foul high over the backstop, gaining a brief reprieve, but went down swinging on the next pitch. His third strike out of the night. Nor did the following two batters fare any better, each gripped the tooth for assurance, then one grounded out while the other popped a short blooper for an easy catch. Same next inning, the drought continued, though two walked, no one hit. Not that they felt jinxed, they still had faith, but certainly frustrated.

Truth was the Badgers were playing heads-up ball. Aside from the first inning their pitching had proved equally strong if not slightly better judging from the score. And after the fourth they'd ceased the personal taunts entirely, finding it had backfired. They dug in and settled down, trying to preserve their one point lead. All cockiness and banter died away. Both teams locked in a quiet, grim struggle.

Deep down Arran had to respect them, the Badgers, no doubt they were playing good ball. And it wasn't that the Badgers were bad guys. In fact he counted some as friends, sometimes played at their houses after school. Liked the boys even though their mothers scowled if he came in to use the bathroom or get a drink of water. Sensing their scorn, he stayed outside most often. Pissed in the bushes and drank from hydrants. What did he care? He'd grown up in the country – shit in the woods and wiped with leaves. No problem. It was their attitude he resented. *Holier than thou* because they had a little money; equated poor with worthless and dirty. Whereas Arran took it as a given that a Clayton was as good as any-*damn*-body anywhere. None better than his family. And he meant to show 'em, prove it at every turn. During the school year he and the better-off boys got along fine. But when summer came all tended to gravitate to their own neighborhoods, to stratify according to parental status and income. While certainly not a stricture or an absolute, it was a tendency nonetheless. A division recognized and felt in a small town. So the rivalry extended beyond the game.

Arran took over pitching top of the sixth. Johnny had done well enough in the fifth, but he'd walked one and allowed a hit and only escaped trouble by a timely double play. In truth he was wearing down, losing his stuff, and admitted as much to Guy. So the job fell to Arran to keep them in the game. His arm fresh, his eye sharp, his pitching was nearly flawless. Good control and moderate speed. Every batter flinched before that nasty side-arm, so deceptive the ball appeared to head right at them before veering across the plate. Having faced Johnny all night, they'd grown somewhat accustomed to his fastball, especially as it slowed through the fourth and fifth innings. Now a change-up, Arran's radical style broke their confidence and they needed to face him a time or two in order to hit.

He didn't aim to give them a chance. Wanted to end the game before the batting order came around again. Wanted to win! But the best pitching in the world couldn't produce a run. Let alone the needed two. So there was dim satisfaction in retiring the Badgers – one, two, three. Now top of the seventh inning, time running out. And considering the long drought of hitless innings, prospects looked bleak. Counting down, about to taste that bitter dust. No more chances no matter what luck was stored in that tooth. Of which Arran was duly skeptical. In spite of two hits and a walk, his last at bat he'd struck out miserably. His own fault, trying too hard.

But whatever his doubts, he still gripped the tooth, seeking an edge, preparing to lead off, he walked to the bat stand and selected his favorite 30 inch "Louisville Slugger." Heard the voice before he turned and saw his little sister Tory , or "CC" as they called her, in the arms of his big sister Carrol standing beyond the fence. Called her "CC" for she invariably asked to be lifted up so she could "see-see..."

"Aee-ren!" she sang out, pointing to him, smiling her crooked little smile, her left eye and cheek still swollen from a bee-sting received the day before.

Carrol beamed "Hi there!" – knew they'd surprised him. "Mr. Reese took over at the ticket box," she explained, "so we hurried up..." Then she added for good measure, "To watch you win!"

Arran brightened, fortified by her words, their presence – he experienced such a burst of joy he gripped the tooth so hard it broke his skin. Handing it to the boy on deck, he saw blood in his palm. Knew it meant something. What? He could not name.

Entering the batter's box, he assumed the stance, took a practice swing and faced the pitcher. Troy Sewter – the very one who'd struck him out. But Arran thought of nothing but *right here, right now*. So eager he swung on the first pitch even though it was well inside, caught it high up on the handle, stinging his hands, and sent the ball spinning down the third base line. Ruled "fair." Not much of a hit but good enough, although it was a footrace, he beat out the throw to first. On base; back in the game; family there to watch. Temples throbbing, in a fever to win, so pumped up he stole second on the first pitch. The catcher's throw was a bit high, allowing him to slide in safe.

Guy hollered for him to settle down and stay put till signaled. "Wait your chance," he urged, for stealing third was way more "iffy." The catcher was no slouch; he'd picked off three so far. Arran nodded, catching his breath, agreed to bide his time.

The boy at bat, Terry Drake, hooked the second pitch to deep left where it unfortunately dropped "foul," returning Arran to second. On the following pitch he struck out. This brought up Johnny, looking cool and confident, though his insides were a torrent. He let the first two go by. One and one. Then he hit a hard grounder directly in front of the runner, which the short-stop bobbled, putting Johnny on first with Arran standing safe at third.

Now Ross was up, and only he, Johnny, and Arran had hit for the Wolves all night. His desire for another hit plainly marked his face. Arran knew that look, a fierceness that actually changed the features, a sure blood-red toughness, inflexible, isolate, reverting to an animal will against which it was foolish to advise or contend. Instinct overpowering reason. Guy saw it too, knew his son. Made a futile attempt, a lame caution to *"Just meet the ball..."* Nothing registered. Obvious from his practice swing Ross meant to bust boulders. At the first pitch, high and outside, he made a brutal stab like a bass leaping for a lure. Blind and flailing, Guy could only shake his head and watch the inevitable. Arran knew what he had to do – *had* to steal home. And Guy wouldn't give the word, unlike Jack, thought it was too dangerous. So he had to decide and couldn't risk a signal. *Had* to steal home whether Ross knew it or not. *Had* to take the chance. He tried to tell him through his eyes, squinting, concentrating with full intent. But Ross looked manic and distant, longing to arch one over the fence.

Arran took a modest lead off third, then sprang, anticipating the wind-up, getting a jump, running for all he was worth, racing the pitch, diving in low, head first, the swoosh of the bat grazing his cap as he slid reaching for the plate in a swirl of dust. The catcher pounced, the crowd hushed, the action froze. Arran lay still. The umpire looked down, hesitant to judge, then swept his arms low and wide as if in blessing, for he spied the ball back of the catcher who in his haste to make the tag had failed to make the catch.

"Safe!" he yelled. Which unleashed an instant roar in protest.

Mr. Tottleson and a phalanx of fathers marched out to have the call reversed – in step, jaws set, bunched to assert influence. Often succeeded in tilting the balance. But the ex-Marine wasn't about to take crap off a pack of citizens captained by a wheedling school marm. Guy stood back amused, watching, waiting to step in if need be.

Fritz reached down and snatched up the telltale ball and warned, "You take your seats or I call this game here 'n now…" End of argument! In the face of which they spat and sputtered and wisely turned tail. Once safely beyond the fence, however, they fired a volley of jeers threatening life and limb, what-have-you. Meaningless crap to one who'd heard Japs calling through the jungle night: *"Hey Yankeez! Marikan Soldiers! Sweet dreams, you boys! Go sleep! We cut you throats!"* No idle threat and he still managed to catch a wink in that viper den. So he turned a deaf ear to the stands, leaned forth and promptly announced, "Play Ball!"

Meanwhile Arran jumped up, happily spitting dust, having tied the score. He gave Carrol and "Seesy" a big wave and trotted over to stand with Tommy and others waiting anxiously to see how Ross fared. Winning run on third. Guy had to admire the little cuss – could've hugged him and could've kicked his butt seeing how close that bat came to his head. Then his thoughts turned to his own son as Ross took a sharp swing and made ready. Guy clenched his teeth and grimaced, "Just meet the ball..."

The pitch was a beauty – waist high, right down the pike – perfect, all a batter dreamed of. And Ross, intent on the kill, jerked his head as the bat crossed the path of the ball, missing. *"Strike three! You're out!"* The words fell like an ax. Ross exploded, hurling the bat then stormed to the dugout, eyes enraged. When mad he hated himself, the world, and everything in it. Passing Arran, he shoved him hard against the fence, venting blame. "Moose, you made me miss!" he shouted through his tears, "I had to swing high!" He wiped his eyes and stomped off to the dugout and sat down on the far bench alone, glowering. High like heck, thought Arran, ya ticked my cap! But useless to argue. Besides he wanted to prime Tommy before he went to bat.

Tommy thought he came for the tooth and started to pass it over. But Arran pressed it back in his hand and told him to keep it. Looking straight in his eyes, he said, "Keep it and you'll hit. I swear..." Tommy nodded faintly, gripped the tooth and slipped it back in his pocket.

Approaching the plate, he no longer felt fat or asthmatic – and if not fully assured and confident, at least willing. Tooth in his pocket, thorns in his palm, he gripped the bat, choking up an inch, took an even, easy swing and waited. Heard his teammates at his back boosting for him, then looked to right field. The memory of his catch seeded his hope. He knew he could hit. The first pitch was low and outside, he checked his swing.

"Good eye, Tommy!" the boys yelled, "Good eye...!"

He cut under the next pitch, fouling it high overhead, the catcher made a brief try before it sailed beyond the Badgers' dugout. "He's gonna hit," Arran vowed, the boys all pressing their faces, gripping the wire-mesh, waiting; "I can feel it..."

"No way Moose. It's over," Ross countered bitterly, but he'd joined them all the same, gazing on.

"It ain't over, Yogie," Arran quietly answered. And left it at that.

Tommy took a deep breath, tried to level out his swing, thinking... *just meet the ball* like the coaches always said. Ready for the pitch. It came in about knee-high, catching the inside corner of the plate for "Strike two!" The Badgers and most of the crowd were all but certain of an extra inning.

Tommy stepped back and flexed his hands, choked up a bit more and glanced again to right field. Saw Johnny poised at third. Heard his teammates urging him on – even Ross now calling for him to *Hit that ball Tommy!* Then he heard nothing but that inner "hum" – a warming surge of nerve, muscle, and sinew as the pitcher wound up and let go. And Tommy saw the ball leave his hand, saw it spin and close and met it with a nice even swing, sending it head-high between first and second, bouncing into right field for a clean hit. He dropped his bat and ran down the baseline like a colt bolting through a spring pasture, tasting that pure moment. Found his doughty center. *And believed!*

Johnny stomped on home plate with both feet, making dead certain, ending the game, claiming victory. Arran led the rush out to greet him. In the next instant hugging each other, dancing around, kicking up the dust when both glimpsed Ross out the corner of their eye, wearing that crazed grin as he leapt full steam in a flying tackle, taking all down in a hard crush. Laughing, jubilant – "We won Slinger! We won Moose!" – he jumped to his feet and gave each a hand up, even Arran, grudges gone, all forgotten, slate wiped clean in victory. In rapture. Loved to win.

Then the whole team swarmed, converging on Tommy. For a moment he thought they meant to maul him, caught in the rough and tumble as they grabbed his arms and legs and heft him to their shoulders and carried him off to the watermelon feed being laid out on tables beneath the tall elms back of the stands. Like a riot of warriors cheering their hero at the victory feast where Johnny, their natural captain, proclaimed him "All time keeper of the tooth!" Thus honored, Tommy plunged in, face to melon, challenging Ross for "King of the feed" – standing toe to toe, belly to belly, devouring the juicy red meat seeds 'n all, like two Vikings quaffing huge goblets of sweet red wine.

THE IS OF THINGS (*from Skin for Skin*)

This knows. This traces the broken web where each is lost to the many and little is known. And nothing is known once each is boxed in the ground, locked away and silent, finished with goings-on. But this knows, this was never boxed away but wrapped in a ragged cloth by the father's hand. Born still, nixed in the womb, flesh kept warm in the mother's blood, keen to the brother's heartbeat, him born to wailing life and active limb. This the shadow twin felt only once the mother's hand, then gently swathed and taken to the garden's edge where a hole was dug and this placed, a stone laid over to keep this safe from hungry dogs and raking plow. Through as many seasons as a boy nears to a man this slept, the wrappings rotted with the flesh till the birdlike bones lay naked in the deep dark soil.

The house fell to rot, the garden to weeds. A rude hand removed the protecting stone and burned the house and barn and again the plow raked the land, the steel blade ripping the earth open to the sky. The sun-touched roots curled about the fetal bones and this mixed with the sap and rose like blood from a wound to join the wind-stirred dust in the whistling grass, twin shadow to goings-on, keen to the brother's heartbeat and other breathings in the is of things. And there is murder to tell. Always murder and hatchings in the is of things...

The sun tips down the dusty sky to spill its last light over the broad horizon then drops like an empty bottle beyond the tall weeds. The wind blows hard at the end of day, leaving line and shadow ill-defined, all relic moments in the ruined dusk. Summer is gone and cicadas have quit their singing while their ghost-husks yet cling to stalks and stems. And the men who shucked corn this day have quit the fields and left their gloves curled on wagon seats till their labor resumes at dawn.

A large-girthed man in crumpled hat and soiled overalls stands before a drab house set in a clump of trees drained of color like the surrounding land. He eyes the road east empty for the past half hour then tosses back a long draught of whiskey he has brewed and dealt over a sum of years. He recaps the pint and slips it in his bib and swallows with a grimace, his whiskers bristling like bunched thorns on his furrowed jowl as his flesh reddens and his squinty eyes burn harsh as lye. For he feels neither warmth nor welcome for the one now turning off the road, dust feathering up from wheeled ruts as headlamps spider forth on either fender of the old Ford-T rolling to a jagged halt.

The engine dies soundless like the figure emerging half-torn in the wind, a leaner man in work jeans, flat cap, and dark wool jacket. Voices torn as well, cool and muted in the initial exchange, words soon heating.

"Came…want…full payment."

"You're a two-legged fool… paid you two weeks back."

"Not so. You paid half on what's owed. We drank on it…you said we'd settle in two weeks this very night."

"Then you was half drunk 'n are full confused."

"No, not half drunk and not one bit confused. I hear you pulled this stunt before 'n you ain't pullin' it on me."

"What fool told you that?"

"My business. Now I want full payment."

"*Full?* By God, I say no!"

"Then damn your no!"

"Damn my…" The large man braces at the other's approach then notes the hand in the bulged pocket and steps back. He stomps to the porch and kicks the door open.

"Come on in here, by God, I'll show you. It's writ in my ledger."

"If that's so then damn your ledger 'n damn your lies…"

No lamps lit, wall-shadows rouse at their hard entry as both cross to the kitchen. The large man reaches for a shotgun leaned by the pantry. But his rival, equally wary, draws a pistol and fires, shattering bone and memory as mute reflex triggers a double-blast that briefly lights the room like a camera flash etching both forms in darkness.

Blank of eye and breath the victim falls facedown covering the shotgun.

Blood pools over the hardwood, enough to mop the floor.

A drawer opens and shuts, then another. Then a pause and a rattle of coins in a tin can and the rustle of wadded bills quickly pocketed. Footsteps pass down the hall and shortly return shuffling under a hefty weight. The door closes.

Outside the engine cranks up and the headlamps arc forth as the car makes a jolting turn and fades the way it came. The house stands quiet in the night. A lone coyote barks in witness.

Where to the murdered one? To the coyote's cry, the waiting stars? No, the shade remains gripped to the cold flesh like the hands gripping the barrel. And clings like a foul breath chilling the air. Clings even once the body is boxed away, so foul no one enters. A shade, not a shadow, for a shadow plays to the wind and moves beneath the bird wing, the sailing cloud, while a shade remains fixed like bloodstains in the wood. And there the foul breath remains. For there is no such in the is of things, only fire, dust-fallings, and this...

PROSPECTS (*from Skin for Skin*)

Faris leads Jack through the pasture gate along the railroad right-of-way, then remounts and rides west. A broad swath of ground lays either side of the tracks good for hunting and trapping with plenty of cover from plum thickets and clusters of sunflowers, iron weeds, and thistles, all dry and brittle in the wind. Occasionally a thistle breaks free and bounds to the north fence, the wind so strong that rabbits couch unwary of the hunter, providing an easy target from his high vantage. Jack, accustomed to rifle shots, merely pricks an ear and holds steady and Faris soon has three rabbits bagged in a gunny sack. Done shooting he packs his .22 in a homemade scabbard twined to the saddle.

That evening after skinning the rabbits, after brushing Jack and doing the milking and other chores, Faris shares a quiet supper with his parents. Ada has pan-fried two of the rabbits, served with mashed potatoes, gravy, and biscuits, the third is left to steep on the stove. Nothing much is said beyond the essential, Brigham often quiets on Sunday eve as if storing up to bluster at work come Monday morning.

Once the dishes are cleared away Faris chances bringing his history book to the table to read by the only decent lamp in the house. There's a work lantern on the porch for use outside at night, otherwise the rooms remain dark to every corner. Brigham and Ada both frown on books, have no use for any but the Bible. Still they say nothing and let him read. Ada washes the dishes while Brigham sits in his rocker, tending the stove and occasionally dropping his hand to pet the old yellow cat curled on a rag rug. By and by Brigham checks his pocket watch, he's heard pages turn every few minutes for the past half hour. He sits up in wonder how anyone can read so long.

"What words you read there, boy? What say they?"

"It's Abe Lincoln's words, Dad. From his First Annual Message, December 3rd, 1861. He says here towards the end something you might like..."

"Does he now..." Brigham leans forth in deeper wonder, even he knows of Lincoln, all but a holy man to most eyes. "What's it he say?"

"He says, *'It is assumed that whoever is a hired laborer is fixed in that condition for life...'* But Lincoln says such is groundless and false, *'for there is no such thing as a free man fixed for life in the condition of hired labor...'* Then further on he says this, *'Labor is prior to and independent of capital. Capital is only the fruit of labor, and could never have existed if labor had not first existed. Labor is the superior of capital, and deserves much the higher consideration...'* You see, I think he's talking about us."

"Why, could be he is..." Brigham nods, suddenly awakened as if Lincoln has spoken directly to him. "Without labor there'd be no railroad, no timber for the ties, no coal to burn or haul. And it takes labor to build a wall or bring in a harvest, it does. But with wages scare 'n low as they is, a man can't build capital by labor alone. No, he can build up callouses 'n break his back, but he can't build no capital. It takes a prospect to make money. Always takes a prospect, remember that."

"Colley has a prospect for me."

"Oh? What might that be?"

"He says...next summer he could tutor me 'n help me get in a college."

"College? What? You hear that, woman?" he scoffs. "If Colley Rose thinks you can do college his hair is curled plum to the clouds. College is for the rich, Faris, now even the rich is poor. *'They that was full hire themselves out for bread...'* That's from the Good Book, ain't that so, Ada?" he asserts in glance to her.

"That it is, the book of Samuel. *'Talk no more so proudly,'*" she quotes, softly noting her son's dejection. *"'The bow of the mighty is broken...'"*

"The God's truth. Why, there's college men as work on the VCCC projects north, has been lie-yers 'n such. There's college men as work with me on the courthouse. Here I am goin' on sixty 'n can outwork any two of them. No boy, college is a fool notion ya get readin' books. Save yer eyes for shootin' that rifle or sightin' a prospect. A man who can grip hard labor in his two hands don't need books or college to pull hisself up. *'The Lord raises the poor out of the dirt 'n sets 'em among princes...'* It's all in the Bible, one book worth readin'. Henry

Ford weren't no college man nor were the Wright boys what first flew. A man knows how to work all he needs is a prospect..."

Faris closes his book, knows there'll be no more reading tonight. Even Ada lays her dishtowel aside. *A fine speech ye be makin' Brigham, let's see how you finish...*

"My first dead man I seen was my Pa shot face down by the tracks. I's twelve years old 'n I did whimper like a pup. But only a brief spell then I stiffened. Eldest of five sons I's from that day the breadwinner. Saw all doors closed to me, even the light 'a day. Took my Pa's place down in the mines, in those coal-black caves where the negro 'n white man is colored the same. Not but a little brass lamp with a tiny carbide flame to light the way. No, no prospects, none. The company store took ever' penny I earned, still I kept us in bread 'n beans. Then one day, three years on, my Ma sent word by my foreman that I's to come home quick. 'Urgent word,' he said, 'do as you will.' My shift not half done I came as called by her, certain a beloved brother was dead or dyin'. No more did I reach our door than I hear the mine explode 'n black smoke rolled up out 'a there. My Ma had the gift of sight, had she not...?" Again he looks to Ada and she gives a solemn nod. "What she'd seen in her mind's eye then happened. Forty men died that day in the explosion. No, there lay no prospect for me, not in the mines.

"I went straight that day to the railroad. Walked five miles 'n hired on as a water boy. Fifteen years old 'n it was less money, but in a year I's the top spike driver on the track crew. It tripled my pay in the mines 'n our family had meat on the table. In another year I stepped up to the train itself, feedin' coal to the firebox. That's when I met Gideon Conroy, the best man I ever know'd. He taught me to engineer, soon had me readin' the gauges, when to pull the throttle, when to brake, when to blow the whistle. By nineteen, when I wed yer Ma, I's assistant engineer. And had prospects of makin' chief engineer 'fore age twenty-five. But one black night it all ended. February the 14th of '03, runnin' down a high curve off the Cumberland Plateau, haulin' too much coal to hold our speed, we derailed. By grace of God I's throw'd clear, but Gideon got pinned in a twist of steel by the fire hole. I seen him try to pull free, but he was gripped as by Lucifer's claw. The flames spread up so fast they swallowed even his screams. Till by dawn there was not a crisp of him in the smoke 'n ruin. Gideon was next a father to me 'n he did not deserve that hellfire. But I dared not ask the Lord why. Again I did whimper…whimpered like a kicked pup through that day and some that followed. To engineer had been my joy, but held no prospect thereafter…"

Brigham stares through the isinglass to the stove fire and the memory, watching it play from flame to ash, then breaks his gaze and turns to Faris.

"So…we moved west, yer Ma 'n I 'n little Hannah, our newborn. In prospect of land we come to Kansas. But what land had been free had already been taken. All sewed up by prior takers. The price was too dear to buy, even worse in the war years. Without money you can own no land no mind how hard you work.

"'Course the war, the Great War, made prospects for some, quite a few made big money, them as already had it. Bet it made a millionaire for each thousand boys dead. As you say you heard Henry Wales tell, war reaps men like a harvest. But listen, from the day the Great War ended, from this very day in 1918 for six months on a million folks died of the influenza right here in these United States. Young men 'n women healthy one day struck dead the next. It weren't so bad hereabouts, but yer Ma 'n I both lost kin back in Kentucky 'n Tennessee. No, there's not only War on his red horse, there's famine 'n plague. And there's always the Pale Rider.

"Men die ever' day workin' mines, cuttin' timber, blastin' tunnels. The Moffet Tunnel I worked chewed up 28 men. I seen six die in one day with my own eyes. We'd but set off a blast 'n I thought it were an echo. But a second blast come a hundred yards on, a misfire that caught men before they cleared. We heard screams 'n shouts and afore we run there they pulled several free. But the rest, those six we dug out had done kicked their last in the dust 'n rubble. Their eyes stared off to wherever their souls went. A awful thing to witness, a poor man alive one minute then starin' dead. But no, I did not whimper no more.

"The last time I did whimper was the day you was born 'n I laid yer brother Joel in the ground, a little blonde boy child what barely filled my two palms…" He holds out his hands and says, "And there I did knell down 'n whimper like a pup. Like with my Pa 'n Gideon, each time I felt myself empty out to nothin' and I did whimper like a pup…"

As he whimpers now, staring to his empty hands with the stove fire reflecting beyond and still sees the baby boy wrapped neatly in a kitchen towel as if awaiting the stork to fly him home to heaven. But no, it was black wings of shoveled earth that bore him underground. Ada lays a hand to his shoulder and he reaches back and covers hers. Faris who has rarely witnessed a tender moment pass between his parents turns away and retreats up the stairs. Only Ada speaks, and only to herself.

Where be yer prospects, Brigham, when ye have so little faith 'n less charity? With you it is all hope…prospect 'n hope. But then betimes I do love thee still. When you do not boast but speak true. Tonight, Brigham, ye speak true…

SEEDS OF HATE (from *Skin for Skin*)

Thanksgiving morning and a clear sky bodes a sunny day. The air warms with gentle snowmelt and runoff; the dead grass buds moisture soon dry in the gusty wind. Ground leaves swirl up and give chase like puppies one after another. Such a bright blue sky it hardly matters whether what spirals or flutters is a falling leaf or an awakened butterfly, not to an old dog's eye or a puppy's play. And to a man or woman each instant is but a daub of color on the canvas of self and others...

Mary Bess carries her share of woe but enters each door like a gust of wind with a fresh aspect and a bold laugh, a bit too immodest for some, yet music to Faris' ear.

"Gosh, Ma, did you see that sun this morning? Pa, Faris? Did you? Like in the beginning, the very first sun ever. We've had clouds, what...three, four, five days now," counting each with a blink of her eyes, "plus rain, sleet 'n two days of snow. When I see that sun, gosh, I gotta keep my hands in close or I'd fly straight up, I swear I would." In her right arm she holds her baby like it's her lone anchor to the earth while depicting her words with her wild left then rests her hand on her hip and looks to them in wonder why they don't share her urge to fly. The only answer she gets is Ada turning from the stove to say, "Come on over here girl 'n let me see our baby Lily..."

Tall at 5'8", Bess towers over her mother, a striking woman of auburn hair and the hazel eyes of her father, eyes flashing with prospect and promise as if this day will bring whatever you wish. Faris wishes she had done better than marry Frank Dodge. Wishes she had bided her time and saved her looks and charm for a man more worthy. But Frank had a car, a job, and in 1928 there were still lots of parties and dances in the offing. Bess was 14 and having Frank's baby bought her a ticket out of Elim. Out of their two-room flat above Winslow Clothing, with a well and outhouse in back and water to bucket up the stairs. While Faris understands the reasons, reason is poor excuse for what should and shouldn't be.

He watches his mother grip her hands in prayer and give voice on high, "Thank ye, O Lord, for the bounty of this day and the joy 'a havin' two of our three daughters home with their husbands 'n little ones here at our table to share this meal..." She's fried up two chickens and two rabbits, providing a good piece of meat for each person along with peas, potatoes, and biscuits, and if that's not enough there's plenty more biscuits either smothered with gravy or buttered and smeared with her mulberry jam. No one will go hungry from her table.

Frank is his usual sloven self, tufts of thin hair uncombed, slump-shouldered and sluggish from his nightshift and hangover. Sober he's quiet and shirking, but drunk he turns mean to Bess and the kids. Faris would like to give him a quick jerk and make him sit up straight, look you in the eye for once instead of cowering like a kicked dog. But Rachel's husband, Race Harlin Sloan, he thoroughly hates. Vulgar, shiftless, he seldom accompanies Rachel to see her parents and likely only came today so he could ogle Bess. His real name is Ramsey, a sometime bootlegger and fulltime anything that offers an easy buck. Their 8 year old son Dylan is of the same breed – Faris caught him throwing rocks at Prince that morning and boxed his ear, so he sits quiet for now.

Of Hannah, his oldest sister, no one speaks a word, twice-divorced at 26 and off with a new man she names Jake or Jerrod, depending, over the last two months she's called from Topeka, Kansas City, Omaha, no telling where they'll end up next or what he does. Faris is certain of one thing, like all the men his sisters have taken up with he's no good. Faris would gladly put a shotgun to each of their skulls and pull the trigger. The world and time wouldn't miss a tick. Not one worth a hair on Colley's head.

"And I'll tell you what's more," Brigham speaking now of Colley missing, having broached the question and preparing to bruit the answer while Ada cuddles Lily-Ann and Ruthie leans close to 'goo-goo' her baby sister, "someone don't want 'im found. You mark my words. It's like the shine boys back in Tennessee, the Rawlins. Any man as got crosswise of them they put a bullet in his head 'n wrapped 'im in thirty foot 'a log chain. Dumped 'im in the river. You wait, the very like has happened here..."

Faris knows there'll be more and refuses to listen to his dad blather to these two fools. He stands and goes upstairs, puts on his jacket, grabs his .410 and a handful of shells. When he comes back down packing the shotgun Frank and Race both turn their heads, suddenly awake to past slights and that dark look in his eyes. But he simply passes on through the kitchen and nods to his sisters, "It was good to see you."

Bess looks up in surprise and asks, "Where are you flyin' off to so fast?"

"Off to hunt birds," he says, knows it seems cold and uncaring, walking out and leaving them. He loves his sisters and would stay and talk if their men weren't around, for it prides his mom to see the family nearly whole. But love can't gloss his hate.

Outside Faris heads straight for the barn to saddle Jack, relieved to see the sky, the sun, to breathe good air. To distance himself from all the tension, the shame and love that binds them. He has reasons to hate the men, especially Race Sloan. As a 10 year old Faris worked a summer on the Sloan farm, Race still farming at the time, till even his old man tired of his sorry ways and ran him off. One evening, early on, Race cornered the boy in the barn where he bunked and tried to wrestle and cajole him into 'snaking the cornhole' as he called it. Pup had warned Faris of such, said there were men that would use a boy and if any ever tried it to fight like a hellcat, which he did.

Faris broke away, grabbed a pitchfork and cried, "You touch me again I'll kill you!"

Race threw up his hands, hadn't expected such fierceness and laughed, "Hey, hold on here. I's only kiddin'. Just horsing around. Wasn't really gonna do it. Hey now, you won't tell Rachel, will ya?"

Faris would never tell a living soul such a thing. Never. But that wasn't why he hated the man so, there lay a deeper cause.

The Sloans owned a chocolate gelding named Tarboy, so skittish from ill-treatment that no one could approach it, let alone ride. Yet Faris, scrubbing each day at the water trough where the horse slaked its thirst, bunking each night in the next stall, talking to the horse or simply humming a song or playing his harmonica, by and by induced the horse to take a halter and lead.

To placate the boy and assure his silence Race offered the horse. "He's yours if you work hard this summer 'n stay mum on our little game." Faris who wasn't about to tell anyone in any case agreed.

From that night on he spent each evening tending and grooming the horse. Even passed up going to town on Saturday nights with Race and Rachel for an ice cream soda or the chance of a movie, preferred the company of the horse. Late at night he'd lie on his cot and reach through the stall and darkness to coax the other near. Without a word he'd draw the horse forth and feel its hot breath on his hand and touch its warm nostrils, all implying an intimacy he seemed to remember but could not name.

By midsummer Faris had trained the horse to run on a long lead in the circle of the corral and jump three barrels in sequence. Soon he added a saddle and bridle and could perform the trick while riding. And shortly thereon he reined about and they jumped the corral fence. Boy and horse, a marvel in motion. On his Sunday's off they would range over pastures and roads for miles around.

At summer's end when he stood to collect his wages at $2 a week for twelve weeks, he received less than half, $10. When he looked up in question, Race said they kept back a dollar a week for board and room, and two more to fuel his lantern.

"What about Tarboy?" Faris asked, ready to ride him home to stable in Elim.

"Hey now, that's a valuable horse. I only meant he was yours for the summer..."

But when Race reached for the reins the horse reared up and ripped them from his hands, tearing the skin. As before, the horse wouldn't let anyone near but the boy. Faris quietly calmed the horse, removed the bridle and set him free in the pasture. He took his $10 and walked home to Elim. Even this, while it fed his hate, had not yet sealed it.

The following winter, a cold January day, Ada went to help Rachael after the birth of her baby. Faris went along in hope to see Tarboy. The Sloan farm lay two miles north of Elim and they walked the full distance against bitter wind and snow. Race had taken the car on a two-day binge to celebrate the birth of his son, Dylan Ramsey. While Ada entered the house to tend mother and child, Faris ran on to the barn, eager to warm his hands on Tarboy's winter coat and simply say his name. But the stalls stood dark and empty, no grain in the box or scent or breath of a living thing, silent except for the wind whistling through the rough planks. Beyond the corral Faris squinted to the north pasture. Through the distant shift of snow he discerned a dark mound slowly take shape to his watery eyes. And walking there he found the carcass, snow spilling off in a stream of wind like a soul carried away. He knelt and touched the black nose frozen hard as stone. The eyes blank. The ribs curled bare like a clawed hand to the raw cavity where coyotes had recently fed. The horse let to starve...

JACK STRAW SAYS (from *Skin for Skin*)

Saturday morning in Pup's Barber Shop, the flow of men slackens towards noon, called to Joe's Cafe for *'Another Pow'ful Good Meal'* – *Chicken Dinner, 25¢*. Though many are back again by early afternoon, picking their teeth, reading a newspaper or magazine in lazy wait of the barber chair. The radio turned low plays a string of favorite carols – *First Noel, Silent Night, Away in the Manger, Joy to the World* – like ornaments themselves tapping deep sentiments of hope and innocence rising in the blood memory along with the scents of hot chocolate, sugared popcorn, and Momma's apple crisp pie, all somehow centered in the ancient evergreen promise to make the old heart new.

Most men listening share the mix of enchantment through the next hour or so and most are soon shaved, trimmed, and gone, leaving only three: old Elmer in solemn snore, Father Nolan soon to take the chair, and Ross Fallon, a stern old Scot-Irish farmer more firm in his politics than his faith, sitting off alone towards the door, does not bandy or trifle, keeps to himself, his gaze fixed, silent, though his neck hardens as Pup turns up the radio to catch Jack Straw and "Old Trusty" speaking common sense to common people. Due to growing popularity the show has gained a slot each Saturday afternoon through Christmas. After giving brief note of the weather and highlights of area events, the voice shifts to a more frank and intimate tone...

"Folks, here we are again in the cusp of two great national holidays, Thanksgiving which predates our founding and was proclaimed in the moment of our gravest peril and disunion...and Christmas, which harkens back centuries to the birth of Jesus our Savior, who calls us forth, each of us, from our selfishness and greed to succor our brother out of love, shared sacrifice, and need. To all listening think of them now, for we all know of a brother, a friend, a neighbor out wandering like a shadow along the rails and roadways, gaunt from want and hunger, hounded by a dark angry wind, in search of a job, a meal, a place to sleep. And those left behind, wives, sisters, mothers

huddled in unheated flats, the coal box and cupboard bare, the babies wail, their bellies empty. Is it so much to ask in this Christmas season that there be a fire in every stove, a chicken in every pot...?"

"Then by God they can go out 'n chop some wood," Ross declares to the radio, "or shoot them a rabbit or pheasant if they're so blame cold 'n hungry!"

"Now Ross," Pup holds out a palm to ease him down, "what you say might be true for folks out here. But in those city slums and tenements there's not a rabbit or pheasant one. Now there are pigeons and I have seen them snared 'n eaten. Did so myself as a boy out of hunger."

Ross sits back hardly placated as the voice of irritation hums on:

"No, there's much to fear in unholy Russia, and I would not trade the American soul for their slavish ways. Not the free soul of our merchants, tradesmen, and farmers, all being stomped by the Giants of finance and industry, these new Caesars who would drain our lifeblood while they feast on plenty. Oh they scream at the prospect of a shared meal as if each tax exacts a pound of flesh. How is it that a man given a shovel and a job is boondoggle while a man given a rifle and sent to fight Sandina in Nicaragua to protect their rich investments is a righteous cause? This old bone of contention has been gnawed on through time and it's high time it was buried. It's not greed and power-lust but our sense of brotherhood, the bread from the sweat of our brow that feeds and defines us, our willingness to lend a hand 'n spare a dime that marks the essential American spirit. A spirit proclaimed long ago in Acts 11:29, 'And the disciples, every man according to his ability, proposed to send relief to the brethren in Judea...and distribution was made to everyone, according as he had need.' This latter part from Acts 4:35 –"

Ross stabs his finger at the radio, "That right there is from Communist Russia! He don't fool me. I knew he was a Red."

"Actually, Ross, I think it's from the Bible."

"Not from my Bible it ain't!"

"Well, I'm no expert, I admit. Perhaps Father Patti will clarify for us?"

Father Nolan shifts slightly, none too eager to enter the fray.

"Yes, yes," he says, "from the Acts as cited. Though I believe he quotes the Douay translation, but you'll find much the same in the King James Version or any you look to. It's a broken quote, incomplete, but provides the gist. Among the early Christians there was as yet no Church, nor a Bible. We only know of them through scattered texts that formed the Gospels and the Acts. As is said in the Acts, *'All that believed were together and had all things in common. And sold their possessions and goods, and parted them to all men, as every man had need...'*"

Ross stares hard and listens but does not yield or blink, holds the Catholics and their priests nearly as suspect as this socialist on the radio...

"Take a stick of gum, any flavor, chew it to a tasteless wad then toss it to the dirt. Better yet stick it under a cafe counter or booth. This is the rich in charity to the poor. They share a few crumbs and a trifle of learning and claim it's enough, these ABCs, their already-been-chewed and throw-aways. It's a wonder the poor don't rise up and take. But given a fair shake they'll gain their own as you would wish, by righteous effort.

"Hear the Scrooges shout, 'Nay, Never! That the poor are poor is their lot!'

"What of faith, hope, and charity? What are we become, a nation that celebrates parsimony and money changers? That shreds Paul's great hymn to charity, that says nay to kindness and yea to suffering? Remember what Peter said to Simon, again from Acts 8:20, 'Thy money perish with thee...'"

"By God I know this much," Ross slaps his hands to his knees and stands, "you'll perish a damn sight sooner from lack of money than by havin' it. And you can have that Red fool and his sermon. I'll take my preachin' in church on a Sunday..."

With that said Ross stomps out. The wreath bounces once at the bang of the door then hangs quaintly framed for the next exit or entry. The colored lights bubble on and old Elmer maintains his deep afternoon slumber, half snore and half dream. Jack Straw shortly signs off, yielding the airwaves to a bright jazzy rendition of *"Jingle Bells"* by the Riley-Farley Orchestra.

Pup finishes cleaning his clippers and with a sweep of the towel offers the chair to Father Nolan. "What say ye, Patti James, looks like brother Ross has bailed."

"Sorry if I ran him off."

"Aw no, he'll be back in by 'n by. Got his hackles up, he'll need a trimmin'…"

WEEDS

Summer ends; the green has gone to dust, spawning a growing bitter wind in late October. A water tower with an unsung name, a stop sign, and a few faded buildings, a dying spot in the road where a lone dog watches puzzled as cars slowly pass, where park swings and a metal slide stand idle to children's play, while the sagging gazebo has long since fallen silent to laughter and damp night waltzes.

On summer mornings old men still gather in the shade of a converted blacksmith shop to listen to the pounding of hammer on anvil that once shaped horseshoes for utility as well as play, where plow shares and sickles are yet honed to cut sod and hay.

– Where do they go in winter…now that they've closed Three Widow's Cafe?

– Oh, with winter coming on they'll go to Sloan's Garage. There's a front room with chairs and a stove. They'll be in there talking.

– Of what do they speak?

– Nothing much, just sit 'n spin like windmills off in a pasture, now 'n then idle, then cranking to life, letting whatever come to mind. But listen close, you'll follow to their time and day. Curious? Then come and see just where, when, and why. They'll be in there surely. The old do well with waiting.

The voice of the old is loud, their nose large and hairy as are their ears; their vision dim as is their memory. The old are humble and shy, more so than the child, for the trial of eighty years whittles each. And as a child is certain of Christmas the old are certain of God and ghosts, yet less certain of man – though they love children, for their budding hearts hold the promise of perhaps a century.

The old exhibit odd fetishes and eccentricities: employ a plural for a singular, nap in the afternoon as would a babe, and are by turns as cross and temperamental as any child. The old love hot stews and recited memories; yet like most amateurs their monologues lack polish, pacing, and are often overlong.

Their clothing is ill-fit and motley, of fiber that defies time. And while commonly clean, pressed, and mended, most bear labels of stores boarded up long ago. And they wear the hat of men who wore hats well: Stetsons with greasy brims and pinched crowns. Their shoes, though fondly polished and shined, are brothers to those enmeshed with thorns, tin cans, and rusty bedsprings off creek-bank junkyards. As if the old no longer change past their bygone youth, largely insentient to convolutions all about them...ignored, unwelcome, cast to the edge of things as are flowers, once wilted, soon passing to weeds. So they remain posed, nearly motionless, like sepia-stained images that vaguely haunt old wallpaper.

Peter (Pete): in manner fawning, yet endearing and good, invariably the teacher's favorite as a boy, possesses a certain fondness in being first to speak.

Henry (Hank): a few years older than Peter, in his early eighties, hard of hearing and somewhat crusty – blunt, brief, and preoccupied in conversation.

(*Interior of a rundown auto garage on the outskirts of a small town, dim-lit, a single gas pump, then weeds surrendering to fields. A chill morning in mid-October. A cluttered desk beyond the entrance marks the office; a middle-aged man sits hunched, checking debits/receipts. Three chairs line the north wall. Just east of the chairs rests an open-flame gas stove.* Peter *and* Henry *occupy two of the three chairs; a young man stands by the stove, sipping coffee. Occasionally the wind buffets at door and window, whistling in, while* Pete *and* Hank *remain oblivious to all but their own breathing.*

Note: being hard of hearing, their speech is a bit louder than normal – also they add a crisp precision to many words, as if underlining each thought and memory.)

Peter: Well now, Henry... (*leans to slap the other's knee*), 'bout time to check the *ant-eye-freeze*, wouldn't ya say?

Henry: Wudn't hurt to check them plugs 'n points neither.

Peter: Oh my yes. That's what the feller on TV calls *win-ter-eye-zing* your car.

Henry: Yep... (*The door opens with a cold gust; a man steps in, fetches a key off a hook then steps out.*)

Peter: Say now, that air's got a nip to it. Ain't it though, Henry... *Hank?*

Henry: I hear ya. Least it's fresh. Clean! Not like that filth in them cities.

Peter: Oh yes, fresh 'n clean, 'cept for the dust... (*purses his lips*). But for Heaven's sake won't this weather play havic with the boys in the World Series though? They say it's rained nine days straight out there in *Cal-ee-forn.*

Henry: All nonsense that. Think they can play the game year round. If they cut this foolishness they wudn't be fightin' the weather. Heck, soon be playin' snowball 'stead of baseball. Now if they done like in our day, Pete...they'd had the series plum run through by late September...with weather fit for it.

Peter: Yessir...

Man at desk (*shares a wry grin with the young man by the stove then frowns at the pair*): Hey, you two old buzzards...what you got against sports? (*They smile shamefaced like two kids caught cussing.* Peter *sits fidgeting,* Henry *less so, each tense and brittle as tumbleweeds blown by the fire.*)

Peter (*draws a careful breath*): Say now, don't get me wrong. I like sports much as the next feller. Played pasture ball when I's a boy, followed each series from ought-three on. In the newspapers...then on the radio since '33. But they've just gone too far.

Henry (*more certain*): What he means...whole country's gone sport crazy. Pay these boys a million bucks to play a game 'n shave their face on TV. Then load these high-schoolers on a blame bus 'n truck 'em a hundred mile on a Friday night to play a game. One game! Plum gone sport crazy!

Peter (*nodding at* Henry's *support*): I'll say so! And there's no need in that...is there, Hank? Why, I think we all agree sports is a wonderful thing. But they've gone too far. Like 'bout anything anymore... (*pause*) No, I enjoy sports, always have... (*pause*) You know though, Hank...I think football is a mite more interesting than baseball. Anymore, I think so, don't you?

Henry: Nope. Baseball is the game for me.

Peter: Well yes, 'cept there's just something about the football. But baseball's fine too.

Henry: Remember that one pitch? What they called the spit ball? *The spitter?*

Peter: Oh yes...

Henry: Wull ol' Clive Williams from over here to Glasco used to throw it for the town team. He's the first ever to throw that pitch.

Peter: Oh, you don't say...

Henry: Yep.

Peter: Say now, how you suppose he threw that? Prob'ly by accident the first time, wouldn't ya say?

Henry: Nope, no accident. Chewed the willow bark. Got the best sap from it, he said. Then he just spit on 'er and let 'er fly.

Peter: Oh my, well. They made 'em stop throwin' that spit ball. Didn't they make that illegal, Hank?

Henry: Yep.

Peter: Well, I wonder why they did that...?

Henry: Dunno.

Peter: It was prob'ly on 'count of danger to the batter. Prob'ly caused the ball to slip off the bat and hit the batter.

Henry: Could be.

Peter: But I wonder why do they still throw the curve ball? Seems it would be just as dangerous...breakin' left or right, you never know which way.

Henry: Bull! Never believed in that ball curvin'. Just a load of nonsense, Pete.

Peter: Oh, but it does curve, Hank. Heard 'em say it on the radio.

Henry: Nope.

Man at desk (*looks up with a weary groan*): What's the matter with you, Henry? They've been throwing the curve for over a century. Everybody knows that.

Henry: Wull, I dunno...

Man at desk: For chrissake, Henry! Wake up! Come in out of the weeds! They can throw a ball that curves. Damn, go to town some night and see for yourself.

Peter: It's true, Hank. They surely can...throw the curve.

Henry: Wull (*still wary, not convinced*)...I dunno.

(*Man at the desk shakes his head in disbelief to the young man by the stove then goes back to working receipts and debits. Wind and silence play for perhaps a minute...*)

Peter: Remember ol' John Goll?

Henry (*pleased at the change of subject*): Long's I breathe air. Finest man I ever met.

Peter: Oh, he was a Captain.

Henry: That he was.

Peter: Fought in the Great War.

Henry: Yep. Dubya-Dubya One...

Peter: And he was the man for baseball. Same as you, Hank. Said it was the one true American game... (Henry *grants a faint smile and nods.*) Remember when we still had the grocery?

Henry: Yep. Clemmon's Grocery...till their boy closed up. Been five year now.

Peter: Why, I believe you're right, Henry. Yessir. But summers back then ol' John would be in most days leaned to the counter listening to a game on the radio. Knew every player by name, too...all their hits and runs. Tell it to you like he saw the very game right outside the window.

Henry: That he did.

Peter: Oh, he was a Captain. Never knew a stranger. Gone to his long home now...what? Three...four years?

Henry: Three year come Feb'uary...the thirteenth! Damn cold day it was.

Peter: Believe you're right...and strange to see him so quiet. Just layin' there... (*Both again silent ...like a moment of respect...*) Saw his boy the other day.

Henry: You mean J-J...the fly-boy?

Peter: Yessir. He's a Major, you know...in the reserve. Flew over in Korea, he did.

Henry (*slaps his knee and chuckles*): And he still flies...*flies low!* That red Studebaker spits a jet trail ever'where he goes.

Peter (*grins back*): Oh my and how. He's some joker...pull your leg. I was out to my mailbox other day...he stops by, leans out with that grin of his and says, 'Think I might be lost, Pete. Help me out. Is this Kansas or Never-Never Land?' I stood there puzzled and says, 'Why, I don't rightly know..." And he says, 'Me neither, Pete. Just asked the price of Foley's 80 acres right south here. Well, he warned I'd need deep pockets, then named his price. I just laughed and said I *never-never* can own that land...'

Henry: A nice piece of ground that.

Peter: Yessir, bottom ground. But the price is sky high. Thirty years ago it would've bought the whole county... (*The phone rings and they pause...*)

Man at Desk (*drops his pen, lifts the receiver*): Sloan here...yeah, sure...doin' okay. Yourself...? Uh-huh...how 'bout the...? No...? Not even with...? (*Voice weakens*) Yeah...yeah...I'll be there... (*Hangs up the phone and grimaces...same as* Hank *as he leans to catch the land price from* Pete...)

Henry: That much...? Why that's crazy... that kinda money. Then these new tractors and combines...bringin' the price of a farm each. Look at 'em...the size of a locomotive. And the debt...all they buyin' is debt, boys these days. Plum cra–

Man at Desk: Can't you two old fools shut the hell up! Just... (*grips his pencil and quiets*). Damn, just give it a rest for once. Can't think... (*he pauses at the growl of an engine starting up in the back shop and looks to the young man waiting*). Sounds like Jeff's got your truck runnin'. Let's go check... (*slaps his* *ledger closed and stands. The young man sets his cup on the desk and glances back in nod to the scolded pair then exits following the other stage left. The wind hums briefly then fades...*)

Peter (*quietly folds his hands on his lap as* Henry *stares to the floor*): A mite prickly today, ain't he?

Henry: Yep.

Peter: Don't suppose he's got debts, do you?

Henry: Dunno. But I say neither borrower nor lender be.

Peter: True. But they got to have it right now... (*pauses in gaze to the window*). You know, Henry...seems to me there's more weeds than used to be. Does it seem so to you?

Henry: Bound to be...plowin' ev'ry last foot a' ground. Like that dern Butz told 'em, *Plant 'er fence row to fence row, boys*. Tear up all the grass...bound to be weeds.

Peter: But they got that *her-bee-cide* now...don't they?

Henry: Don't do much good. Still got weeds. And you bet it costs a pretty penny.

Peter: Why yes, they even spray from aero-planes. Seems the wind would carry it off?

Henry: Pissin' in the wind, you ask me... (*they nod to one another as the wind gusts and trails away...*) But tell you what...T.C. Rose was the man to deal with weeds.

Peter: Oh, I'll say he was...always up 'n at it.

Henry: Yep, ol' Thaddeus Claude hisself...reaped 'em with that hoe a' his. And he didn't carry no debt, neither. Paid cash money for ev'ry inch a' ground he owned.

Peter: My yes…and owned a bunch before he died. Lived to be a hundred, didn't he?

Henry: Nope…a hundred 'n one. Buried 'im in August '61.

Peter: Why, I believe so. Hot as blazes it was…awful windy 'n dry. I recall the dust on his silver casket…dust to dust… (*again a brief pause of respect*). Remember…how ol' T.C. would walk to town most days his last years? A whole mile each way to fetch his mail and a pint of buttermilk at the grocery. 'Cept he never lingered to catch a game, no sir. And always carried that hoe along, cocked across his shoulder.

Henry: Yep…bent half double from years a' work, he was. He'd stop now 'n then…hoe a few weeds…in the ditch…a field or pasture. Never idle, that man.

Peter: No, reckon not. I asked him once, there along the road…I said, 'T.C., why you always hoeing them weeds? There'll still be hundreds tomorrow…' (*shakes his head at the memory*). Well, he just reached out with a quick jerk of that hoe…cut a weed clean at the root. Then grins to me and says, 'That'un won't be!' (Sloan *enters from the shop and stands baffled as they laugh and repeat in chorus*): THAT'UN WON'T BE…!

(*Presently all fall silent; action freezes; the room dims like an old tintype. The stage slowly darkens…for a night, a year or more. When it lights up again, the chairs and desk are gone, the door and window boarded shut, the stove stands cold. All utterly quiet and empty except for the far wind and two tumbleweeds set stage center.*)

BOB'S CAFE

Many years ago in the heady '60s I was a student at a typical state university. A good school by its own measure, full of nihilists, idealists, iconoclasts, and ranters...the rest were eager youths and co-eds, seeking entree to the stable strata. I of course was among the wildlings, a skeptical free spirit, raging with my own brand of individualism.

On this particular day I had risen, as was my custom, in the afternoon; if not pious, certainly taking advantage of scholarly prerogative. My tongue was swollen and numb, my throat coagulated, for by and by I had become wholly addicted to cigarettes. I shall always remember walking from my bedroom to the bathroom mirror and viewing my dull pallor, my posture oppressed by alcohol. I felt like a bedlam consumptive. How I would anguish! The sordid squalor of student slums! How eloquent my righteous indignations! Simply, I lived in poverty adequate to my need, as now, and though I felt the spears of persecution, I suffered merely from post-adolescent delights: alcohol, tobacco, irregular hours, inconsistent ideas, and lastly the physical and psychic ordeal of erratic exposure to sex, oscillating like the weather that winter, now hot, now cold. I would shower and shave, brush my teeth, dress (always the same denim jean, jacket, and shirt, whether hot or cold), grab my favorite text (usually Tolstoy), my pen and private journal, then enter the day, confident, refreshed, vital, prepared to expend my energies in filial devotion to my present grandmaster of the word, seeking to usurp his brand of esthetic to help ballast my barroom poetics and eager scattershot prose.

Thus out the door, down the street, I would walk past children, houses, churches – princely as the young Apollo who has but lately acquiesced to his beauteous Venus – on past the trees and the park. I breakfasted daily at Bob's Cafe.

It served no large clientele. The counter edged over a half dozen frayed, padded stools. There were about five booths of worn vinyl upholstery, the color of dried blood. To the back stood a garish pinball machine, blinking, easily tilted, where junior-grade hoodlums hung out, the usual twelve-year-old combination panhandler, mamma's brat, Huck-Finn types whose habitual villainy, in schoolyard parlance, entailed "playing hooky". To use the restroom you had to ask first then pass through the kitchen where the hunchback worked to a narrow broom closet, standing room only, always wise to lock the door behind you for the single sink and stool served both sexes. Above the counter read the intimidating blast, "Pay When Served!" Outside a newspaper rack stood next to a telephone booth, the receiver yanked out about half the time.

Bob's Cafe stayed open around the clock, closed on Mondays. His menu was the usual quick-order, greasy-spoon fare, durable like leather and denim and the gratuitous smiles of lonely women. But his breakfast was outstanding, praised in the most effusive terms throughout the student quarter. The pancake, eggs, sausage, and hash brown special was so agreeable in fact that it was famously known as "Bob's Breakfast." His customers were nearly always hungering for breakfast, be it high noon or midnight. And his grill and waitress were so expeditious they seldom garnered a complaint beyond a jocular gripe or groan. Finished, a modest tip was adequate and welcome.

Besides the comic puffed-up little hoodlums, various working men came at mid-morning and mid-day to drink Bob's coffee – perpetually perked, black, thick, rank and steamy, a brew that offers brief comfort and anodyne to all the whiskey, boredom, and despair working men the world over face and endure. Bob's coffee, a sometimes friend, ever hot and certain to leave its foul opinion on your breath for hours, was also talked of about town, but in terms more infamous than laudatory.

There also gathered at Bob's Cafe in the early evening and the gray Sabbath noon a most peculiar sect – gnomes of tenement belfries who guarded no treasure beyond that of each other's existence. Called like the twelve apostles, though here there were only five to my knowing. A genial black dwarf of bright smile and broad hips, a broom-thin albino with his pinhead sister, and a sunbaked tan-man – all called by the hunchback in the kitchen. As the Pope and St. Peter are heir to Christ on earth, this one was heir to Quasimodo – his flesh utterly wrinkled as if by some horrid curse or sin, resembling that of Michelangelo's flayed skin in the Last Judgment. And observing them seated in their world apart, I wondered at the cruel taunts these wretches had incurred, all the mortifying insults, the daily spite of eye and tongue, enough to make crucifixion seem merciful. Yet they sat calm, unfazed in their inner sanctum, sharing repast in their separateness, humble and meek, certain of their fated lot, if nothing more.

There was no trace of February in the air, the day as warm and propitious as April, so I was not at all surprised upon entering to find I would be the sole customer. On such days men are likely to enjoy their work, young rogues apt to frequent river banks, and the ill-cast and ill-begotten more prone to gather on a sunny park bench to wave on their wee friend the tan-man running past, barefoot and shirtless even in winter.

Bob and the waitress were seated side by side at the counter sipping coffee. I took the booth nearest the window, laid out my present study and journal in prescribed ritual and prepared to receive my meal as the day's sacrament. The waitress, Liz, brought me my coffee and asked softly, "The usual?" As I nodded she shot a worried glance over her shoulder to Bob and said, "He hasn't been well today, not at all well."

She wiped her hands on her apron and walked back to the grill to ladle out some batter and crack a couple eggs. Soon she added sausage and hash browns, all the while taking care to remain as silent as her task would permit, always keeping an eye on Bob's slumped figure. I noted from his shaky balance and mumbled phrases that he was drunk. Occasionally the hunchback would appear clinching his broom, shyly look on and shake his head then disappear. Although there was little movement of his lips I could hear him hoarsely intone, "Poor Bob, poor Bob...," with the firm conviction of one who knows well the pained posture of an anguished soul.

Gradually I became aware of the moment, its vibrant drama. The man at the counter was not merely drunk, he was tragic. The silence closed around like mortared brick.

"Wah duz'e knoe, huh?" he blurted in protest, then louder, "*Huh!*" snarling like a wounded animal. "Tell me, Liz! Wah 'n hell'z knoe? Five years, he saiz...ooh God!" This last he uttered like one forsaken then sunk his face to his hands and sobbed, tears soaking his shirtsleeves, bawling desperately as if gazing into his grave.

When Liz brought me my meal her eyes were moist and frightened and seemed to be searching for an explanation. She sighed and said, "That poor man. He hasn't slept all night, you know. And I can't stop him drinkin'." It was then I realized she was not seeking an explanation, nor apologizing in any way, she was asking that I participate, at least acknowledge if not play a part in the drama. My opening line:

"What's the matter with him, Liz?"

"Oh honey, he's got the cancer."

"Of the lungs?"

"Yes, and the doctor says at the most five years. Bob just found out yesterday and he hasn't slept a wink 'n I can't stop him drinkin'. Poor man..."

I didn't know what else to say and started to give an awkward condolence when Bob slipped off his stool and fell to the floor. As I rushed over and helped Liz lift him back on his feet I could feel his body trembling from fear, fatigue, and alcohol. He struggled for footing, his legs rubbery, stomach ill-mannered, and his eyes resented me being there, resented my youth and strength. I returned to my booth and started to eat.

Liz stayed there, propping him up, comforting him. He cursed her and flung out his arms. She started to leave but he called her back.

"Ayme sarry! Ayme sarry!" he pleaded, reaching for her. "Dun go, Liz, yur my baby...huh? Dun leef ol' Bob."

"I won't leave you, hon. I'll stay."

"Yu'll be my gurl-fren, Liz?"

"Yes, I'll be your baby."

"Wah duz tha Doc knoe? Huh?"

"Nothin', Bob. They don't know a thing."

"He cant tell uh man 'es gon die. Naw! He cant do tha!"

"There now, Bob. You're gonna have to get some sleep, dear. Let me take you upstairs."

"Oh God, Liz! Yu'll luv me thoe, huh? Won cha? Yur my gurl, huh?"

"Sure, Bob. I'm your girl." She rubbed his neck and gently leaned to his shoulder. He cried again but less violently, beginning to quiet and weaken under her caress.

"How duz'e knoe? How? Hows'z knoe I got canzur? Huh?"

"He doesn't, Bob. Doctors don't know anything 'cept how much they charge."

"Oh God! Yu'll luv me, huh? Liz?"

"Yes dear, I will."

"Dun leef ol' Bob, Liz."

"I won't leave…"

I suppressed my hunger out of a certain respect one shows at times, like stifling a sneeze at a funeral. Simply looked on, I and Quasimodo, the latter quietly intoning the same hoarse phrase, "Oh Bob, poor Bob…" Observing Liz, I admired her intense concern and tact. This warm and rather witless woman had a great heart that somehow guided her toward the right and necessary act. Tall, big-boned, buxom, of ruddy complexion and raw Nordic stock – I wondered how many there were like Liz in restaurants and bars across the country. They always seem to sense when your glass is empty or your heart in ache, these large-armed matrons who through sheer prowess convince men they are still boys. The guardians of our truest self, the very pulse of being that still longs for the womb. Often poor in marriage and unwelcome in bed, but in bars and cafes they are esteemed. Men tithe them wages and express jovial regard – these sisters of mercy along the road to our shared demise.

Eventually Liz succeeded in coaxing Bob upstairs to his bed. And I don't know, perhaps she slept with him, which would have shown utter fidelity on her part. Women like Liz don't receive men's lust so much as share their sorrows and accept the task required of them. Whatever happened I do know that she nursed Bob back to some level of function.

When I rose to leave, the hunchback was waiting to collect my tab, his big brown eyes like those of a dog certain his master was dying.

"Ain't it too bad though…" he offered with grave acceptance as if the fates had already decided and carried out the sentence, "…bout Bob. Poor Bob."

For an instant I felt subsumed, somehow fallen, naked, in sync with Bob, Liz, and Quasimodo...and I was grateful I had the exact change. I did not care to remain such an integral part of humanity that day.

Soon thereafter, not predilection but circumstance drove me out into the streets, down the dusty byways and winding roads. I drew close to the dreamy rim-land of my childhood simply because I had no place else to turn, suddenly married, without a job. But with each day the familiar faces and scenes grew less tenable and urged us on. As a young father and husband I thought less of divine liberty and looked more to my duty, to my wife and son, less certain of my thoughts, but more certain of my heart, at last leaving the errant trail of vainglory and reverie of which I was once so fond.

After trying the mountains and several other locales we returned once more to the university town, drawn not by nostalgia but the grim pragmatism of the laborer who moves for the sake of work and money. And by and by, driven by a whiskey hangover and another weary day, I returned to Bob's Cafe. I better appreciated the coffee, though the breakfast had grown stale and more expensive. And the apt and ample Liz had been replaced by a dour stick of a woman with dark piercing eyes, pointy ears, sharp nose, chin, teeth, and tongue. She flitted like a sparrow from task to task with erratic quick steps, her arms awry – a mistress of spite, changing mood like a crazed chameleon. Her one relatively laudable trait lay in feeding her tip change to the jute-box.

Walking back through the kitchen to use the john, I met with her male version, a slight, surly man noisily scrapping dishes stacked in clutter next to the sink – his apron soiled from weeks of scouring, as was his stringy hair and yellow teeth. When asked if the john was open he cast a smirk and said, "Have at it..." It was open alright, near to overflowing, hadn't been flushed for hours and I wasn't about to try it. I checked my breath and wondered what had happened to the hunchback? Hopefully Quasimodo had found sanctuary sweeping floors in some quiet church. Of the others, who knows?

Back at my booth, cupping my coffee in callused hands, I reflected on the state of things, all the transitions in self and surroundings – feeling more inclined to Steinbeck than Tolstoy by then, wry and wary, wore the outlook of a Joad. My coffee grown cold and bitter, I signaled for a refill. Miss Sparrow splashed it full. Then Bob made a brief pass through to check the register and gather his mail, noticeably thinner, eyes mute and glassy, afflicted by cataracts. He moved vague and slow as a ghost, ignoring all as he faded on upstairs, resigned and imprisoned by resignation. No longer questioned, knew his time was near. Probably felt pretty sick.

When I left the cafe that afternoon I never even considered its future, relieved to escape its mortared walls, the sign above the door already flaking. You hear it said you can't go back. So it seems. Even now, many years on, I recall driving down the street, thinking, "That's one bridge burned…"

BLACK MOON

The pickup was loaded with furniture which he planned to sell in town. He drove slowly down the highway so the canvas tarp wouldn't blow. There had been some rain that afternoon and he knew the old dealer would pay less if the furniture was wet or in any way damaged. Having talked with him earlier that day, when asked if he bought used furniture, the old man's eyes had glazed with practiced indifference as he absently replied that he'd have to see the 'stuff' first. So the young man promised to return with the furniture before the store closed that evening.

He glanced to the rearview mirror, checking the tarp, and remembered the dogs running behind the pickup, lost in the trailing dust. That morning he'd dumped the dogs, a yellow Lab and a white Spaniel, near a little town too small to have a dogcatcher where he hoped they'd find a home. Some years before when his father moved the family off the farm, he remembered the dogs dumped along a desolate road, how they'd circled and sniffed the air then ran after the car. There were other times in his youth when grownups came in the night to haul a stray away; they might as well have lynched his best friend. He could never understand the gruff ease with which adults performed such acts. Now, however, he realized if you live long enough, sooner or later you'll likely commit every lame act you felt incapable of as a child.

Later in the week he would leave his wife and young son, another betrayal, though only for a short while, till he could resettle. Still, an uncertain sadness quarreled with his thoughts, indistinct as two children quarreling behind a barn, faint and defiant as a distal, nostalgic scream. Too much was passing from him, too many attachments forsaken in a day. He felt more and more a traitor with its sour pang and hunger. It was dangerous to feel so empty. The home he had searched so anxiously and hopefully for, his wife, child, family, and friends, who were more than people to him, all members of a holy tribe living off a harsh yet cherished land, all betrayed.

There was another reason he drove slowly. He wished to savor the land, its contour and color, its varied texture and scent, take it all in and etch it deep to give assurance he would one day return. So he drove silently asking of the land its forgiveness – far easier to apologize to the vast face of the prairie than be griped by the pleading condemnation of his young wife's wounded eyes.

It was one of those transitional days of late November, the air full of melting snow and mud odors, the atmosphere gray, oppressive, as pale sifting stratus clouds distorted the anchoring sun in a purplish haze, yellow-rimmed, shrouding the sky. And over all the land stretched a black sea of mud with islands of filthy snow scattered here and there, waiting to die. In the fields, arthritic stalks of milo and corn huddled, gnarled and bent by wet snow and high winds, their tumescent fruits hanging isolate, untenable, also waiting to die and to rot. One of those near-winter days of car-heaters and stoves half ablaze, the smell of over-boots on damp floorboards and gloves let to dry.

Many farmers had come to town, their cars and pickups lined the streets, no parking space left in front of the bars and cafes where the men sat talking over their coffee or beer while their women-folk shopped at IGA or Boogaarts.

As he drove down the street he could hear their talk, the men, already knew their words. How it would have been a record milo crop. How the pheasant hunters out from Kansas City and up from Wichita had done enough damage dragging their big-ass boots and shotguns through the fields. No respect. Then the early snow and high winds had hit, knocking the buxom feed to a muddy mattress as sure as the little woman got hers. And there she lay in all her ravaged splendor, ripe and ready, the richest grain ever, and you couldn't get to her lying there in the mud. *No damn way! And di'ja hear, some took over 90 bushel an acre before the snow!* This really sparked some ripe words. He'd heard it all, their pool-hall parlance, the county had been fairly abuzz with it for a week. He had it memorized, the piss and moan of each wagging tongue.

That ought to slacken their fat bellies, he thought, wondering how many new pickups orders would be canceled. But to those in the bars and cafes it smacked of sin, an unharvested crop, something like thievery or adultery to their eyes. Like the Holy Virgin set before them, ever-merciful and kind, yet her loving mercy was forever out of reach, which made man's doings all the more desperate. For the well-healed and their boosters he had no sympathy, only bitter distain. They hadn't any need, nor were they luckless. Year after year the big landowners had pilfered the prairie then dissipated their gains in vain bellicose consumption. Having tilled the land for less than a century, yet in this mere span they'd rifled the grass and soil in many places clear to the rocks. So he viewed the storm cryptically as the Indian nemesis...or dirt farmers blown to the wind. For there was a bitter pulse about the land and in himself if he'd admit it, an angry sullen spirit which knew of other harvests left unfinished and other lives left untapped. And if the current gentry were not pleased with their substance then they could leave like all the others had through the years. All those they'd helped chew up and spit out...the jilted daughters and abandoned widows and sons. No, he had no sympathy for the overlords and bankers, only for the victims of their usurious, cunning ways. And of the latter he knew a good many, knew their worries and shared them. Knew also that they wouldn't be in the bars and cafes, or even in town – for they bought their whiskey early and would be parked in old pickups along the county's back roads. And their thoughts with each drink would turn to their pending debts, after each bottle to their children, and with each passing day to themselves and to their wives alone at home dreading the anger, rage, and despair that would return come nightfall.

He longed desperately for the past – a past before all the looming thresholds of decision and anxiety when at times the sadness of the entire world seemed to collapse and descend upon a man's lower gut like some deadly black cancer, an effluvium of despair like a day-after's breath of alcohol and tobacco. He would like to have gone to the little cafe in the south part of town where his friends would be drinking coffee, their words always full of mystery and play like rowdy children born of riddles. And he would have joined them like a child in their theater of the absurd, shared in their cuss and laughter, and thus briefly escaped the environs' as well as the mind's hostility, instead he turned east up 4th Street. He headed on past Lincoln where he could have turned, then circled the block and parked in front of the used furniture store.

The old building had once been the local Nazarene Church and retained the faded red lettering above the door; this epitaph merged with another more recently daubed on the wood and so juxtaposed the old dealer's sign read "Nazarene Used Furniture Store." It served somewhat as the county repository, shoddy, dilapidated, no larger than a one-room schoolhouse which it resembled, containing all the unharmonious clutter in which the communal soul abides. Whereas the Nazarene had been a carpenter and went into Judea to become the Messiah, his church now housed the unfired corpses and chipped remains of his former craft.

The young man stepped in and found the old dealer with another customer. So he stood back and let his eyes drift over the soiled mattresses, springs, and bedsteads, tables, chairs, halltrees, and lamps stacked about the floor and up the walls in indifferent array. There was a desk child-scrawled with crayons; a mirrored bureau in the far corner which a delicate old lady may have owned before she passed away. A strange expression he thought, *pass away*. He always envisioned a person walking over a pasture hill into the distance with the nimbus of evening serving solemn witness to their passing. An old scythe hung like a crucifix on the east wall, the veins of its handle long sealed by the dirt and sweat of earthy labor. The implement as ancient as the Nazarene himself, and he wondered if the user had reaped just reward in final harvest. Close by stood a woodstove, its metal hide pitted by rust and ashes, the grate and flue unfired for a decade now. A set of narrow bedsprings stood against the wall, bent and warped as if by fevered nightmares. He wondered if the heat that had framed this tension had been of death-throes or passion. To the side, behind a chest, he spied a swirl of glass tubing that spelled the word 'Cafe' – a ghostly haze haunted the cold, dead neon trapped within. And there were mirrors along the aisles, some with quaint filigree and frosted pictures, one cracked, others gazing up off tables. He had long been superstitious of mirrors, not only for their reflections but for the memories inherent in their silver-lined surfaces. Avoiding these stares, he stayed by the gas-heater for warmth. Nonetheless the old building and its contents oozed a chill, damp breath. A gray winter day, the sky one omniscient cloud with no shadows, the only thing sustaining the world was a raw, hungering sense of the spiritual, seemingly lost as well. Even the walls, naked and stained, bore ghosts of vanished scenes rather than the wallpaper itself.

To avoid the haunt he decided to walk outside and await the old dealer on the front steps. No longer was he drawn to the past and its certainty, rather it was the future he yearned for. Time for a journey, time he stepped past the various thresholds and shed his angst and dread. Life now seemed absurdly transparent, brief and metabolic, whereas it had once appeared dense, mysterious, and dramatic. No matter, whether toward peril or promise, he would choose a path and go. His grandfather, a veteran of the Great War and the trenches, had told him that when crossing a narrow plank bridge to never look down, always trust your instinct and look straight ahead. Was this the way to cross life's voids and uncertainties? To keep running in sweat behind one dim headlight beamed through the darkness, with bone-faith and trust your only guide? Was this what his grandfather meant, that we must always run blind?

Presently the old dealer came out and sent his other customer on with a perfunctory word. He turned his vague blue eyes to the one waiting, gaze and intent blurred by thick bifocals. He gave a nod and hunched his gray jacket against the damp air as they silently crossed to the street. At the pickup he pulled back the tarp, peered in briefly then stepped back, coughed and spat, preparing his gambit.

"How much you take for the lot?"

The young man thought a moment and said, "Fifty dollars."

"Nope," the old dealer winced in parry. "Cain't do 'er. I'll give ya twenty for the works. And that's my offer."

"Hell, those chairs alone are worth five bucks each, which comes to thirty. Then there's the couch, the table, the bed…"

"I know that, son. I know all that," the old dealer wheezed, dismissing the youth's indignation. "But I got to turn a profit. Pay for my trouble. Now I may sit on this stuff a year before I can turn it, and that costs me, son, in storage, heat 'n electric. Plus I charge fair prices, I'm reasonable. Don't like to hike my customers. Now twenty dollars is my offer. If ya don't like it, don't think it's fair, go somewhere else."

"No place else buys used furniture."

"Suppose so," the old dealer shrugged, frank, impatient, "then take 'er home or to the city dump. I can't pay much for it, son. Heck, I get more every day. Stuff like that."

"How about forty dollars," the young man persists.

"Whoa now!" the old dealer laughs, genuinely amused. "Think to bargain with me, eh? Well, I never change my mind once I make an offer. That's it. Twenty dollars, boy, take it or leave it."

"I need the money."

"Then swing yer pickup over round here 'n help me unload. I'm an old man…"

They worked quickly, unloading and stacking the furniture, and he listened as the old dealer complained about his back.

"No sir, I never wished nor whined," he gasped, breathing heavily. "Don't get much out of this, boy. Do it sort of as a service, ya see. Naw…" he paused lifting another chair to the porch, catching his breath and rhythm to better match the young man's occasional concurrence and nod, "should rest myself, 'stead I drive down here twice a week from Rynal. That's sixty miles. You know where Rynal is, don-cha?"

"Can't say as I do," the young man answered blankly.

"Well, it's up off 36 Highway. 'Bout ten miles west of Bellville," the old dealer again paused, blinked his eyes, cleared his throat, briefly searching his thoughts before resuming. "I do an antique business up there. Fine stuff too. Not like this ol' shit here. No sir, get tourists from New York, California, all over the country stop in there. Have some fine quality articles. But since Clair died, that's my wife, there's no one to really care about, no one to worry. She'd never let me do this…drive this far and this much more work 'n all. But as I's saying, do this more as a service. Lots of folks ain't so well off, can't afford to pay much for furniture. So…" heaving another load, "I give 'em a fair shake. Keep prices reasonable. Though, takes a lot out of me to drive, and I really don't make all that much, ya see…"

This last trailed off as the old dealer noticed the young man had turned away, not listening, avoiding as much his breath as his words. The old dealer straightened with a grimace and began slowly ascending the steps.

"I got talking there," he said. "Forgot 'bout your money. Suppose you want cash."

"Yes," the young man answered, turning to follow.

Inside, the old dealer carefully counted out a score of dollar bills then casually asked the young man if he was moving far.

"Yeah, I'm going back East," he replied.

"Say now, that is a goodly distance. Do you have work out there?"

"No," the other answered quietly. "I write songs. Want to make it with my songs."

"Oh, you one of them guitar players, like ol' Hank?"

"Yeah, somewhat."

"Say, I sure wish you luck, young feller. Yes sir..."

With that the young man said thanks and started to leave, but before he could reach the door the old dealer called him back.

"Just need your name here. Got to keep records for Uncle Sam, ya know," he added with a chuckle.

"Clayton. Lee Clayton," the young man answered, reluctant, bitter at the deal and now being detained.

"Clay...Clayton...?" the old dealer repeated, trying to recall, as if thumbing through the pages of a telephone directory. "Did you ever have relatives up round Oakvale?"

"Yeah," the young man answered warily, for he knew, knew better than the harvest talk in the pool-halls and cafes, the question that would follow. "My family farmed north of there. We moved away when I was six."

"Your father named Faris?" the old dealer asked, examining the other more closely.

The young man noted the recognition in the old dealer's eyes, knew that he shared his father's features, the same posture, the same wry, dark look.

"Yeah. That was my father. Did you know him?"

"Sure. Sure nuff did," the old dealer said. "Knew your father 'n mother and you kids. You was all young then, of course. No sir, knew your father right well. Ya see, I ran the sale-barn up to Mankato and cried sales all over them parts for years...before I got too old –" the old dealer stopped abruptly, again regarding the young man.

"Your father, he took his life, didn't he?"

It came like a blast of ghost-heat from a furnace or white steam off a train engine, long, panicky, all the fear, thought, guilt, and repressed screams that cloaked the years began to churn like hot gravel through his gut...*yeah old man, took his life. Had to t'save it. To save his spirit. My father's spirit, old man. That deep heart of him wrapped warm like a babe in a blanket, cuddled and nestled to his chest, took it and faded over the hills, lurching from shadow to shadow, yet wanted to scream...'cause there was all kinds of lyin' bastards out to get him! Running low and hunched, silent through the slumbering dusk...yet wanted to scream! Hell, he used hot lead to fill the vacuum of his dreams and left his life dissolving on the floorboard of a 1940 Ford sedan! And dire words, old man, depict the act – the rank dust, despair, and body odor mixing with the pale dross and singed flesh, burnt gunpowder and dried blood – but memory holds it dear. Killed his life to save it! And the only garden to surface that spring was asparagus and onion, then only the wild and fibrous. And the preacher said only that he was a desperate man and should not be blamed. Then after weeks of drought it rained at his funeral, hard into his grave. So God must have been pleased. He passed away, as they say, if not his spirit, then the man, his footprints, and all the moments up to his last act on this earth. And the three unities of his drama like the holy trinity lie shattered in the clutter of this remnant church.* Yeah, old man...he exhaled slow and easy, releasing his anger like a child does its breath when attempting to blow a bubble bigger and bigger.

"Yeah," stated evenly, "he shot himself that next spring down by Asher."

"So that's where it was," the old dealer drawled. "Yes, I recall now hearing such." Then he asked, a bit more tentative, "This don't bother you...to talk about it?"

"No, not at all," he lied, "it's all long gone, in the past."

"Well, yes, it's been quite a while. But sure, I knew Faris. Knew his cousin too."

"Arlan?"

"Yes, Arlan was his name. Knew both them boys, and liked them too. And they thought the world of me, yes sir. Why, I's the one what cried the sale for Arlan before he moved out to Kentucky, I believe it was. You recall that?"

"No," he lied again – it was the day before his third birthday, the train depot in Mankato, and he remembered hugging his cousins good-bye. "No, I was too young."

"Suppose so." The old dealer raised a hand to his lips, delving into his thoughts. "Something else, you see, I always been a little hurt...oh, nothing big, ya understand. But yer dad, Faris, told me I could cry his sale too. It seemed he promised. But come time he got the Wilke brothers up to Superior. And I helped both them boys, a fact I did, and they thought the world of me..."

The young man tensed. *Like the twenty bucks you gave me you damn leech!* He wanted to scream, *Five more seconds, old man, I'll bust you like a broke bottle!* Edging to anger, he caught himself and gripped a chair. *Hold it, hold...!*

"The day of the sale I tried to talk to Faris but he was right short with me. I asked why didn't I get to cry the sale like he promised. But like I said he just wouldn't have a thing to do with me. Like he didn't know me, or I him. And for quite a while I was hurt by that 'cause I was close to those boys. Then later I heard what happened and of course forgave him. 'Cause it's an illness, ya see, they can't help themselves. Why, you never know. People seldom do. Heck, the best friend life ever give me took his own life. We rode this country and cried sales together for twenty years and I never guessed it. But later, looking back, a man knows. They don't talk so much, kinda short with ya, and don't laugh much towards the end. Course no one blames..."

Within his heart the young man felt his deep voice awaken and cry, *You vulture, vulture...I am not yours to feed on!* Yet the bubble did not burst and he ceased to listen to the old dealer quickly as cocaine numbs the face. His dark anger no longer threatened even though his heart still pulsed a bitter portion. He turned and made his exit.

Outside, he learned what he'd only feared and guessed at before. What others had seen and already known, his father and all those lost like strays down byways and back roads. An enlightenment he did not want or call for – he felt its surge and damnation as his bitter cry again welled forth – *Vulture!* – and he saw what made the land vengeful and heartless and the past, present, and future visible and ubiquitous as the evening shadows. In the western sky an imminent sphere, a black moon of despair that hovers both above and within the wounded soul. Anger and reverence poured forth before the unbidden orb, this palpable singularity drawing all light and life and reflecting none, cratered by the haunted ones impacted there. It hollowed his gut and drained his eyes, offered to kill his flesh and save his spirit, draw the latent self to it. A sky hinting no twilight before dark, which reigns empty and numb, sucking your vital marrow; a doubt that freezes thought and action, your very life; a hard, vicious wind that howls about your house and through its walls like they were made of paper.

The same fear that comes with puberty when the hair appears upon your legs and under your arms, the tempting, anxious pleasure that drives and imbues your loins. But this fear wholly unwelcome and consuming. Not wanting to grow or remain. Crying in panic for a never-never promise never to be.

He stood in gaze, close to empty, dangerously so. Felt it suck him dry, cold and alien, as if balanced on the legs of a corpse. He wondered how empty his father had felt leaving the farm. Had he sensed this dark apparition roiling the atmosphere, chilling his bones? He was frightened now and knew he'd better find his friends fast and share some warm whiskey and laughter before this darkness claimed him utterly.

COLD SHOWER

(For Dalton Howard – Vietnam vet & singer of heartfelt songs)

It was my first day in-country, Nam '68. Arrived the evening before. Bunked down. Slept. Awoke in a sweltering heat...soaked through. Went to shower. They had those barrel showers, y'know, jacked-up on stilts...worked okay, but water was cold. Well, I's dancing there, shivering, sudsing up, a guy comes in. God, grungiest dude I'd ever seen. Filthy. Dirt caked in layers, hair stuck out like a crazed maniac...all wild-eyed, mean and lean. I stood utterly dumbstruck at the sight, wondering how the hell he got so dirty? So I ask:

"Man? Where have you been?"

"Cambodia...ninety-day patrol," he grumps and walks over to the next stall, pulls the cord and stands calm as you please, comments on how warm the water is. Christ, I gotta wonder at that. And ask again:

"Cambodia? What the hell you doing in Cambodia?"

"Just seein' what's movin'" – all matter-of-fact as he looks me over and asks:

"So...what you been up to, buddy? "

"Nothing. I mean, I just got here. First day."

"What's your MOS?"

"Clerk..."

"Ah, sure..." he turns away, mumbling, "you're a *REMF*..."

"A what?" Green as hell, I'd never heard the term.

"Rear echelon mother fucker," he casts back a grin.

"Oh..." I give a lame shrug.

"Hey man, it's cool...best not hump the bush. But tell ya what..." he squints my way, considering, "I got friends in artillery. Could help ya transfer...you could see some action. Now you might go deaf. But at least you won't die!"

SNAKES!

They worked sometimes north of the river, sometimes south, or in its loop and bend, they'd be east or west. But no matter where in its meandering course, they faced the similar landscape of rock, rubble, and sunbaked soil. Like the surface of the moon, a construction site. The only sign of life lay in the river snaking beyond the tree line or in a new growth of weeds in a trash-heap dozed along the perimeter, that and the occasional flit of a bird or an insect in sweaty buzz and drone.

Each day right about sunrise the crew arrived, the quiet soon broken as diesel beasts cranked up belching black smoke in dogged slog to reshape the terrain, and men cursed and jerked ropes on portable generators, then saws and drills whirred alive. While down by the river, as if to mark the day's long toil, the loud clank of steel on steel as a crane hoisted a 7-ton hammer driving 40-foot pilings through the muck and silt into bedrock. Man and insect joined in timeless struggle to carve a niche, perhaps more of will than understanding, amid the rude face of things.

Rude, like the surface of the moon, yet to men burdened by tool belts, the hot sun and the day's labor, gravity grew greater, not less. No one skipped along like astronauts in grainy film, half buoyant, in apparent frolic...except maybe Jesse, quick, agile, tireless, the lone black skin on an all-white crew. He'd blow in each morning, not a minute to spare, hop from his little Dodge Dart in a cloud of dust, smiling like he'd just set the dayspring. Gold tooth and all.

"C'mon, fellas, Mister Cousins don' pay us to stand round, les git it on..." nearly late and swaggering like he was straw boss. Dave the foreman and other Missouri boys would just shake their heads at his strut and gall. All worked for Mr. Cousins, a hard driver, owner of Cousins Construction – he contracted mostly floodplain, waterway, and heavy foundation projects, keeping a dozen crews of 8 to 12 men busy, often 7 days a week. Though each foreman kept a core crew, other men were shuffled like cards, intermixed, broken up, depending on project, skill set, and need. And Jesse most of all, dealt around like a wild card.

"You're our token you-know-what," men would joke. And Jesse would answer back, "Yeah, the black fly in white milk!" Always with a laugh, though grudgingly. But they kept him on, whether in nod to equal rights or happenstance.

Then too there was "Shotgun" – Corel "Shotgun" Willims, a black laborer who'd been with Cousins Construction from the beginning. He'd been tagged "Shotgun" because he was often riding around with the boss man. Mr. Cousins liked his easy banter and soon entrusted him with all the petty errands that saved time and money and forestalled favoritism among foremen and crews. "Just send Shotgun," he'd tell them. By now most of the old hands had retired or died off. To the new-hires, when asked about his name, he'd frown and say, "I kilt a man. Shotgunned 'im for messin' wit my woman..." Then wink to those in the know and confide to the few he trusted, "Keeps these white boys more respectful of this black man," recalling the razing he'd endured as a *step 'n fetch it* early on.

He'd been with Cousins Construction now twenty years and set to retire within a month, his 60th birthday. In fact the week prior they'd held a little event for him in the construction trailer, served pizza and cold pop and stretched lunch beyond the usual half hour to a full 40 minutes. Mr. Cousins was there and handed him a nickel-plated pocket watch for his years of loyal service. Shotgun smiled politely and thanked him. Took it home and tossed it in a drawer – "Just a damn Walmart work watch," he later groused, having hoped for something finer with a gold band he could flash on his wrist. *"Shee-it..."* – twenty years a go-fer and almost gone.

But Jesse was a carpenter, brash and cocky, like a fast gun, hammer out and ready. Any man that offered a nail challenge, the others would gather round and say, "Watch this..." – Jesse would pounce and have a nail set before his opponent bent a knee, then nail 2 or 3 more, tap-tap-tap, spin around and holster his hammer, flashing that gold-tooth smile, "Always bet on black, baby!" About five foot five, spidery and spry as a lightweight, moved like he was 20, though now pushing 50, his sole concession to age was an elastic back-brace to firm his spine, which only made him that much fiercer. Clint, the foreman's right-hand man, who counted himself the best hammer man in the state of Missouri, packed a 28 oz. "California Framer", the handle honed with a tar-pitch grip, came the closest, but still only buried 7 to Jesse's 10. And he was ten years younger, a lean six-foot, blue eyes, bristled chin, even held that Eastwood squint, and would never concede, simply spit a wad of tobacco to the dust and say, "Get you next time." And though Clint couldn't best him with a hammer, he'd draw even on the jive, pretty quick-witted for a slow-drawling hill-boy.

"How is it you a black California transplant come by a great outlaw name?"

This stumped Jesse for a moment, always ready for a slight, stood sucking air then protested, "Hey! We got outlaws in California too! I's in a gang even. They called me PM!"

"Why's that? You never wake up till noon?"

"No...shit no! PM...that's Psycho Man. Anyone start some shit on a brother, I go berserk, grab a brick, bottle, anything...hurt 'em bad. Cuz if you didn't they'd hurt you. Maybe kill you. See this?" He lifted his dew-rag and pointed to a long scar above his brow. "See it?"

"Yeah, I see it. What happened? Get caught in Dave's zipper?"

"Aw, that's dirty, Clint. That ain't right. Tell 'im, Dave..." looking to Dave to help square things. But Dave and the others, all on break, remained leaned back in the dirt, grinning, enjoying the exchange.

"So you's in a gang, huh?" Clint followed up.

"Sure, had to...to stay alive."

"So what'd you do?"

"Oh, just stuff. Steal some liquor, radios, mostly fight. I's the wheel man."

"Wheel man...?" Clint smirked, not impressed. "Like Bloods 'n Crips, eh?"

"Naw, we's way before them. Called us the Blue Devils. Even had signs, like so..." He held up his trigger finger and pinky then pointed straight, "Means –"

"You take it up the ass?"

"No, listen...means attack like a bull! All in, baby. And this..." he thrust out his thumbs, like hitch-hiking both ways, "means heat's on, scram, scat, outa here!"

"That's right," Dave interrupted, "you called it. Breaks over, time to hit it," rousing the crew back to their task. But Clint jumped up with one last dig.

"Hey Jesse, check this out. A sign from down home…" he clawed his hands and screwed up his face and angled forth like a spastic scarecrow as all gawked in question. Then he stomped, snapped his finger and said, "It means you better stay back, my dog's got rabies!"

Even Jesse high-fived this as all hustled back to work.

Dave ran a tight ship, kept a crew of ten to twelve men hopping day in and day out. Burly, good-humored, relentless, set the pace and never slackened except at break and lunch, then skip those as well if there was concrete to pour and work right on through till sunset. But he'd make up for it next day, give the men an extra 15 minutes for a mushroom hunt or the like down a gully or under a bridge, and on Monday morning he often had a large sack of pan-fried fillets, bass, pike, or crappie, fresh from weekend fishing and shared out to all the fellows, even Jesse, who'd smack his lips and gush with pleasure, "Damn, them bad boys are good!" Dave would nod and say, "Here, grab some more," ever blunt, generous, all around good guy. Definitely Mr. Cousins' most productive foreman.

And in concession to which he was allowed his own errand boy, his step-father who he called Pap or Pappy, alternately affectionate or perturbed, snapping orders to go fetch this or that at the company yard or a hardware store, and Pap, a grizzly little man of sixty was right there in his shadow, ready to run and grasp whatever like a loyal squire, while grumping at the horrendous pace, "Dang, he's like this even days off, up at 4 a.m. to catch blame fish, I swear…!"

Dave was a knight for labor, always questing forth, leaning in, demanded a lot from his men by giving all himself. If there was material to carry, he'd shoulder a double load, or one-hand a metal form that other men double-teamed, then slog on through knee-deep mud, radio in his free hand, shouting orders to the high-loader for a couple tons of fill-sand or "Bring that water pump pronto then another bundle of 2 by 4s! Where? The southeast corner where we left off Friday! Christ, wake up, Slim! You still breathin' bar fumes?" Jovial, cursing, jutting his massive jaw, somewhat awkward, cumbersome in built, like he wore armor, leading them on to the next project like he was charging an enemy pill-box.

Clint, as mentioned, his right hand man, and several others formed his core crew and all hailed from a small rural town sixty miles south of the city. Drove in early each day, home again late each night. Rode together like they'd played ball together back in high school. Even had their own preacher, Clay McKay, a lay minister in a one-room bare-floor church. Wood heat in the winter, open windows in the summer. Real downhome, no quaint hymns with piano and choir, they'd shout their praise in raw song, pray and testify. He preached a fundamentalist gospel, but never dour, buoyant, happy, always up, filled with joy of loving Jesus. Good looking, active, wore overalls, smiled like a movie star, constantly smiling and chewing gum. Could quote any passage in the Bible pertinent to his faith and belief. And believed everything he heard on talk radio: "They couldn't say it if it wasn't true," he'd assert, "could they?" Like the good word, couldn't believe any voice of authority could bear any message but the truth.

Theirs a tight-knit group bound by life and faith to which Jesse among others could never belong. And he knew it – "Like a black fly in white milk!" But he'd been with them nearly two years, tolerated, more or less accepted for his spunk and effort, like a mascot or favored dog. And his favorite trick was nailing.

"What we got goin'?" he'd shout, "I can git with it!"

And they'd sic him on a task, his arms and legs spread, angling, scurrying quick as a crab, nailing here, there, and often in the wrong direction. Or wrecking out, he might jerk a plank right out from under you.

"Damn! Watch it, Jess!" – cracked like a whip past his ear.

"I know, I know...got that bad boy!" he'd answer up, hustling on, anxious to make amends with the next effort. "Talk to me! Talk to me!" he'd yell above the growl of the generator, awaiting measurements for boards to brace up a wall, often cutting the 2 x 4s long or short, but no matter, he'd re-measure and cut in a snap, keep three or four flying through the air like a juggler in a circus or tossing ears of corn in an old-time husking contest. They'd watch him cut and weave up on the embankment, his constant sass and spin, then spare a laugh, "Yep, Jess is one hard worker. Give his black ass that..."

Dave, mostly patient of him, could also grow exasperated trying to make his requests understood. Such moments were often surprising and unpredictable. For instance, the time he called for Jesse to measure out and set a line 20 foot parallel from an existing wall. Jesse looked up, *"Pair a'what...?"* absolutely flummoxed, had no idea what that meant. Dave groaned to the man standing by, "To think he gets paid the same as you 'n me."

"Well, you do get foreman's wage," the other noted. "And he probably dozed off through geometry like most us boys...or never had it."

"Yeah, maybe so..." Dave wearily conceded then called to Jesse, "Come out twenty feet either end of that wall, drive two stakes 'n set a line!"

"Right, got it, Dave! Got that bad boy now..." And in a snap, 1-2-3, he had the stakes driven and the line stretched twenty feet parallel, more or less...always wise to check it.

Never fired or laid-off, Jesse remained highly unwelcome, not quite outcast, but kept on edge, in question. And there were other outliers on the crew, not due to race, but rather to age, origin, or predilection. Loren for one, a lumbering loner from northeast Kansas, a red-leg Jayhawker, a whole other breed, somewhat relic and suspect to Missouri boys. While there was no enmity between them, he was more stolid than jocular, and solitary as a bear. Yet a competent, reliable hand, so Dave usually assigned him his own project, off and away. He never said much and never swung a fast hammer, just a steady tap-a-tap, then pause and cock his head like a bear picking through a plum thicket.

They'd call out and needle him now and then to see if they could get a rise.

"Hey Loren! Keepin' busy over there?"

He'd slow turn like a tree shifting in the wind and answer, "Heck yeah..." his voice quiet and raspy like passing through dry leaves. At a company picnic earlier that summer he'd brought his wife along, an amazingly attractive woman.

"Hey Loren!" they called out the following Monday, "You

got a pretty good lookin' wife!" He cast a slow broad grin, "Yeah, not too shabby..." which kept them laughing the rest of the day. *Not too shabby*...guess she liked the quiet type.

Then there was Buckeye. He drove 130 miles from central Missouri every day – up at 3:15, back home by 8:30 or so, barely time to eat, shower, and sleep, then back to work. He'd topped over 400,000 miles on his little red Ford Ranger and vowed to retire once it hit a half million, to the moon and back. In his early sixties, oldest man on the crew, older than Pap, so Dave usually put him to lighter tasks, had him follow up and make certain everything was copacetic, like checking Jesse's work or nailing form clamps and braces or building bulkheads – or when readying a big foundation pour, he might holler, "Buckeye? Got them pencil rods snug?" And Buckeye would give a screw-clamp another tap and drolly answer, "Tighter'n a skeeter's ass stretched over a rain barrel, Boss..." Seldom spoke but when he did he'd cap it with an old saw, colorful, to the point. Like speaking of the current president, George Jr., "Ol' Dubya's got us in two new wars. That boy's about as sharp as a dog's dick!" He'd fought in Vietnam and had no faith in the scenario unfolding in the Middle East. And when younger men would rib him and call him "Biscuit" for soaking up all the gravy, the easy tasks, he'd answer, "That might be, but I's sure as hell no biscuit over in Nam..."

Of course Buckeye wasn't his given name, born John Reed Clemmons. But from the time he could remember his dad called him Buckeye. "Told me I's lucky to grow up on a farm, always somethin' to do. Me, hell, I thought he worked me like a slave. But guess he's right, cuz I love that old place and why I drive in each day rather'n move close by. S'pose I's always lucky, even when I's unlucky..." he chuckled quietly – this during a rare lull, crouched down out of the rain, confiding to a fellow worker...

"Got my draft notice first summer outa high school. Passed the physical, 1-A. Kinda excited, kinda scared, approaching the Monday of induction. That weekend, helping the old man put roof sheeting on the barn, I slipped off 'n fell a good ways, busted my ankle. They canceled my induction and I thought I's home free. Started focusing on cars 'n girls, then six months later, all healed up, got my second notice. Somehow they knew, didn't feel so lucky. Off to boot camp, infantry school, then straight to Nam. Some of them boys really got into the fight, couldn't get enough. Me, I just wanted to git through. Lucky even there, cuz the odds weren't good, pretty rough at times. Each day dealt another black card…the enemy, friendly fire, the jungle. That monsoon heat so heavy you could hardly breathe…hotter'n two rats fuckin' in a wool sock. The stink 'n decay, the rot in your crotch 'n feet. Still got some of that, but hey, made it through. A hundred times thought I's a goner, clutchin' the ground so hard your fatigue buttons felt big as apples.

"In my ninth month, not quite a short-timer, but seemed I'd used up all nine lives…VC pinned us down, the lieutenant, our fourth by then, not a bad kid, but green, clueless, about as wide between the eyes as a day-old inchworm…anyhow, he called in an airstrike. And that first strafe cut tree limbs right above our heads like a giant weed whip. I feared the next pass they'd drop napalm 'n we'd all be char-babies. So I says, 'LT, don't ya think it's time to put up some smoke, let the flyboys know we're here…?' Damn near too late, but he did so, and those bombs dropped just outa range…still close enough to feel the whoosh 'n heat and smell VC flesh burning.

"And it wasn't but two weeks later, during a sweep, we got lost, separated, shit happened. Same lieutenant, still alive, led us around in circles for two days, ripe for ambush. He'd check his map, try his compass 'n curse, totally bewildered, lost…but gettin' better at it, the cursing. A real clusterfuck. Earlier on, I'd been through that area and sensed I knew a way out…y'know, the homing instinct, like an old hound lost in the night hunt that straggles in a day later. So I told him I had a hunch, thought I could lead us out. He said, 'Go for it, Buckeye…' There was some luck for ya, took us a good twenty hours, but we snaked through the enemy back to our own lines. Hell, they gave me a little bronze medal for that…for just finding a way home. And finally made it home. Damn lucky, 'n lucky every day since. Like Mom always told me when I'd grouse at Dad sending me out to chore, 'Son, what can't be enjoyed, must be endured…'"

As Buckeye was prone to remind one or another of the crew, for they were apt to grouse, habitually groaning before work in stretch and yawn, bitching at the hot weather, lack of a rain-day, at Dave's frantic pace, and groaning at day's end of the next day to come. But they saved most of this for break-time and lunch, finding common ground, griping about wives, ex-wives, and girlfriends, most conceding, "That's the fuckin' ya git for the fuckin' ya got!" Then on to sports, naming all the overpaid, underperforming athletes, never happy with the home team unless they brought home the championship, finally tossing out their two cents on politics and the economy, while never missing a chance to curse lawyers and the damn bankers. And Jesse would jump right in the mix, welcome or not.

"Tell ya what, what chaps my black ass. Couple years back, in slack time, wanted to start me a bizness. Went to a banker, hell, even had my own name 'n slogan...Fast Hammer Construction, *'Honest 'n on it!'* Yeah, needed me an ol' truck, a bobcat 'n trailer. Figured 'bout fifteen grand. They turned my ass inside 'n out runnin' through all my shit. Still no loan. I said, man, I got co'ladral, my own home. They said, no deal, bad location. Shit, me'n my people been here, fought 'n died here, long as anyone. Most time can't get a loan for a damn thing. Why's that? Huh? Makes me so angry...like to cap that banker's ass!"

This brought a rare nod of sympathy, all agreed they'd like to shoot a banker. Encouraged, Jesse extended his rant:

"Now these Mexicans floodin' in. Ain't even Americans 'n they git loans left, right 'n center...stealin' jobs all over. Steal yours too, you don' watch it!"

Again he scored a general nod, all union men, and though Missouri was not yet a "Right to Work" state, pressures were building, chipping away at union wage and status. One man, however, sat looking doubtful, Mark Haven, a business school dropout who favored carpentry and coon hunting over numbers – lost the hearing in his left ear hunting one night when a sharp twig stabbed his eardrum. He cocked his good ear at Jesse's conclusion, shook his head and declared:

"There's a reason for that. Mexicans are hard workers and

pay taxes. Not like so many that expect a free ride."

"What you talkin'? I work, man, I work..."

"Sure you do, Jess," he grinned matter-of-factly, "but there's plenty others that don't...and won't."

"Yeah, there's reasons for that too! You talk it, I walk it –"

"Just look at the Indians, for instance," Mark deflected, trying to avoid another black-white shout-out. "What do they contribute? Been over hundred years and we're still paying their keep on the reservations!"

Clint, who'd been sitting back gnawing an apple, enjoying the exchange, suddenly sat up, taking exception to this ex-college boy in his designer jeans and know-it-all manner that marked him nearly as suspect as Jesse's black skin.

"What d'you mean? Indians gave a lot to this country. Every damn inch!"

"Aw, come on," Mark scoffed. "Name one Indian that ever contributed one actual thing."

"*Sacagawea*...by God! Without her Lewis 'n Clark would've left their bones on the upper Missouri. And the Russians would've grabbed the whole Northwest."

"Aw, don't feed me that...just a fairy tale on some old Indian squaw."

Clint griped the apple he'd been nibbling and arched it ready to throw – "You take that back! Take it back or I'll hit you with this apple! I mean it! Sacagawea is my blood kin...an honored ancestor –"

"You Indian?"

"Part so 'n damn proud," and whether conjured or imagined, he had dark red skin and black hair and spoke ready vengeance. "Now you take that back or I'll hit you! Sacagawea was a great woman..."

Mark laughed nervously, glanced side to side, and seeing no relief, answered, "Alright, alright, Jesus...I take it back. Sorry..."

Clint gave a confirming nod and said nothing more, leaned back and continued eating his apple. No one spoke for a time as the wind caught a swirl of dust like a spirit roused and soon settled as if appeased. Moments ticked by, and Clint, perhaps to amend for the threat and knowing Mark bred and trained hounds, asked about his dogs.

"Hear you run a fair line of Blue-ticks. Got any comin' on?"

"Oh, a couple. A little green yet. But they should be ready by fall."

"What d'they go for?"

"Oh, eight hundred to a thousand, depending."

Clint chewed his apple and considered, "Not a bad price for a good hound." Others of the crew also gave a nod, many ran coonhounds, an old tradition.

"Hey Loren?" Clint asked, again ready to bait and banter, "You need a good hound?"

"No-o-o, don't s'pose. Got a German short hair...suits me."

"You hunt birds?"

"Yeah...hunt birds," Loren confirmed with a wary smile.

Clint tossed his apple to the weeds and laughed, "That figures..." He let it rest a second then jerked his head, "What about you, Clay? You could use a good hound."

"Naw," he grinned, chewing his gum, "think I'll stick with the ones I got."

"Those ol' mutts that Moss breeds...still got 'em?"

"They tree a coon don't they?"

"That they do..."

Time ticked on, the wind blew, most of the crew done eating by now, a few nodding off, Jessie sat itching to speak.

"I got dogs," he said, getting back into play.

"You hunt coons?"

"Clint, don' you git started. Naw, pit bulls...call 'em Bad 'n Mad. Male 'n bitch, got 'em for protection."

"Pit bulls, eh? Hear they're a mean, nasty breed."

"Naw, they good dogs. Just a bad rap is all."

"Sure, there hasn't been a pit bull mauled a child...in what? Last four or five minutes?"

"Hey, you don' know my neighborhood!"

"No, but I can imagine."

"That's right, I need 'em to protect my property, gone t'work all day."

"S'pect you do."

"These bad boys, I mean real bad boys, down the street

from me, last winter they tossed a Shepard over the fence. Big Shepard, a black 'n tan. Didn't last a minute 'fore my dogs tore 'im apart. Blood, fur 'n pieces all over the snow..."

Clint had no quip for this, the words and scene depicted left a sour taste in everyone's stomach. Except for Luther, a dour man on all occasions, who looked on with a sullen smile. He ran the backhoe, precise, accurate, dug all the trenches. And like many exacting souls, he never forgave another's faults. A stanch son of the Confederacy, devout admirer of Bedford Forrest, even resembled the famous cavalryman, reddish-brown hair, gray eyes, though his features were more stern, coarse. And unlike Forrest, he was literate, yet of all he read, including the Bible, what he quoted was hate. And he hated Jesse. Didn't say it, but it oozed through his gray eyes. Like the day he found Jesse's dew-rag left hanging on a grade stake, drying in the sun, he picked it up and examined it like some foul animal hide then dropped it in the dirt.

"Left to me," Luther sliced his words, eyes fixed on Jesse, "I'd round up ever' pit bull 'n shoot 'em."

"Don' shit me, Luth. I know who you'd shoot, you 'n your Klu-Klux boys!"

"Whoa now," Clint said, trying to temper things, "those days are long gone."

"Yeah, sure, long as it's daylight. But come sundown I step outside this city them boys in white sheets be waitin'."

"Ah, Jess, that all died out years ago. They put the sheets back on their beds and joined the party of Lincoln. Ain't that right, Pap?"

Called out and named, Pap sat like a man on the hot seat, these questions of what was and now is were tricky.

"Well," he grimaced in glance to Dave as if asking whether he ought or ought not speak, "things have changed considerable since I's a boy. The Ku-Klux would march on Veteran's Day, Fourth of July...and the coloreds...er, the blacks...why, they couldn't even walk on the sidewalk. Had to keep to the gutters. Same in most towns around, ain't that so, Buckeye...?" – tossing him the hot potato.

But Buckeye had had his war and wasn't about to be drawn into a war of words, he simply gave a quiet nod. Remembered those days and those ways, and even as a boy he didn't think it right how black folks were treated, many of them were neighbors, good people. But ways change slow, and what can't be changed must be endured.

And endurance was what they needed for the day's big concrete pour, trucks due to start rolling in by one. With but a few minutes left for lunch, Clint didn't want to end on a dull note and decided to push Jesse's button once more, caught his eye and grinned:

"Hear Joey was asking about you the other day."

"Joey who?"

"Joey Cousins, the boss's son."

"So what'd he want?"

"Wanted to know if you was a midget."

"What's that shit?"

"I said, 'Naw, he's no midget. He's at least an inch taller'n a midget.'"

"Oh, that's wrong, that's wrong –"

"Yeah, but about the right height for a queer."

"Hey buddy!" Jesse jumped up and grabbed his groin. "I might be some shy of six-foot, but I got a nine-inch black snake here I'll lay up against any of yours. C'mon, whop it out if you think I'm lyin'. Yeah..." he nodded, strutting about, too pumped to sit. "Yeah, always bet on black, baby. Like that horse in Santa Anna, Night Dancer his name, 'n odds thirty to one. Only black horse in the race. I bet five hunnerd 'n won fifteen grand! You believe me, I don' care. Always bet on black, once you had black you won' go back. Bought my right girl a diamond big as a dime. Put that on her black hand, it shine, shine..."

"Sure, Jess, sure," Clint and the others ever doubtful the horserace tale, "shine like a diamond in a billy goat's ass."

"Hey, watch it now! I got that diamond 'n I got the duds...shiny silver suit. Man, I dress when I go out. Look like a million bucks, me 'n my lady..."

Already striding off, fully energized as Dave calls them all to their feet, back to work, and Jesse out in the lead, swinging his arms, he'd told them and showed them, yeah. But Dave's sonorous voice had ended the bull session and dominated thereon, firm and cajoling, directing trucks, shifting men where needed, hustling them on, no afternoon break that day, had over 200 yards of concrete poured by 4 o'clock, then every back bent, cutting keyways, setting anchor bolts, and finishing the surface on through till sunset. Another late night home.

The next morning, Friday, promised a fairly easy day, mostly wreck out, removing and stacking wailers, braces, and clamps. They'd leave the forms in place for the concrete to cure through the weekend then finish the day prepping footings for a new wall. Dave set a casual pace and come break time the motors shut down, even the pile-driver in lull, down 40 feet, awaiting the weld of another 20-foot section in hope to reach bedrock. All quiet, the dust soon settled and the air cleared of gas and diesel fumes, while a warm south breeze redolent of ripe plums wafted up from the river. They could see crows and other birds in the thickets squabbling over the fruit, and some of the boys wanted to go down and join in the harvest, so Dave gave his okay and even tagged along.

A short while later they returned, caps and hardhats brimful, enjoying their booty, savoring the plums. Dave had both hands cupped, his broad jaw ginning ear to ear, "Look what I caught!" he announced, showing the few stragglers who'd stayed behind a big green bullfrog, throat puffing, eyes bulged in wonder of its new environ and fate. At his approach Jesse jumped up, his eyes bugged out even more than the frogs.

"Ge-get that thing away from me!" he stammered, backing off as Dave moved closer, hands held forth to offer a better look.

"It's just frog, see? Can't hurt you…"

"NO! Stay away!" Jesse flailed his arms and shot back another good twenty feet, barking like a frightened dog, "BACK…BACK! I don' like repitles! Frogs, snakes, lizards…I don' like 'em!"

The boys all laughing as Dave grinned in disbelief, "It's only a frog…" and Clint added, "Christ, Jesse, we eat them, they don't eat us. Ever have frogs legs? Like fried chicken…"

"I don' care…keep 'im back! Reptiles is slimy!" – hands stretched forth in plea and warning, voice quavering, eyes full of animal fear – "Don' like 'em, don' want 'em near…"

Dave desisted with a quizzical shrug, carried the frog over

and freed it in the weeds, while others in the crew continued to laugh and point at Jesse. Except for Buckeye who looked on and shook his head, knew the poor fool had let them smell his fear, all now roused like hounds scenting blood.

Sure enough, at lunch, after gulping down sandwiches and iced tea, Clint and Clay hurried off toward the river ostensibly to pick more plums, though they were really after another frog or lizard, something slithery to drop down Jesse's shirt and watch him dance. But they did one better, caught a six-foot long black snake, non-poisonous yet quite aggressive, though they mercifully stomped its head, forgoing the notion of tossing the writhing creature on their unsuspecting victim. Snake in hand, they hurried back, game to spring their great surprise.

High noon, the sun well up, the hot wind as well, stirring dust devils over the stretch to the river. No one suspected the devilment approaching, only two dark forms, indistinct, gradually coming into focus through the wavering heat. Buckeye noticed them first, guessed something was up as Clay elbowed Clint, both grinning wild, gripping something behind their back, then he spied the dangling tail and thought to warn Jesse, but he was in half-nod, head slumped forward, elbows to propped knees, and in the next instant a breath of excitement rippled through the crew as Clint rushed up and dropped the snake around Jesse's extended neck with a mocking laugh, "There! A black tie for your silver suit!" while Clay echoed, "Always bet on black, baby!"

Results as expected, in a blink Jesse flexed up in a shriek of terror, choking and gasping like he was caught in a black noose, arms and legs akimbo, attempting to shuck the fearsome thing, the snake whipping from neck to arm and leg before he finally kicked it to the ground and skipped away, struggling to catch his breath, heart beating to summon all his blood to fight or flee, glancing to each and all like they'd just lynched him then cut him free to taunt and laugh, which they did. And he glared back at them, at Dave foremost, his eyes fraught with fear and anger and cried, "Why'd you let them do that? WHY?!"

His protest did little but whet their amusement and they simply shed his accusation, reluctant to leave their hoot and holler as he turned and limped to his car, didn't dare stomp or kick, having strained his back in frantic effort to escape the snake. But their laughter slowly ceased as Buckeye walked over, picked up the dead snake and flung it to the weeds.

"Y'know," he said in a wryly casual tone, "may have gone a bit too far this time…" Coming from an old hand and war veteran, they took their chastisement in silence, though still smiling as they settled back, pleased at the prank and their pranksters.

Buckeye moseyed over to check on the victim. He paused by the driver's door, window rolled down, peered in at Jesse staring out through the windshield, his chest heaving like a frightened bird. Buckeye had dealt with panic, his own and others' a thousand times in Nam.

"Best ease up there," he advised, "take some deep breaths, slow 'n easy…"

Jesse didn't answer, but his breathing soon slowed and deepened. Finally, still staring out and away, he said, "It could stop a man's heart, don' they know that?"

"Doubt they were thinkin', Jess. Like boys with a hard-on."

"Yeah 'n I the one gits fucked."

"Well…" Buckeye slowly drawled in glance to the crew stirring now to return to work, "you gonna be alright?"

Jesse nodded, got out and went back to work, faced them, but didn't turn his back, kept a close eye on Clint and Clay, Dave and Pap, on Mark and Luther. He mostly bucketed clamps and, despite his back, toted 2 x 4s over to the sawhorses for Buckeye and Loren to clean and oil. No joking, stayed mum, collected his check at quitting time and didn't say a word as Dave urged, "Hey now, don't go away mad…" His little Dodge Dart was the first one out the gate, spewing dust and gravel a good eighth of a mile right back at them.

But back to work again Monday morning, bright and early like a slap in the face, swerved to a halt in a cloud of dust, as usual not a minute to spare, jumped out, donned his back brace and tool belt and marched right in, jaunty, full of sass and swagger, greeting one and all like there'd never been a frog-scare or snake-dance, nothing. He'd been in the union twenty years working with nearly all white crews, suffering similar slights and events, generally gave as good as he got and wasn't about to be run off. Mr. Cousins kept him working almost year round. In another five years he could take his twenty-five and out. A good pension, his own life, do what he wanted.

And at break Dave opened a big thermo bag full of fried catfish – "Here, get ya some," he offered all around, "you too, Jesse, here, dig in...still warm, the wife fried 'em up this morning."

Jesse wasn't shy, fisted one piece then another, and didn't hide his relish.

"Damn, Dave, these damn fish are good!"

"Fresh from the river, caught 'em Saturday."

"Man, like to catch me summa these bad boys."

"Hell, ya oughta come down 'n go fishing with us," Dave suggested, in part to make amends, in part curious to see if he'd bite. "Got us a sweet spot there on the Mar d'Sane" – actually the *Marais de Cygnes*, the name given its own twist by the locals, none of them too keen on French – "Yeah, a nice little river."

"Really, you mean that?"

"Sure, come down next Saturday, only about an hour south. Another weekend off, old gas line needs moved, holding things up."

"Shoot yes, Jess," Clint chimed in, "get you out of the city. Take you fishin' on the river like ol' Huck Finn?"

"Naw, I dunno," he allowed, doubt creeping in, "might feed me to the fishes, you 'n them KKK boys."

"What?" Clint sounded offended. "After all these months, you're practically one of the gang."

"Yeah, the one you gang up on."

"Aw Jess...there'll be none of that. Besides, there ain't but a few of the Ku-Klux left. All old-timers in old folks' homes...all pinned up in diapers."

"I like that...pinned up in diapers!" Jesse laughed. "A pretty good one..." Then he frowned, again skeptical. "That's a river though. They'd be reptiles."

"You bet, a lil' girl snake for your black snake...maybe copulate."

"Fuck that, no way I'm goin'!"

"Jess, you folks come from the jungle plumb full of reptiles 'n snakes."

"Hey, I ain't from no jungle, I'm PM from LA 'n you try any snake shit on me again I'll go Psycho Man on you! All out...I mean it!" – laughing, though making it clear he wanted no repeats.

"Okay, had our fun...one 'n done," Clint vouched, slapping a high-five.

"Well, I dunno..." still wary.

So it went all week, joshing back and forth at every break and lunch, them trying to bait him into fishing, and Jesse tempted, playing coy.

"Heck, I ain't even got a pole," he'd say.

"No problem, Jess. We got poles aplenty. Bait, tackle..."

"But they's reptiles. Still them reptiles..." he'd shake his head.

"Sure, there's reptiles. But we've got a nice grassy bank to fish from. Brush all cleared. They won't bother you if you don't bother them."

"What 'bout turtles? Any turtles?"

"Yeah, there's a turtle now 'n then."

"Now I like a turtle."

"Well, there ya go. C'mon down 'n catch some fish..."

More tempted each day, he'd nod and grin, still non-committal. Finally, afternoon break, Friday, Dave said, "Time to fish or cut bait. You gonna sit at home or come down?"

Jesse drew a deep breath, time to decide.

"How do I git there even?"

"Easy as pie," Dave answered. "Just jag over to 71 and head south. You know Highway 71, right?"

"Yeah, cross it comin' 'n goin' ever' day."

"Okay then, that'll take you most all the way. From Lee's Summit 50 miles south to Butler, then another 6 or 7 miles you'll hit the Mare d'Sane. Now about a mile before that you'll see a road sign for Athol. We call it *Asshole*, just a spot in the road that once was 'n ain't no more. Little ghost town."

"Ghosts?" Jesse's eyes widened and Clint laughed.

"Tain't no ghost, only haints down our way."

"Haints?"

"Yeah, sort of a Southern-type down-home ghost. Thick as flies –"

"Ah, button up, don't listen to 'im," Dave grumped, could see Jesse getting spooked and Clint not helping. "Ain't no haints, ghosts, nothin' of the kind. Just good fishin'. We're lookin' catch catfish, right? So, directly you cross the river, you exit on a little country road. Try to time it about 2 o'clock. Pap'll be waitin' in his blue pickup, he'll guide you in. Got it? Easy as pie…"

Jesse licked his lips, blinked his eyes, thrilled as a child poised at the brink of something wild and wonderful.

"That's it! I'm in! Two o'clock, I'll be there!"

They were all thrilled, frankly, a big event, taking Jesse fishing. Though Buckeye begged off, heading home for some serious R & R, "Rest 'n more rest," he said. And Loren, when asked, answered, "Naw, don't guess so…" To which Clint laughed, "Gonna bird dog that pretty wife, I bet!" Loren just grinned, "Yeah, might do that…" But most others were in and hustled around to make final plans.

Walking off something caught Jesse's ear and made him pause, a certain tone, somewhat conspiratorial, as someone mentioned "Lanterns."

"What's that?" he spun in question. "What's that you say?"

"Lanterns, Jess. Relax," Dave explained. "We use 'em for night fishing. Hang 'em over the water, they come right up to the light…then you spear 'em, hook 'em, or grab 'em by the gills. Lots of fun. You're welcome to stay 'n night fish. Up to you?"

"Might. Just might do that," he shared a grin with Loren then jogged on to his car. Damn, Friday and not a bit tired…going fishing with the boys. Could hardly believe it.

Up by sunrise Saturday morning out of habit, brewed coffee, fed the dogs, then cleaned the house and took his clothes to the laundry and shopped a week of groceries. Even called his right lady to tell her he had business with the boys and couldn't take her out that evening. She didn't mind, a hair stylist, had to work till 3 and said, "See you tomorrow, but better rest up, boy!" He laughed hearing that, after a long string of wrong ladies, had the right lady now. Each had their own job, own house, own money. Independent, no hassle.

Yeah, had his chores put away by noon, then stuffed his little Styrofoam cooler with summer sausage, longhorn cheese, a gallon jug of Mountain Dew, all packed in ice – a box of

Nabisco snack crackers and a can of bug spray kept high and dry. Nearly set, he'd gassed up his car night before, didn't want to get way-laid in some Red-neck town hunting a gas station, no sir. He locked the doors, set Bad 'n Mad free in the back yard.

Property secure, he headed south at a quarter till one. In a short while he passed through Lee's Summit and in the next ten miles left the suburbs and city behind. Hadn't been in the country, not really, hardly ever. Years before he'd ridden a train from LA to Kansas City and aside from an occasional worksite had kept to the inner-city all his life. He loved how the country opened up to farms, pastures, and rolling hills. He felt like Sammy Davis Jr. in an old cowboy movie. Loved those Westerns as a boy. And Sammy too, about the same size, and both quick – fast hammer 'n fast gun. Yeah, they'd have made a pair...

Riding south through new territory with such thoughts, he forgot all about his lone trip to Colorado. Longed to see the mountains and working with a good guy that summer, a white fellow who owned a hunting cabin, Jesse mentioned as much and the fellow said, "Here, take the keys and drive out for a week," but cautioned him not to go into town, "It's full of cowboys and you wouldn't like it..." So Jesse said alright, grabbed his right lady and took off in the heat of August, headed for the mountains. And it was great up in that cabin, crisp fresh air, clear spring water, and standing there gazing up at the snow-capped peaks. Good for about three days then cabin fever set in and he decided to take his right lady into town and dine in a fine restaurant. He was a citizen and taxpayer, no one could stop him. They found them a nice place named "The Longbranch" just like in "Gunsmoke." Went in and sat down in a fancy leather booth, a set of longhorns above the bar, a big buffalo head mounted on the wall, elk head too, and in between stretched a bear hide. At the far end they spied a fireplace, flames aflutter. A real nice place. Only a few patrons, yet the waitresses never glanced their way. He slapped the table and said, "Can we get some service, me 'n my lady are hungry." No one seemed to hear. The waitresses disappeared in back. He slapped the table once more and said, "I got money...cash money!" The bartender continued wiping the bar, never looked up. Then Jesse noticed outside, through the window, pickup after pickup began to arrive, big cowboys lumbering out of each, stepping to the sidewalk, all staring in like Zombies wakened from the dead. He grabbed his right lady's hand and said, "Let's git!" –walked out with a friendly nod to the Zombies, flashing a grin, then straight to the car and out of there, careful to hold the speed limit while a line of pickups trailed them like following up a funeral – *his!* Beyond the city limits he sped away, stopped at the cabin long enough to collect their suitcases and lock up, then raced down out of the mountains and never looked back...

But he had no thought of this at present, only of himself and Sammy Davis, fast hammer 'n fast gun, with such fantasies at play he covered the distance in a snap. Never even glimpsed the road sign to Athol, but saw the river, and there just beyond sat Pap's blue pickup, and he had to break hard, nearly missing the exit, but made it and followed on. A gravel road, dust billowing up, kept his windows rolled tight and the whitish dust still drifted in, ghostlike, settling on the dash. In a couple miles they turned off the road, crossed a bumpy field and came to a halt just shy of the timber alongside two other pickups belonging to Clint and Dave.

Jesse hopped out and slung his cooler by the rope lid, greeted Pap and they followed a path winding about a hundred yards through the timber. Easy going, nice and quiet like a park and opened up to a grassy clearing, as Dave had said, right above the river. Dave and Clint were already setting poles and had a little fire going in a round of rocks. They waved him over, thrust a beer in his hand, and soon had him rigged with his own pole, a long river pole with a 30 lb. test line. They showed him how to work the reel, to lock and free the brake, then baited the hook with chicken liver, attached a cork bobber, and helped cast his line to a slow swirl of current about 40 feet out.

"Got us the best little fishin' hole on the whole Mare d'Sane," Dave winked. And it surely was – grass sloped gently down to a steep cut-bank where the river slowed in a horseshoe widening out nearly 50 yards. One might be tempted to dive on in, though hardly wise, a deep channel with treacherous under current. Besides, they'd come to fish and they soon set their poles, braced in the mud, a rock cleft, or crook of a limb. But Jesse kept his gripped in hand, eyeing the bobber, at the least nibble he'd jerk and reel in. Nothing. Bait again and cast out.

"Gotta be patient," Dave advised. "Let 'em take it way under before you try 'n set the hook."

Jesse'd nod, barely breathing, finger checking the tension on the line, eyes fixed on the bobber. No one yet catching anything of note, only a couple one pounders they released, and Pap hadn't even had a bite, though not a bit worried, leaned back, gazing from the water to a drifting cloud, best part of fishing for him was to simply relax and not hurry. Clint also sat relaxed, toothpick in his mouth, while Dave chewed a cigar, never lit it, and never chewed one at work, only when fishing. So after about an hour Jesse eased back and stabbed his pole handle in the mud like Pap. Cast his eyes about, taking in the scene, all the strange novelties, birds, butterflies, plants. Noticed some vines growing up and down the bank, on into the trees, with tiny clusters of purple fruit dangling among the leaves.

"Hey, is them grapes?" he asked vaguely.

"Is the sky blue?" Clint laughed. "You bet, wild grapes."

"They poison?"

"No, you can eat 'em," Clint assured then reached over and picked a cluster, popped a couple in his mouth and tossed the rest to Jesse. "Go ahead 'n try 'em. They're pretty tasty. Not much fruit, mostly skin 'n seed. Folks make jam out of 'em, even wine."

"Really?"

"That's a fact..."

Jesse tasted one, then nibbled a couple more, spat out the seeds and said, "Hey, they good!"

"Like I said. And Indians mixed 'em in with dried buffalo meat to make pemmican. Them 'n dried plums, all pounded together into a mush, added some bear grease, buffalo fat, then stuffed it in leather bag...a parfleche. It'd keep for months. A main staple. Kinda like your summer sausage there."

"No shit?"

"No shit..."

Jesse rolled another grape in his tongue, thinking about

those Indians and their pemmican and what it tasted like.

Just then Dave yelled, "Jess! Your pole!"

He glanced around and saw his pole bent double to the water, line zipped tight, the reel clicking wild, and the handle about to escape its hold in the earth. He dove down and grabbed it up and all gathered round, coaching him on how to land that fish.

"Ya got a big one, Jesse!"

"Okay, give 'im some line…now reel in!"

"Easy now, don't rush it, let 'im tire…"

The fish, long as a man's arm, would surface, its wide flat head and back nearly the color of the muddy water, then roll showing its creamy underbelly in attempt to dive again. "More line!" they'd shout then "Reel 'er in!" all the while Jesse nodding, "Got it! Got it!" laughing like a kid on a carnival ride, up, down, out 'n around, trying to snag that fish. Till finally it tired and he hoisted it up over the cut-bank, landed in the grass, gaping air.

"What we do with that bad boy?"

"Skin 'im 'n eat 'im. What else?"

"How we do that?"

"No sweat…" Clint reached down and caught it by the gills, took out his pliers and plucked out the hook. "Follow me…" he said and walked over and plopped it on a broad tree stump. "Alright, Jess, see that hammer? You're the hammer man. Take 'n whack him about three good ones, else he'll flop around and stab us with one of them thorns."

Jesse picked up the old blood-rusted hammer stowed there for just that purpose, then whack! whack! whack! did as he was told. The catfish stiffened briefly, quivered, then went limp.

"Good…now take that old spike there," Clint pointed to a large rusty nail stuck in the loose bark, "and drive it through the head. Not too deep, just enough to anchor whilst I skin it out…"

Jesse tapped the spike through the head into the stump then stood back as Clint snapped open his Buck-knife, made several deft slices then stabbed it in the stump and again used his pliers to peel skin, fins, guts and all back to the tail and with another quick slice tossed the bloody bulk aside. Last, he placed the blade back of the head and pressed down through the spine, then held up a large slab of shimmery white meat.

"There, ready to eat!"

"How we gonna cook it?"

"Hobo-style…in that bed of coals," Dave said as he ripped out a length of aluminum foil. "Wrap it in this and let it fry in its own juices. Be tender, sweet 'n ready to eat in about an hour."

"Hot damn!" Jesse slapped his hands together, "Hot damn!"

He looked down on that catfish head still spiked to the stump, at least 8 inches wide, thorns jutting out a good 4 to 5 inches either side. A monster fish, proud of his catch, wished he could show the world.

"Where's them other guys? Mark, Clay…thought they's gonna come?"

"Well, Mark thought he'd come," Dave said, "had to tend his hounds," then added with a sly wink, "but he may have gone line-dancing instead. And y'know Clay, likely stalled out writing his Sunday sermon…always searching God's word and such. Then Slim 'n Jordan, hard tellin' about those two…may have stopped by a tavern for happy hour…then roar right on till midnight."

"What 'bout Luther?" a keener concern he'd rather not see.

"Aw, forget Luth," Clint frowned. "Nearly always a no-show. Bet he's out covering ground with his metal detector, huntin' shell casings, bayonets 'n other relics from the Northern Invasion. War-crazed, won't leave off until he finds the bullet that killed Lincoln."

"You got that right," Dave affirmed. "War-crazed since he was a boy…"

A notion that left Jesse slightly unsettled – but his unease passed as they chatted on and watched the river flow. By and by Pap pulled the fish from the ashes and pronounced it baked and ready. Tin foil opened up, all knelt and dug in with knives, forks, fingers while Jesse divvied up sausage, cheese, and crackers, and Dave tossed him another beer. But the prime feast was the sweet tender catfish. *And damn!* he'd caught it.

Bellies full, they sat watching the sunset. The wind died,

the birds quieted, the only sound was the big heavy sigh of the river flowing past. All calm, a real peaceful feeling, Jesse thought, one he'd like to grip and hold onto. Yeah, glad he'd come and said so as he stood, making ready to head back.

"Thanks for havin' me down, fellas."

"Don't mention it, Jess...our pleasure," all happy campers at this point. Then Dave added, "You stick around, once it's good 'n dark, we'll do some night fishin' by lamplight, lots of fun. Have you outa here by 10 or so. Back up to the city by midnight. Up to you?"

Jesse stood silent a moment, thinking he ought to go but itching to stay, try some more of this. "Damn," he said, "think I will...just do that. Yeah..." Sat back down and watched the sky pass from red to deep blue and purple, then the first twinkle of a star and soon others started to appear sparkling in the black velvet night. Taking it all in, like magic, as Pap stoked the fire to keep the mosquitoes at bay, a gentle breeze brushing through the trees while up out of their dark form and sway rose the full moon, so big and close he might reach up and touch it. Or so it seemed as his gaze drifted from there to the long chain of stars hanging like smoke from the earth to the high heavens.

"What's that called? That far smoky light?"

"The Milky way..."

"I be damn..." he declared, so much of the sky never visible in the city.

Beer rushing through him, he walked to the edge of the clearing to take a long leak. Back turned to the fire, watching his own shadow dancing, cast up by the flames, him pissing like a lone wolf, marking his ground...*Yeah, I'm diggin' this*, he grinned as he shook off and zipped up.

Turning around something caught his eye like a slip of moon off through the timber, silently floating his way. Shortly, he spied another, and two more, all in advance, lanterns held luminous next the sheets, sprouting like mushrooms in eerie glow. "Wh-what's that?" he stammered scrambling back toward the fire, "That there!" pointing to the ghostly forms.

"Where? I don't see anything," Dave answered blankly, Clint and Pap simply shrugged, both mute.

"You blind! There, there 'n there!" aiming his finger like a six-gun and wished he had one, fear rising in an adrenaline rush as he discerned eye slits and mouth holes from which rose a chorused groan: *"Coon! Coon! We smell coon!"*

"Shit! That's the Ku-Klux! DAMN!" Limbs in flex, coming unglued, now running down the bank, his heart throbbing to his neck and ears, numb to words in flight and panic, couldn't hear Dave yelling, "It's a joke, Jess...a joke!"

Too late, already jumping in the river, then quiet, submerged, and back up, dogpaddling, gasping for air, caught in the swirling current, kicking for dear life. And he'd never really learned to swim, no pool in his neighborhood, what little he knew, to tread water and dogpaddle, he'd gained in one day-trip to the YMCA, "Nuff that wet stuff," he told them, "get me into boxin'..." And he was fighting now, fighting for every breath as he heard them up on the bank, Clint, Dave, and the boys in white, their makeshift hoods pulled back, all yelling:

"Keep your chin up, Jess!"

"For Chrissake, keep a'kickin'!"

"C'mon, you can do it," Dave urged as Pap readied a long limb towards the water for Jesse to grab. And he recognized their voices, the whole crew of them white bastards, he grinned and gasped, somewhat calmed in his struggle, thinking heck of a time for a swimming lesson, but pulling for him, yeah, friends of a sort them honky hounds, but encouraged, *Gonna make it, gonna do this...*

Clint stood foremost, cheering him on, watching him fight the current while Pap leaned out over the bank, Dave grasping the back of his belt as he extended the limb barely a yard shy of Jesse's hand.

"Don't give up, Jess, fast-hammer it!" Clint yelled, and to fuel the final kick he shouted, "Don't ya know there's snakes out there!"

What's this...? Jesse gasped, fear rising like fish vomit, biling up, choking him. *Snakes!* At the very thought he felt the current coil around his arms and legs, one giant dark mass wrapping him, seizing his heart, his eyes froze big as thunder as the river swallowed him whole in writhe and terror to its muddy depths.

"Jes-se! JESS!" Clint barked twice more like a cannon shot, hoping to see him break the surface, but nothing rose or appeared, only the limb Pap dropped to the water, carried off in the swirl of the broad deep current, sibilant beneath the tremor of cicadas and the hushed wind.

"Sweet Jesus...Lord have mercy," Clay murmured, others silent.

But Dave thinking, always thinking ahead to line them out...a prank gone wrong, no way they'd read this right, the authorities and others.

"Listen boys," he said. "Shuck them sheets. Pap, you burn 'em. Squat by that fire and make certain not one thread escapes the flames." No sooner said than Pap gathered up the sheets and set them blazing gold and yellow, shrinking to blue-white ash that blackened in the red embers. Each man's face reflected the lowering flames as Dave further instructed: "Here's the deal. You all arrived late 'n he saw your lanterns comin' through the timber...and spooked. Jumped in the river. We tried to call him back. He drowned. That's the story...and that's the truth. I don't wanna hear another word..."

All stood numb, gazing out at the starlight rippling on the river snaking off and away. All except Luther, who held that sullen smile and a gleam in his eyes.

THE EVER POND

This is a tale of the ever pond whose waters form the medium of our lives, where cells are etched and born, where the very synthesis of salt and blood occurs. Surrounding the ever pond are trees and grasses and all the tiny animals that feed upon its sustenance, its liquid salve and generative mirth, to then die, decay, and feed it in turn. These waters draw from a hidden spring, live-giving, ether-fed.

Each day a little dog and his boy play about the ever pond. The dog we may call fate, circumstance, or Raxas...his boy, Abe, our forebear in allegorical disguise. Their elements combined form the power or force that rules our lives in equal portions good and bad. Perhaps they are halves of the old one, Abraxas.

Herein arise myriad forms of existence. Flat-shaped rocks, of which I am one, jut along the shore. I have a friend who is a cork, another is a grasshopper, and still others are water spiders, wasps, dragon-flies, even dung. Of course there are the untold beings commonly glimpsed, ever present – the birds, frogs, mosquitoes, worms, and such. In the depths swim leviathan catfish, and near the surface turtles, bass, and crawfish. About the shallows snails move imperceptibly, cleansing the debris of our lives from the algae and moss...these arbors which snag hair, nail, and fin and other flagella of being.

Now, there are certain factors in this our existence that must be explained. The layout is not the sylvan paradise it may seem. The object of our lives, or rather survival, is to nurture in proximity of the pond without becoming immersed. For once immersed, one's life is ended. We are faced again with the perennial ambivalence and paradox, the very medium that grants and sustains our being is also the deathly quagmire and ultimate burial ground of our lives. A situation shared by the medieval alchemists, who, in their attempt to derive from mercury the sorcerer's stone and secure immortality, ended up poisoned by its vapors. And since we are all relatively blind, myopic creatures, the rhyme and reason, the how, why, and what escapes us quite completely. Each left to the indifferent mercy of the little dog and his boy, their caprice and play, the rapt mischief of jaw and hand.

So we languish, embraced by our lady mantis, relenting

before our destined turns.

As a rock it would seem I'd be well guarded, safe in the anonymity of sheer number whose appearance is nearly the same. Yet there are days I'd swear that the little boy Abe has a favorite among his rocks, namely me. Repeatedly I am grasped and whipped side-arm, skipping across crescents of tiny waves. At each dizzying splash I strain and leap, propelled by dire need like a duck in early take-off flailing its webbed feet as I cleave the air, assuming the most aerodynamic form, reaching for every last whiff of momentum to complete my flight across the groping depths of demise and negation. And damned if he doesn't seek me out again. The last flight I nearly didn't survive, several mighty leaps and successive quick-steps, the abating thrust, verily I was shedding tackles as I skidded chest-to-chin across the water up onto the shore. Even as I rested, revamped by the lucid sun, a ripple of insanity lapped drolly at my feet.

I have a friend, as I have said, who is a cork, wine-soaked and prone to muse. Witness with me the advent of his frantic undulation and hapless bounce. One day while lost in thought, Raxas sniffed him out and Abe plucked him up to use as a bobber on their fishing line. So fastened with hook and bait, they flung him to roost upon the madcap waves, prey to any hungry phantom that may rise to drag him under. Down he goes then up again. But his buoyant struggle continues and he may yet escape the embracing waves to puzzle and bask in safety of the shore.

Another friend who is also a cork submits willingly to the waters, which exhibits both faith and audacity, savors at once the humility and mystical intimations gleaned in vying shoulder to shoulder with fate, tasting of death. Some call this foolish, but we are all foolhardy. Besides, such daring may prove heroic, if short-lived.

I've also a friend, spry and dapper, with two spindly legs. This one Abe and Raxas would like to catch and use for bait. Yet they are easily distracted, the little dog and his boy, and thus far the grasshopper eludes his captors.

The water-spider I know well. He skims over the surface of despair, chiding each muffled grief and terror-reeking malodor. He laughs and mocks, this spider, firing fierce invective at the dark waters. Confident, aloof. One day he may find the tongue of some fat toad noosed about his neck and gag.

And there are the wasps and dragonflies that I admire – the former for its potency, the latter for its color and flight. But all this is frail and non-enduring, for soon the little dog and his boy will cast them to the waves. Whereas many abide witless, hard-shelled and blessed, left unknowing, numb to the futile pain of their lives.

Then there are those of the dung, of whom I have known a few, though none counted special, mere acquaintances. Their flesh and soul as much called by the moist rumblings of the nether world as by the diamond radiance of the sun. With their lives they feed every last want, barter and apportion their meat. They alone never suffer death in its fullest measure. Quite simply they are one day gone and no one notes their passing, nor even the little dog and his boy.

While of the rest I know little. I know that some of them reach the waters of the ever pond second-hand. Some of the flies and mosquitoes are snatched up by the frogs and lizards. I know also that many pale worms are exhumed as bait by Abe and Raxas. All in all it simply cannot be fathomed – this knowing fixed fore and aft to each moment, and whether of feather, scale, or hand, each lent one to another, fated to its own pleasure, act, and pain amid the play of the little dog and his boy.

For certain we will all die. Eventually our skeletons will end at the murky depth, silted over, silent. Occasionally the thunder will shake our bones or a seismic tremble raise us up a bit...and these may be the dark incantations of a future person's memory affecting us...perhaps a far progeny...or a professor recalling our particular generation, its peculiar traits and habits.

As long as the waters remain we will never be wholly separate from the living in our death. But ultimately the waters of the ever pond will leach out and evaporate, exposing all the skeletons, including those of the little dog and his boy. The dark basin will stretch like a dry skin in crack and curl and thus will end the process of everything. When all the reasons and why are laid bare in the nameless dust...

(*Told by a lone traveler met on a journey once, as a little dog and his boy looked on.*)

THIRTY YEAR SUMMER *(an essay on work and writing)*

When the last of the snow melts away and the grass turns green underfoot and the bite of the air warms and sweetens with flowers, were I in conference with God I would have to look about me and seek a more active prayer. For if in the beginning was the Word, it is the Word made flesh that we live by, and our flesh must cast its shadow beneath the sun to find its essence – an urge deeper than belief or faith, our need to grasp and mold the dust of which we're made. In a word a man must work and sweat, like a child must play. Returning to work in the spring is like raking dead leaves from the soul, letting all sprout anew.

I'm a carpenter, a construction worker. To be honest I've dreaded most mornings like a punch in the nose, or a jab to the kidneys, for the lower back is where it hurts the worst. But by mid-morning, warmed by the sun and labor, muscles and joints shed the ache and resume the play, the cuss and shout, all the raw poetry fit therein. Foundations laid, I've built houses, barns, and privies, hospitals, schools, and churches, hung sheetrock, fit doors and windows, erected staircases, tacked on siding and shingles, and run miles of trim – base, casement, crown, and chair-rail. I've milled rough-cut lumber to specified width, length, and thickness. Even cut timber in the mountains, later sent to mills.

I've worked construction off and on for over thirty years. Construction has been my patron, what allows me to write, and more, it has forged my hand and framed my view. I write between stints of work and change of season, at the least opportunity, like a stubborn weed that roots in cracked sidewalks and foundation walls. I worked my first summer as a carpenter at age 16, certain it would be my last, filled with dreams of aerospace and cocksure adventure. And again at 19, building concrete forms and tying steel, certain I would stoop no more, spare my hands for finer things. I had entered the Air Force Academy a year earlier, but disillusioned by the war, the cadet regimen, I resigned, determined to become a writer and experience the world from the ground up. A headstrong, arrogant youth, I thought to bend life to my will and walk where and how I pleased.

The following summer found me considerably humbled, married, with a child on the way, working curb and gutter off Pennsylvania Avenue in Washington D.C., learning to swing a pick and sledge alongside the progeny of slaves, men who had never known any options other than manual labor, crime and prison. One hot day the foreman seized a young worker by the throat and in a few seconds took him down and choked his breath, then grabbed a brick and made to strike as another worker lunged to deflect the blow, screaming, "Don' kill the boy!" Why the foreman's murderous rage? The boy had mouthed him when asked to dig. I kept my mouth shut and learned the rhythm of work and saw the sweat bead on my flesh the same as theirs.

This marked my first year of construction. With the change of seasons I headed west, traded a pick and sledge to work a jackhammer on a crumbling bridge through a cold Kansas winter. Observing my early efforts, the foreman, an ex-Marine and leaner cut of John Wayne, stepped up, took the jackhammer from my hands, stabbed the mass of concrete and shouted, "Gotta use it like your pecker, son! Use it like your pecker!" Then he strode away and laughed, leaving me to wrestle with the task, the notion. And yes, the concrete did eventually yield, but not in so sensual a way as a young man might wish.

Concrete, that mute mud of man, has formed my view as certain as it forms the basis of all we build; at once the most common and exacting of materials, it requires pain and patience, and like a rush of words, demands your full attention until it sets. I've formed concrete for bridges, water-treatment plants, for containment walls on nuclear reactors, for war memorials and bank vaults, for sidewalks, driveways, basements – poured and finished concrete on scores of different structures for as many different ends. Bent to the mud as if pulled by a deeper gravity. And the ache is always there, and the dread. And the relief once it's done, as I ease my grip and stand.

Through all the variety of time, place, and task, I've worked alongside a thousand different men. There is no one kind of man that labors. Some are of burly heft; others lithe and agile, highly athletic. And regardless of stature, their hands are uncommonly strong, socketed, geared for gripping. Many are drinkers, prone to grip the bottle; a few are fallen scholars, conversant on nearly any topic. While most have a quick grasp of matters at hand, some are plainly slow-witted. Yet I've learned something from each and every one – a tick or trait, a wry observation. And whatever their intelligence, I would chance to say most were grudging students in school, due in part to a lack of interest, a certain bent towards the practical, an instinct that leaves them wary of the written word, of reading. But they can size up a man, read one another, you and me, with a clarity and bluntness that is telling. With the spoken word, rooted in life and locale, they are masters – and the oral tradition lies at the very heart of human existence, compared to which the written is of recent origin, we only think it ancient, when in fact it is hardly older than the digital. If in the beginning was the word, it was the word spoken around the fire and on the hunt. The word still spoken by the working man as he grapples, spits and cusses, declaiming for or against, trading stories, jokes, gripes, depicting the moment, the task.

As an old worker reminded me one cold morning when he heard me lamely wish for quitting time, "Wish in one hand, shit in the other 'n see which one fills up first…" So the worker keeps his logic grounded, learns as he grips the shovel, the hammer, feels his hands blister, bruise or break, learns that there's a consequence to every act, and to words. For words can lead to clinched fists and bloody noses, for damn sure to a heated exchange from which there is no exit. Take the ghetto youth nearly beaten to death in face of the foreman's dark fury – *"You mouthin' me, boy?"* – I'll grant him this: he landed two good punches before he went down. And when he came to, choking and gasping for breath, he made no excuses. Back to work the next day he dug when and where he was told. Learned his lesson, as they say, "Don' trouble trouble…" Such words define a moment, a drama. Whether delivered in a Southern drawl or the staccato yip and slur of the ghetto, words born of experience pack a truth and meaning that may lack for nuance, but are as certain as the sweat that sustains them. They are the words of ballads and songs carried through the centuries, words of fable and parable and all the old saws. Common words spoken by common men.

Though few laboring men are lettered or read more than the sport page or want ads, no few have a genius for coining a phrase. And of genius or any such airy notion a gruff old mason may declare, "It's worthless as a cup a' cold piss!" Graphic, vulgar, and to many ears offensive, but you get the gist and you'll not forget it. Or a boast, and this more elevated and appealing: "I can weld anything but the crack a' dawn an' a broken heart!" A phrase I first heard voiced by a welder in Tennessee and years later by a welder in Kansas. Who was the originator? – I have no idea. Perhaps one of the anonymous thousands who welded on troop ships bound for Europe during World War II, over whose seams an inspector chalked "Kilroy was here!"

Which leaves one to ponder all the wretched dawns and broken hearts from that war and the mess of wars since. By and large it is working men, their fathers, brothers, sons, and now daughters, who fight our wars. They carry the wounds in their mind and flesh. Their words surge from the gut, raw and rude as their wounds. And their suspicions. Sadly, the cause for which they spill their blood often proves as worthless as a cup of cold piss.

When my grandfather returned from World War I, so shaken in his faith from having seen men torn and butchered, rolled under like corn stalks by that merciless plow, he never again bowed his head in prayer. Went from a devout Christian to a *backslider*, as he called it, in one dark season. Still, he never preached his nonbelief; he took his children to church and waited outside. He served as a medic, tended to the wounded and carried off the dead. After seeing the trenches, he returned to the farm, immersed his hands in labor and lived out his three score and ten. Rarely spoke of the war. Preferred to talk of baseball, crops, and weather. Once, full of a boy's curiosity, I asked him of the war and what it was like to see men die. His eyes fixed to the distance, he slowly said my name, adding, "There are some questions you should never ask."

To my grandfather every worthy man was "A Captain" – and those less so, like certain questions, were best not mentioned. From him I learned to work at whatever task at hand, whether pulling weeds, tamping posts, or stacking bales, a boy was meant to shadow and learn, and if he wanted to learn to drive a tractor he must first learn to blister his hands. Work was not to be shunned; it was a matter of pride and worth, of manliness. I watched my grandfather work alongside other men, each holding steady, loathe to let the other down, certain to do their part as if each movement were an oath or vow. There was no grousing, no task disdained, whether mucking manure or reaching inside a cow to pull a calf. Never a thought of not doing what was needed or asked. Yet a job was never rushed, and he always took time to talk to a man. He had a slow, easy cadence that savored the moment and spoke to the root of things. He taught me to listen to what a man said, and more importantly, to what he didn't say.

An ethic passed from generation to generation. And a generation later, an ethic I've passed to my sons, making certain each learned to sweat and labor even as I urged them to strive and study, so they would know that the pride in becoming a man is rooted in work. Eventually I saw my sons become soldiers, one in Army Special Forces, the other an Air Force pilot, both veterans of our recent wars. Now returned from their grim duty, they take on the fonder role of father and husband, raising their families. Like my grandfather they wrestle with the dubious nature of war and its aftermath. Whatever their fate, I know he would count them each "A Captain."

Oddly enough, there are men, accomplished men, who envy the worker's more free and relaxed manner. There is even one, a friend who prompted me to write this by accusing me of having lived *a thirty year summer*. Granted the irony of passing a good deal of that time knee-deep in snow, I admit as much. And smile, for there is something to what he says, something implied in working outdoors, in the sun and rain, in the wind and winter, grubbing in the dirt and mud, grappling with lumber and tools that veers close to playing hooky from our modern age. Escaping the modem, the conference room, the quarterly report, to indulge in horseplay, in sweat and swagger, like soldiers on leave, a rowdy, questionable lot. Unruly, gnarly, like weeds.

Across the urban landscape, at every construction site, on heaps of sand and upturned earth, you find weeds. And workmen: Rednecks, Blacks, Mexicans. Like weeds we stand in contrast to the surrounding edifice, to whatever is being built, cultivated. At every storefront demolition, or office walled-off and remodeled, ours is a rude, riotous presence. People give us wide berth. And often ask, "When will you be done?" Meaning: "When will you be *outa here* and cease this filth and racket?" For we are brusque, sweaty, and like spiny weeds our bodies bristle with sharp tools: chisels, saws, claw hammers. Our voices are sharp as well, seldom tame or welcome.

I've stood with my fellow workmen and watched corporate types file past, each in a trench coat, bearing a leather case, their hair coiffed and trimmed, all deferent to the gray-haired CEO. We smile and shake our heads – better to age in the sun, grow leathern and wry, than have our manhood pruned. While they in turn are no doubt grateful not to dirty their hands or stoop in brutish labor as they give a jaunty nod and rise like patricians to their respective cubicles to plot and plan our social course. So men sniff and scorn one another.

But the truth is more complex and thorny, and envy flows both ways. There are workers who will do most anything, even walk on their mothers, to escape labor and rise in status, as there are men, perhaps as many, who forsake their professions and escape to labor. I've known architects who've turned to carpentry so they could achieve by hand what their minds conceive. And I've seen their brethren at the firms bent over blueprints, counting light fixtures for a high rise, their dreams of grand design let to lapse – or perhaps they sketch their Monticellos at night and on weekends. Or take Jefferson himself, our greatest patrician, who praised the yeoman farmer and rugged tradesman, while I admire much of his life and intent, I would admire him more if instead of extolling such virtues he had freed his slaves and farmed by his own hand. It took Lincoln, the rail-splitter, and 600,000 American dead to address the question our founding fathers could have settled had they listened to the wisdom of their untutored hearts. Or better yet, the whispered longings of those who worked their fields and their fine gardens.

But mine is a contrary voice – and yes, we will always need the tutored mind to design and govern, to parse the law, mend our bones, and lay our dead to rest. As we need the rougher type, to man our trenches.

It is an active life. I grasp a thing and place it there; I kneel, reach, and climb. I hear it said that working men wither quickly once they retire. How else could it be? They are what they do. The carpenter and iron worker, the farmer and rancher, are all defined by their task. They grip, they heft, the fruit of their efforts ever at hand, with few abstractions between self and ends. The farmer plows, the carpenter hammers, the iron worker walks a high beam and in one misstep he falls. A consequence constant as gravity to which I give brief testament: while working on a cooling tower one day, a rotten timber dropped from the span above and struck my head – were it not for my hard hat and being belted to a crossbeam, I would have fallen impaled on rebar fifty feet below. Height makes you focus. As does chance.

Farmers, those closest to the ground, suffer accidental death in numbers equal to any occupation in the country. Equal to firemen or policemen, and in most years, to soldiers. They face the hazards of weather and markets and poor yields. Still, most fight tooth and nail to stay on the land. And many, like my own father who scratched out a meager living on a tenant farm, choose self-murder when faced with leaving. You find this stubbornness in most workers, a hankering for the elemental, a devotion that often defies logic and bewilders their women. With each step that removes them further from the land, from their accustomed task, they feel a slippage in the soul. Trapped like a wolf, they will gnaw off their leg, even end their life in defiance of any other meaning. I took instruction from my father's act and learned that a man carries his own definition and is as he sees himself, not as others would have him. And learned to write of the world I see, not of the world I'm told.

Of workers I have known, many carry on their father's fate, take on his battle even as they decry his fool words and failings, make those words and acts their own, wary of all cushy paths and fine positions as if they would somehow deny their fathers. And I suppose in a way I do the same. Even as I watch my step.

No, I do not farm like my father and grandfather. I have crossed a divide between country and city, a divide as old as the banding of man. But it is a shared border, and while there are distinctions and conflicts between the two, there exists a degree of overlap and understanding. Whether you hoe beans or haul hod, you grip a wooden shaft the same as a hunter grips a spear, your ends and means as direct and as physical. But there evolves a further divide in our modern age as processes grow ever more abstract.

Dexterity of hand at a keyboard, in clicking a mouse – can this really compare to the skill of a tradesman manipulating tools and material? To a farmer seeding the soil? We learn through our hands as well as through our minds and are shaped by what our hands shape and do. There is a contention, an argument implied here. Is anything truly integral to our flesh shaped by typing letters onto a digital screen? By the vast sweep and harvest in cyberspace? Is something not lost in removing ourselves so utterly from the physical, from traditional tasks? Is it not essential to our nature to delve like Adam, and if so, is there no way to reclaim it short of becoming Luddite fools willfully subject to the perils of nature from which man has only recently climbed? Or are we hoist on a technological petard, left without choice, fated to fall back into the mud?

No doubt I ask too much to answer. Man has always found himself somewhat out of place no matter his time or task, in need of some greater meaning, longing for yet unable to grasp it. Always falling short, ultimately stumped. And in face of this question, this search, the sum total of human understanding still counts for very little. Of all that is known a skeptical worker might say, "Put in a thimble it'd rattle like a pea in a boxcar."

Working intimate to the earth, the flesh, you feel its consequence every day, the burden of labor and age. And seeing your blood and sweat drip into the soil, how can you hope to crawl up from the dust? It's enough to crawl out of bed each day. Once it rots, you cannot restore the integrity of wood, or return a plank to the tree to drink sap from the roots, to branch and flower. In youth I filled many notebooks with mighty words and big questions of which I've forgotten the greater share. Now I seek trusted words apt to my hand and experience. After thirty years of labor my thoughts grow firm and terse, like a tree in winter.

What does an old tree know? It knows its roots and where it stands, remembers many storms and whorled wounds, and is grateful for the sap and bud of spring. So what do I know? I know that I long for the sun on my skin like a child warms to the blessing of its father. But while the sun begets our warmth, indeed is essential to all life and growth, it is not a human warmth but a vast storm of fusion, and if you seek to embrace it you will die as surely as if you stepped into a hellish fire. Work twelve-hour days beneath the August sun tending a hot-tar kettle and see if you don't numb your flesh with cold beer and howl in lust for the moon's cool light. The sun is not merciful. And likewise whatever impetus gave birth to the world and time, whatever thought was involved it was not human thought, and its love is not human love, it is as partisan and as indifferent to the spider, the snake, to man or whale, and lends equal witness to a supernova as to a lit match. Any judgment or salvation is consequent to every act and is as brief and temporal as our lives. Forgiveness is our own, as is hope and love. Virtue, or worth, is the staff that goads and directs, wielded by the hand that leads, by the hand that hammers and toils, by the mind that reasons and dreams at the base of a towering ideal that may one day crumble, in an instant as we watch and grieve.

Or is it really so harsh and lonely, this life?

Something made implies a Maker. That seems to be true. But what does it say of the Maker if it is often slipshod and tragic? And what does it say of our mortal selves, this weary husk? Are we grateful and worthy? Many times, my hands numb from work, I rub away the ache and wonder at what little I have done, and looking back over the years, wonder what it is I've been making? These calloused hands, what fruit do they bear? I am grateful to have loved a fine woman and proud to have raised two worthy sons. Yet looking to the distant stars, the dust at my feet, I too long for greater attachment and meaning. My sons, are they and I seeds of that hidden soul? No, I do not believe, yet the question is there, present, like the shell about the egg. Again I look to my hands and remember my father's and grandfather's hands, their strength and sinew, their scarred, bent joints. As my hands age and weather I see the same knuckles, tendons, and veins, like the ridges and rivers of an old skin map, a gnarly root clawing the earth. And I sense that as well, the earth's fond gravity calling to me from the deep, dark blanket of winter where their hands lay folded, at rest in their graves.

Alas, my long summer ends, I can feel it in my bones. And approaching the winter of my life, I take most winters off, shut myself away and craft words. I love winter, the solitude and reflection. My body rests in witness of my mind at play, like a ghost in envy of the flesh. At the moment I conceive and begin a story, constraint of time and space recedes; I grow ecstatic, sense a raw purity like the utter silence following a fresh snowfall. With first breath of inspiration I grip my pen and write, rooting like a desperate seed in quest to flower. As weeks pass through periods of freeze and thaw, as the snow turns to muck and slush, the words slow and the labor grows intent, dark, unending, like the depths of winter. Finally, I write in grudging rhythm, striving to end my tale, my task, while the root is deep. For when the sun warms and the trees bud and bloom, I hate every thought and word and hunger to put my body back into play, to stomp and shout and work up a sweat, lose myself in the physical, and fear I would go mad if I could not.

Why? Why do I love work that so many shun? For I truly love to grub in the dirt and build. In the shovel I see a spear, in the hammer a war-ax, and gripping each, I feel instinctual, like a warrior set to meet his foe. I swing like Casey at the bat, driving stakes with a nine-pound hammer. Drive them into the ground one after the other until I gasp for breath, and catching my breath, drive some more. Take a stance, whip my body, heave my shoulders and snap my wrists. Why? Because it feels good. Maybe it's a male thing – to drive, stab, slash, and thrust. It feels good. If the weather is cold, work warms me; in the heat of summer my flesh is lathed in sweat, soothed and basted by the effort. It feels good. Like hitting a baseball deep into left field, like sacking a quarterback, like tagging an opponent with a hard right, or being tagged in turn – and though this may not feel so good, you can bet it *feels*. Our scars and wounds are marks of pride and experience, like tattoos they adorn and exalt out flesh. And why work feels good like sport, play, and conflict, is because it speaks to our bones, like a tuning fork humming to the ear.

But spasms of joy, like all pleasures, are brief then I slump into drudgery and look to end the day. The deep satisfaction comes when the job is finished, the season done. When I can turn away and write. In late autumn when the sky lowers and rains blacken like ink in icy pools, I long to grasp my pen and stab the page. Seek a truth and meaning beyond daily ends and means.

There is nothing quaint about the carpentry I do. I do not frame pictures or make fine furniture. I frame buildings and form structures. I work in the guts and bowels of factories. Rub up against the abrasive edge of man and machine, glimpse the bones and underpinnings. And I did not come to write in one fell swoop. It took years of ragged effort and false starts punctuated by bouts of drunken inspiration when I'd stumble home to jot down a crude thought or lyric. I attempted my first novel at age 22, but lacking the will and experience, I gave up on prose for another fifteen years. Still, I continued writing songs no matter what the circumstance. I'd wake from a hangover and voice my regret; at work, tear open a nail sack and scrawl a verse, a chorus, then rush home, grab my guitar and hunt down the chords. At night I sang my songs in taverns and bars; by day I'd play the lyrics off my tongue, taste them like the dust and wind, like oaths and curses, share them with fellow workers, for songs are the common man's literature, old and enduring.

Only after this long oral apprenticeship did I return to writing prose, and then only by chance. Laid off one winter I wrote a song – but words, scenes, and characters continued to spill forth like rummage from an old trunk. Next day I sat down and began to write a novel with no greater thought than to prove I could. Each day I wrote until my head grew wooden, grasping words, building sentences, erecting a scaffold, a plot, scaling the wall of doubt. By spring I had shaped my tale. Scaled that wall. And I have written nearly every winter since.

I write like I labor, to exhaustion, because it feels good. No matter the frustrations, I feel whole and rooted, for every memory and experience is given meaning as I draw upon all the lives I've known, all I've witnessed and been told. There lies the chief pleasure of writing. And its chief burden: deciding what to say, what gist or trait to reveal. There is a deep responsibility in telling a story, in giving it pulse and life. And pride and sadness once it's done, like seeing a child grown and gone.

In writing this I had hoped to construct a shiny sphere of thought, a lucid condensation of thirty years of labor. But I feel a frenzy crowding in, a ruder more romantic sense demanding a say, and see I've come up with something rather unwieldy, more of Frankenstein than Apollo, like a giant mud ball rolled through a cornfield, left oblong and misshapen, with stubble and leaves sticking out, and here and there a work boot or leather glove, or a crumpled portion of the husker himself. And examining this mud ball, not in slow, minute dissection, but bringing its full crude mass to bear, what have I learned from work that bears on my writing? I could claim many things, that conjunctives are like hinged doors, they close off one idea and open to another, build an elaborate metaphor using items of construction as my grammar, but it would be sheer artifice. For I tire of words. Tire of spelling like I tire of sorting nails. I tire of "a," "an," and "the." Yet the point is not so well taken without their use. In youth I sought out adjectives in want to make my meaning soar. As I age, more and more I favor verbs; I see them do the work of language, no matter the regal subject or prized object, it's the verb that gets things done – that hammers and saws; that weds, murders, destroys, and constructs. What I've truly learned is to give each man and moment, each particular, full measure: how a nail is set, where a comma is placed. No building or story is finished in one stroke, they take time, endurance, and discipline. And looking to the end result will not achieve the task, let alone one day's work.

Solitude to a writer is like water to life, essential, like going deep in the ground, down to bedrock, before you build. To write a novel is like being buried alive. You leave the sunlight to enter the darkness and become the soil, immersed at the sentient root of things. Terrible at times to lie there as in a grave. And under that grave weight you labor, grappling, nearly immobile, slowly gaining strength and movement, and bit by bit you work your way to sunlight and air and at last break through to the grassy surface like old blood resurgent in the purple bloom of grape hyacinth. And the only way to move while buried is to become the soil, a mix of elements that conceive and sprout like a seed seeking nourishment and growth in the fertile dark – for to focus on the flesh, the self, while creating, is to remain there compressed like a fossil, a corpse, that will never again breathe, run, or sing. Whatever thought is most vital and stirs the blood, that can wedge free and reach the light, forms link after link in a great chain, and in the moment the story ends, the thought ceases, the chain is broken, and the flesh is free. Free to stand once more, full and primordial, void of the word. I know it's spring when tufts of wild onions thrust green above dead grasses, when dark storms sweep the prairie and birds trill manic, alive, and flowers burst their colors. The wind sings warm and I am tempted only to scent, see, and listen. And name not a thing.

I tire of words, like I tire of work; I can feel it in my bones. And as my long summer lengthens to the biblical forty, I gradually step from the pit of labor and take my labor to my wife's garden, mend and improve our house, chop wood for winter. At last turn away from the bluster and shout of rough men and harken to the joyful shout of our grandchildren, lend an ear to their words and questions, smile and share my own.

There are days I feel young as ever, fit and frisky. And there are mornings I gaze in the mirror and wince at my gimped self. I laugh. Ever notice how babies all lookalike, the same with really old guys. They all wear the same expression, rheumy-eyed, perplexed, as if bound in the cusp of time and question, seeing their sentiments grow relic like horseshoes taken down and tossed on Fourth of July and Labor Day then hung back on a nail and let to rust. No matter if they've lived a life of achievement, crowned with the laurel of wisdom, they are ultimately stumped, captive to their frail, failing flesh. Make one wrong move and the hip cracks like a vase, or the heart goes "Pop!" like bubblegum and their lips stick tight forever as they lay in their casket while others pass by commenting on how they don't quite look themselves this day. The vision blurs along with the mind. *What was that thought?* they ask. *What was I saying? Was it yesterday or fifty years ago I first caught her smile?*

Confused, bemused by age. Yet even then there is delight and play. I've seen old men basking in the sun, gazing to the trees and singing to the birds – trees they might have climbed when young, birds they might have hunted. Is theirs not a purer moment, a deeper appreciation and wonder?

Melvin Litton has published three novels: *CASPION & the White Buffalo; GEMINGA;* and *I, JOAQUIN* – all from Crossroad Press. His stories and poems have appeared in *Chiron Review, Mobius, Foliate Oak, Floyd County Moonshine, Pif, First Intensity, Broadkill Review, The Literary Hatchet, Bards and Sages,* among others. He has two poetry chapbooks: *From the Bone* (Spartan Press) and *Idylls of Being* (Stubborn Mule Press). He is a retired carpenter and lives in Lawrence, KS with his wife Debra and their shepherd Jack. He also writes and performs songs as The Gothic Cowboy and with The Border Band: www.borderband.com